Uncle John's

ULTIMATE BATHROOM READER

The Bathroom Readers' Institute

Bathroom Readers' Press
Berkeley, California

Cover design by Michael Brunsfeld

Uncle John's Ultimate Bathroom Reader
by The Bathroom Readers' Institute

Bathroom Readers' Press ISBN: 1-879682-65-6

Printed in the United States of America. First printing 1996.

"Honey Bucket," by John Foley, originally appeared in *Alaska Magazine*,
Copyright © 1992 John Foley. Reprinted by permission of the author.

"Origin of Halloween" from "HALLOWEEN: 5TH CENTURY B.C. IRELAND"
in PANATI'S EXTRAORDINARY ORIGINS OF EVERYDAY THINGS by
CHARLES PANATI, Copyright © 1987 Charles Panati. Reprinted by permission of HarperCollins Publishers, Inc.

"The Puppet Master" from *Biography of an Idea* by Edward L. Bernays, Copyright
© 1965 Doris F. and Edward L. Bernays. Reprinted by permission of Harold Ober
Associates.

"1995: The Year of the Toilet" originally appeared as "Gone to Pot: Movies Flush
with Bathroom Scenes," by Mick LaSalle. © SAN FRANCISCO CHRONICLE.
Reprinted by permission.

"Knifestyles of the Rich and Famous," from *Marie Claire* magazine. Reprinted by
permission of *Marie Claire* Magazine/Hearst.

"Dave Barry's Flaming Toilet." Dave Barry is a columnist with *Tropic*, the Sunday
magazine of the *Miami Herald*. Reprinted by permission of *the Miami Herald*.

"Killing Mass Transit," "Good News for Hitler," "Morgan's Swindle," "Into the
Mouths of Babes," originally appeared in *It's a Conspiracy!* by The National Insecurity Council. Text © 1992 by Michael Litchfield. Published by EarthWorks
Press. Reprinted by permission of EarthWorks Press.

Selections from *Primetime Proverbs*, © 1989 by Jack Mingo and John Javna.
Reprinted by permission of the authors.

"Millennium Madness," "The Great Criswell," "Is It 2000?," and assorted inserts
on the year 2,000 from *The Bathroom Readers' Guide to the Year 2000*. Copyright ©
1996, by Eric Lefcowitz. Reprinted by permission of EarthWorks Press.

"Who Cracked the Liberty Bell?" Reprinted by permission of AMERICAN
HERITAGE Magazine, a division of Forbes, Inc. © Forbes, Inc., 1973.

"Food Questions: How Do They Do That," by Trish Hall. Copyright © 1987 by
The New York Times Co. Reprinted by permission.

THANK YOU!

The Bathroom Readers' Institute sincerely thanks the people whose advice and assistance made this book possible.

John Javna
John Dollison
Lenna Lebovich
Gordon Javna
Erik Linden
Melissa Schwarz
Sharilyn Hovind
Larry Kelp
Andy Sohn
Michael Brunsfeld
Sherry Powell
Benjamin Brand
Gary Morris
Jennifer Massey
Chris Rose-Merkle

Gordon Van Gelder
Eric Lefcowitz
Leni Litonjua
Morgan Smith
Max, Lucy & Alice
Julie Roeming
Lonnie Kirk
Paul Stanley
Bennie Slomski
Gordon Javna
Thomas Crapper
Jesse & Sophie, *B.R.I.T.*
...and all the bathroom readers
Hi to Emily and Molly!

Special thanks to Leder Norahs

☆   ☆   ☆

PREDICTION FOR THE YEAR 2000

"When Jane cleans house she simply turns the hose on everything... Why not? Furniture (upholstery included), rugs, draperies, unscratchable floors—all are made of synthetic fabric or waterproof plastic. After the water has run down a drain in the middle of the floor (later concealed by a rug of synthetic fiber), Jane turns on a blast of hot air and dries everything." —*Popular Mechanics, 1950*

CONTENTS

NOTE:
Because the BRI understands your reading needs, we've
divided the contents by length as well as subject.
Short—A quick read
Medium—1 to 3 pages
Long—For those extended visits, when something
a little more involved is required

☆   ☆   ☆   ☆

AN ARTFUL HOAX

On display: Vincent Van Gogh's ear (that's how it was labeled).

Where: In New York's Museum of Modern Art in 1935, during the first exhibition of Van Gogh's art in the U.S.

Background: Hugh Troy, a New York artist, suspected that most Americans were more interested in Van Gogh the man than they were in Van Gogh the artist. To prove this, he mounted a shrivelled object in a velvet shadow box and wrote: "This is the ear which Vincent Van Gogh cut off and sent to his mistress, a French prostitute, Dec. 24, 1888." Then he visited the Van Gogh exhibit, and when no one was looking he put it out on display.

What Happened: The "ear" was mobbed, while Van Gogh's paintings were virtually ignored. It wasn't until later that Troy admitted that he had fashioned the ear out of a piece of chipped beef.

INTRODUCTION

Well, here we are again. Another year, another bathroom reader.

We're wiped out. As usual, it was plenty of work pushing out this latest edition. But it was also a gas.

We at the BRI often feel we have the most *satisfying* job in the world. We get to spend the year poring through old magazines, newspapers, and obscure books, looking for off-the-wall subjects to write about...and then we get to "field-test" the materials.

Amazingly, after nine years—and over 2,000 pages—of *Bathroom Readers*, it's still easy to find new things to write about. The material keeps on flowing. In fact, we already have almost enough information floating around now to roll out our *next* volume—our 10th Anniversary Special. (Keep on the lookout for that.)

If you're a longtime Bathroom Reader fan, you've probably already noticed that this edition is bigger than our previous seven volumes (not including *The Best of Uncle John's Bathroom Reader*, of course). We've gotten plenty of requests to add as many pages as possible, so the book will keep you company through more sit-down sessions. And we've done our best to comply.

Keep those cards and letters coming—let us know what you like and send us your own favorite bathroom reading material. We can always make use of it, one way or another.

Happy reading—and *Go with the Flow!*

—*Uncle John and the Bathroom Readers' Institute*

BRAND NAMES

You already know these names.
Here's where they came from.

CLOROX. In 1913, the Electro-Alkaline Company of Oakland, California, started selling bleach in jugs carried by horse-drawn carts. A supplier pointed out that their name sounded industrial—even dangerous. He suggested combining "chlorine" and "sodium hydroxide" (two of the product's ingredients), to create *Clorox.*

BRILLO. From the Latin word *beryllus*, which means "shine."

LEE JEANS. At the turn of the century, Henry D. Lee was one of the Midwest's biggest wholesalers of groceries, work clothes, and other items. In 1911, because he wasn't getting shipments of work clothes on time, he decided to build his own factory. In 1924, he started making jeans for cowboys. In 1926, Lee's made the first jeans with zippers.

FORMULA 409. The two scientists who invented the "all-purpose cleaner" in the late 1950s didn't get the formula right until their 409th attempt.

CONVERSE ALL-STARS. Named for Marquis M. Converse, who founded the Converse Rubber Company in 1908. He introduced the canvas-topped All-Star—one of the world's first basketball shoes—in 1917.

BAUSCH & LOMB. In the 1850s, Henry Lomb invested his life savings ($60) in an eyeglass business run by John Bausch. By 1908, they were selling over 20 million lenses a year.

TURTLE WAX. In the early 1940s, Ben Hirsch mixed up a batch of car wax in a bathtub. He called it Plastone Liquid Car Wax, and started selling it around the country. Several years later, he was walking along Turtle Creek in Beloit, Wisconsin, when "he made a mental connection between the hard shell of a turtle and his product." *Plastone* became *Turtle Wax.*

Why did Japanese scientists invent "square" watermelons? They stack better.

THANKSGIVING MYTHS

Historian Samuel Eliot Morison says that "more bunk has been written about Pilgrims than any other subjects except Columbus and John Paul Jones." After reading this, maybe you'll agree.

It's one of American history's most familiar scenes: A small group of Pilgrims prepare a huge November feast to give thanks for a bountiful harvest and show their appreciation to the Indians who helped them survive their first winter. Together, the Pilgrims and Indians solemnly sit down to a meal of turkey, pumpkin pie, and cranberries.

Just how accurate is this image of America's first Thanksgiving? Not very, it turns out. Here are some common misconceptions about the origin of one of our favorite holidays.

MYTH: The settlers at the first Thanksgiving were called Pilgrims.

THE TRUTH: They didn't even refer to *themselves* as Pilgrims— they called themselves "Saints." Early Americans applied the term "pilgrim" to *all* of the early colonists; it wasn't until the 20th century that it was used exclusively to describe the folks who landed on Plymouth Rock.

MYTH: It was a solemn, religious occasion.

THE TRUTH: Hardly. It was a three-day harvest festival that included drinking, gambling, athletic games, and even target shooting with English muskets (which, by the way, was intended as a friendly warning to the Indians that the Pilgrims were prepared to defend themselves).

MYTH: It took place in November.

THE TRUTH: It was some time between late September and the middle of October—after the harvest had been brought in. By November, says historian Richard Ehrlich, "the villagers were working to prepare for winter, salting and drying meat and making their houses as wind resistant as possible."

Every Thanksgiving, Americans consume 45 million turkeys—one for every 5-1/2 U.S. citizens.

MYTH: The Pilgrims wore large hats with buckles on them.

THE TRUTH: None of the participants were dressed anything like the way they've been portrayed in art: the Pilgrims didn't dress in black, didn't wear buckles on their hats or shoes, and didn't wear tall hats. The 19th-century artists who painted them that way did so because they associated black clothing and buckles with being old-fashioned.

MYTH: They ate turkey.

THE TRUTH: The Pilgrims ate *deer*, not turkey. As Pilgrim Edward Winslow later wrote, "For three days we entertained and feasted, and [the Indians] went out and killd five deer, which they brought to the plantation." Winslow does mention that four Pilgrims went "fowling" or bird hunting, but neither he nor anyone else recorded which *kinds* of birds they actually hunted—so even if they did eat turkey, it was just a side dish. "The flashy part of the meal for the colonists was the venison, because it was new to them," says Carolyn Travers, director of research at Plymoth Plantation, a Pilgrim museum in Massachusetts. "Back in England, deer were on estates and people would be arrested for poaching if they killed these deer....The colonists mentioned venison over and over again in their letters back home." Other foods that may have been on the menu: cod, bass, clams, oysters, Indian corn, native berries and plums, all washed down with water, beer made from corn, and another drink the Pilgrims affectionately called "strong water."

A few things definitely *weren't* on the menu, including pumpkin pie—in those days, the Pilgrims boiled their pumpkin and ate it plain. And since the Pilgrims didn't yet have flour mills or cattle, there was no bread other than corn bread, and no beef, milk, or cheese. And the Pilgrims didn't eat any New England lobsters, either. Reason: They mistook them for large insects.

MYTH: The Pilgrims held a similar feast every year.

THE TRUTH: There's no evidence the Pilgrims celebrated again in 1622. They probably weren't in the mood—the harvest had been disappointing, and they were burdened with a new boatload of Pilgrims who had to be fed and housed through the winter.

McDonald's sells "McSpaghetti" in the Philippines and "McLak" salmon burgers in Norway.

SPECIAL AFFECTS

*Here are a few unexpected ways that movies have
made their mark on the American public.*

COMA (1978)

"In 1978," writes historian Scot Morris, "there was a reported 60% drop in human organs donated to U.S. hospitals, as
compared to the previous year. Why?...The decline in donors occurred just after the release of *Coma*, a film in which hospital patients are murdered so their organs can be harvested and sold."

FORREST GUMP (1994)

The title character carries his favorite book, *Curious George*,
around in a suitcase. Later, he gives a copy to his son. In the first
three weeks after the film's release, sales of *Curious George* books
jumped 25%—and have stayed high since.

IT HAPPENED ONE NIGHT (1934)

Clark Gable took off his shirt in the Oscar-winning comedy, and
America saw he was bare-chested underneath. Overnight, under-
shirt sales plummeted.

E.T. (1982)

"In one of the film's more dramatic moments," writes Carolyn Wyman in *I'm a Spam Fan*, "the alien opens up his clenched fist and
out drops—not the expected weapon—but brown, yellow, and
orange pieces of both boy and extraterrestrial's favorite candy"—
Reese's Pieces. "Those few minutes of screen time sent sales of
Reese's Pieces into outer space. Sales increased 65%, causing the
company to keep two factories open round the clock."

LOVE HAPPY (1949)

The Marx Brothers' final film was so badly underfinanced that the
producer had to invent what is now known as "product placement."
He devised a rooftop chase scene where the characters jumped
from one neon sign to another. It was one long commercial and
corporations paid to be a part of it.

"Republican" and "Democrat" are both towns in North Carolina.

PLITZ-PLATZ I WAS TAKING A BATH

As kids, we were all told that trains go "choo-choo" and cars go "beep beep." Check out the sounds they make in other languages.

AAH-CHOO!
Portuguese: Ah-chim!
German: Hat-chee!
Greek: Ap tsou!
Japanese: Hakshon!
Italian: Ekchee!

SPLASH!
Hindi: Dham!
Russian: Plyukh!
Danish: Plump!
Spanish: Chof!
Greek: Plitz-platz!

EENY-MEENY-MINY-MO
Arabic: Hadi-badi
Italian: Ambaraba chichicoco
Japanese: Hee-foo-mee-yo
Swedish: Ol-uh dol-uh doff
Polish: Ele mele dudki

CHOO-CHOO!
Chinese: Hong-lung, hong-lung
Danish: Fut fut!
Japanese: Shuppo-shuppo!
Swahili: Chuku-chuku!
Greek: Tsaf-tsouf!

ZZZZZZZ...
Arabic: Kh-kh-kh...
Chinese: Hulu...
Italian: Ronf-ronf...
Japanese: Gah-gah...

UPSY-DAISY!
Arabic: Hop-pa!
Italian: Opp-la!
Japanese: Yoisho!
Russian: Nu davai!
Danish: Opse-dasse!

KITCHY-KITCHY-KOO!
Chinese: Gujee!
French: Gheely-gheely!
Greek: Ticki-ticki-ticki!
Swedish: Kille kille kille!

UH-OH!
Chinese: Zao le!
Italian: Ay-may!
Japanese: Ah-ah!
Swahili: Wee!
Swedish: Oy-oy!

BEEP BEEP!
Chinese: Dooo dooo!
Hindi: Pon-pon!
Spanish: Mock mock!
French: Puet puet!
Japanese: Boo boo!

CHUGALUG!
Arabic: Gur-gur-gur!
Hindi: Gat-gat!
Hebrew: Gloog gloog!
Russian: Bool-bool!
Chinese: Goo-doo, goo-doo!

Native Americans spoke more than 133 different languages.

FAMILIAR PHRASES

Here are some origins of everyday phrases.

K NUCKLE UNDER
Meaning: Give in to someone of superior strength.
Origin: Today only the joints in your fingers are known as knuckles, but before the 14th century *all* joints in the body were called knuckles. In those days, "knuckling under" meant getting down on your knees before your master or conqueror.

BRAND-NEW
Meaning: Obtained very recently.
Origin: The German word for "fire" is *Brand*. Horseshoes, as well as other items that were fresh from the fire of a blacksmith's forge, were said to be *brandneu*, or "brand-new" in English.

DOUBLE-CROSS
Meaning: Betray.
Origin: Comes from boxing and describes a fixed fight. If a fighter deliberately loses, he "crosses up" the people who have bet on him to win; if he wins, he "crosses up" the people paying him to lose. Someone is betrayed no matter how the fight turns out; hence the name *double*-cross.

FINISH IN A DEAD HEAT
Meaning: Tie for first place.
Origin: Racing term from the days when horses ran several races, or "heats," to determine a winner. (A horse had to win two out of three, three out of five, etc.) When two horses tied in a heat, it was considered "dead," because it didn't count.

HAVING KITTENS
Meaning: Acting hysterically.
Origin: In the Middle Ages, when a pregnant woman experienced severe pains that didn't appear to be labor pains, people thought she was bewitched and "had kittens clawing at her inside her womb." A common excuse given in court for obtaining an abortion was "to remove cats in the belly."

Q: When did cars first come with seatbelts?   A: 1950.

HERE'S THE STORY...

Inside facts on The Brady Bunch, *the syrupy TV sitcom that aired from September 26, 1969 to August 30, 1974. Like* Star Trek, *it was never very popular in prime time, but has become a monster cult show.*

HOW IT STARTED

In 1964, while TV producer Sherwood Schwartz was working on his hit show *Gilligan's Island*, he began fleshing out ideas for a new family sitcom.

In the mid-'60s, the standard *Leave It to Beaver* sitcom family was already out of date; you had to have a gimmick to have a hit. So Schwartz came up with the idea of making the wife a widow, and the husband a widower. It was a TV first—a blended family, with three kids from the dad and three from the mom. He called it *Yours and Mine.*

Schwartz wrote the script for a 1/2-hour pilot episode in which Carol and Mike Brady get so lonely on their honeymoon that they return home to get Alice and the kids. He showed it to the networks and got a mixed response. NBC liked the idea, but thought the pilot was unrealistic (who'd leave their honeymoon to be with kids?); ABC wanted Schwartz to expand it to a 1-1/2 hour TV movie (he refused because it would be too boring); CBS rejected it outright—they had their own widow-marries-widower show in the works (it never aired). So *Yours and Mine* was dead in the water.

Then four years later in 1968, Lucille Ball and Henry Fonda starred in a fairly successful movie with a plot similar to Schwartz's show, called *Yours, Mine, and Ours.* It reminded someone at ABC of the pilot they'd seen in 1964; they called Schwartz and bought the program. Once ABC was committed, Schwartz had no trouble getting Paramount TV to finance it. The show was on its way.

INSIDE FACTS

Name That Show

Paramount immediately ran into a problem with the name. A lawyer for the owners of *Yours, Mine, and Ours* threatened to sue them if they kept the title *Yours and Mine.* Schwartz wanted to fight— he'd registered *his* title first. But no one else thought it was worth

---

America's four favorite leftovers: pasta (including lasagna), pizza, chicken, and meatloaf.

the effort. The choice came down to *The Brady Bunch*, or *The Brady Brood*. "Bunch" sounded like juvenile delinquents; "brood" sounded like a horror flick. Finally, they just picked one and started production.

The Bradys vs. the Censors

• It was officially established in the early episodes that Mike Brady was a widower—but the fate of Carol's first husband was never discussed. Why? Schwartz wanted to leave open the possibility that Carol was a divorcée, even though the network wouldn't allow it explicitly.

• 1969 was the peak of the "sexual revolution," and Carol and Mike joined in. They became the first TV sitcom couple to actually sleep together. Until then, censors had always required twin beds—even for married couples. But the Bradys had…a double bed!

• One thing the Bradys weren't allowed to have: a toilet. ABC removed the toilet from the Brady bathroom, leaving only a sink and tub. The running joke on the set was that the Bradys used the restroom at the corner gas station.

The Blended Family

• Schwartz interviewed 464 boys and girls to find the Brady kids.

• He wanted the sons and daughters to have the same hair color as their parents. The reason: he didn't want viewers confused about which kids belonged to whom. But when the Brady kid auditions started, Schwartz didn't know who was going to play the parents. So he hired two sets of Brady kids—blonde and brunette. When Robert Reed and Florence Henderson were hired as the parents, he fired the blonde boys and brunette girls.

In the Cast

• Barry Williams was the most popular Brady kid. He was an instant pop star, getting 6,500 letters a week in 1971.

• Robert Reed didn't want to play Mike Brady. A classically trained actor, he had the lead role in the Broadway play *Barefoot in the Park*. He wanted to star in the TV version planned for the 1970 season, and only took the *Brady Bunch* part after ABC decided that all the actors in their *Barefoot* sitcom would be African Americans.

WHEN YOUR HUSBAND GETS HOME...

Here's a bit of advice taken directly from a 1950s Home Economics text book. It was sent in by a reader, along with the comment: "Times have changed!" No kidding. Believe it or not, this was part of a course intended to prepare high school girls for married life.

Have dinner ready: "Plan ahead, even the night before, to have a delicious meal—on time. This is a way of letting him know that you have been thinking about him and are concerned about his needs. Most men are hungry when they come home and the prospects of a good meal are part of the warm welcome needed."

Prepare yourself: "Take 15 minutes to rest so you will be refreshed when he arrives. Touch up your makeup, put a ribbon in your hair and be fresh-looking. He has just been with a lot of work-weary people. Be a little gay and a little more interesting. His boring day may need a lift."

Clear away the clutter: "Make one last trip through the main part of the house just before your husband arrives, gathering up school books, toys, paper, etc. Then run a dust cloth over the tables. Your husband will feel he has reached a haven of rest and order, and it will give you a lift, too."

Prepare the children: "Take a few minutes to wash the children's hands and faces (if they are small) comb their hair, and if necessary, change their clothes. They are little treasures and he would like to see them playing the part."

Minimize all noise: "At the time of his arrival, eliminate all noise of washer, dryer, dishwasher or vacuum. Try to encourage the children to be quiet. Be happy to see him: Greet him with a warm smile and be glad to see him."

Some don'ts: "Don't greet him with problems or complaints. Don't

---

A record: 60.2% of the U.S. TV audience watched the last episode of M*A*S*H in 1983.

complain if he's late for dinner. Count this as minor compared with what he might have gone through that day."

Make him comfortable: "Have him lean back in a comfortable chair or suggest he lie down in the bedroom. Have a cool or warm drink ready for him. Arrange his pillow and offer to take off his shoes. Speak in a low, soft, soothing and pleasant voice. Allow him to relax—unwind."

Listen to him: "You may have a dozen things to tell him, but the moment of his arrival is not the time. Let him talk first."

Make the evening his: "Never complain if he does not take you out to dinner or to other places of entertainment. Instead, try to understand his world of strain and pressure, his need to be home and relax."

THE BEST & WORST TIPPERS

According to a poll in Bartender *magazine:*

• Lawyers and doctors are the worst tippers. Normally, doctors are the #1 tightwads. In rougher times, it's lawyers. The reason: "There are more lawyers and less work."

• The biggest tippers are bartenders and "service personnel."

• As smoking gets more restricted, cigar and cigarette smokers —who are now forced to smoke at the bar instead of at restaurant tables—are becoming notably good tippers.

• Other leading tightwads: teachers, computer people, musicians, professional athletes, and pipe smokers.

• Other top tippers: hairstylists, mobsters, tavern owners, regular customers.

• Vodka drinkers are good tippers. People who order drinks topped with umbrellas are bad tippers.

• Democrats tip better than Republicans.

One in 500 humans have one blue eye and one brown eye.

FAMOUS TIGHTWADS

For some bizarre reason, really rich people are often the most uptight about spending money. Here are a few examples of people who've gone over the deep end about loose change.

MARGE SCHOTT, owner of the Cincinnati Reds. Told her staff in 1995 she couldn't afford Christmas bonuses and gave candies instead. They turned out to be free samples from a baseball-card company …and they came with coupons inviting consumers to "win a trip to the 1991 Grammys."

CARY GRANT. Nicknamed "El Squeako" by Hollywood friends, he counted the num ber of firewood logs in his mansion's garage and used a red pen to mark the level of milk in the milk bottles in his refrigerator, both to keep his servants from taking them.

FRANKLIN D. ROOSE-VELT, U.S. president. Mooched dollar bills off of his valet to drop in the collection plate at church.

GOUCHO MARX. Wore a beret, which became one of his trademarks, "so he wouldn't have to check his hat."

CORNELIUS VANDER-BILT, American financier. When his doctor told him on his deathbed that a glass of champagne a day would mod-erate his suffering, Vanderbilt —then the wealthiest man in America—replied, "Dammit, I tell you Doc, I can't afford it. Won't sodywater do?"

J. PAUL GETTY, oil baron. Installed a pay phone in his mansion to keep visitors from running up his long-distance bill; put locks on all the other phones. "When you get some fellow talking for ten or fifteen minutes," the billionaire ex-plained, "well, it all adds up."

LEE IACOCCA, former head of Chrysler Corp. Threw himself lavish holiday parties and charged the gifts to underlings. Popular saying at Chrysler: "If you have lunch with someone who looks like Iacocca and sounds like Iacoc-ca, rest assured—if he offers to pick up the check, it's not Iacocca."

The G in *g-string* stands for "groin."

ALLENISMS

Truths from one of America's leading wits, Woody Allen.

"Sex without love is an empty experience, but as empty experiences go it's one of the best."

"I am at two with nature."

"There's no garbage in California. That's because they turn it into television shows."

"To *you* I'm an atheist; to God, I'm the Loyal Opposition."

"The difference between sex and death is that with death you can do it alone and no one is going to make fun of you."

"The lion and the calf shall lie down together…but the calf won't get much sleep."

"More than any other time in history, mankind faces a crossroads. One path leads to despair and utter hopelessness. The other, to total extinction. Let us pray we have the wisdom to choose correctly.

"Death is one of the few things that can be done just as easily as lying down."

"I took a speed reading course and read *War and Peace* in twenty minutes. It involves Russia."

"When I was a little child, I was breast fed from falsies."

"I will not eat oysters. I want my food dead. Not sick—not wounded—dead."

"I'm not the heroic type. I was beaten up by Quakers."

"What if everything is an illusion and nothing exists? In that case, I definitely overpaid for my carpet."

"I never want to marry. I just want to get divorced."

"Why are our days numbered and not, say, lettered?"

"The worst thing you can say about Him is that basically, He's an underachiever."

"I should have stayed in college…I was in the black studies program. By now I could have been black."

CELEBRITY SWEEPSTAKES

There's an old saying in advertising: "If you haven't got anything to say about your product, have a celebrity say it for you." Sometimes celebrity endorsements work, sometimes they don't. Here are a few examples.

ROSEANNE AND TOM ARNOLD

In 1993, CelebSales, a clothing manufacturer, hired the outspoken couple to endorse a line of large-sized clothing.

What they wanted: A positive image. Roseanne had TV's #1 show and she was unapologetic about her size. "I think the sexiest thing a woman can do," she said, "is be as fat as me—or fatter." Roseanne also attracted publicity. *People* magazine, for example, shot an entire fashion layout for the line, with Roseanne modeling the clothes herself.

What they got: A lawsuit. A week before the clothes were to premiere in a fashion show, Roseanne pulled out of the deal, obtained a court order canceling the show, and sued CelebSales, claiming they owed her $750,000 in licensing fees. CelebSales countersued for $24 million, arguing that the Arnolds "not only reneged on agreements to market the clothes on television, but generated publicity so vile that nobody would want to buy their product."

What happened: The clothing line was canceled. In 1996, a court awarded the Arnolds the $750,000 they said they were owed. By that time, they weren't even a couple anymore.

CYBILL SHEPHERD & JAMES GARNER

In 1986, the Beef Industry Council announced that it had hired Shepherd, an ex-model and star of TV's "Moonlighting," and Garner to represent them in a $30 million "Beef: Real Food for Real People" campaign.

What they wanted: To change beef's image as an unhealthy food. "We're thrilled that two stars of such magnitude have agreed to join the beef team," one council spokesperson told reporters. "I don't think we could have two celebrities and an industry more suited for one another."

What they got: Egg on their face. A few months later, Shepherd was interviewed in *Family Circle* magazine. "Asked to name her latest beauty tip," said a news report, "the star was quoted as saying, 'I've cut down on fatty foods and am trying to stay away from red meat.'" Shepherd claimed her publicist had made the quote up. "The comments attributed to me were released by my publicity office, but they were not entirely correct," she explained. "I do avoid 'fatty foods,' but I have retained red meat in my diet."

Then, in April 1988, Garner underwent a quintuple bypass surgery to correct clogged arteries. Was beef the cause? "It could very well be due to something else," a beef board spokesman protested. Newspapers reported that Garner was recovering. "According to his spokesman," said one, "he is 'beginning to eat a normal diet.' No word on whether beef is included."

What happened: The Beef Industry Council pledged that it would stand by Shepherd and Garner...then quietly dumped each of them when their contracts expired.

JACK KLUGMAN

The star of TV's "Odd Couple" and "Quincy" was hired as spokesperson for Canon USA copiers in 1982.

What they wanted: A recognizable TV pitchman

What they got: Unexpected competition. In 1984, Minolta hired Klugman's "Odd Couple" co-star, Tony Randall, to endorse its *own* line of copiers. Randall played a compulsive cleaner on the show; Klugman played a slob—which was why Minolta wanted Randall, as *Fortune* magazine reported in 1985:

> The Minolta ads, which according to his agent riled Klugman, played up the Odd Couple stereotypes and even made a thinly veiled reference to Klugman when Randall ad-libbed, "Of course, I'm not a slob like, uh..." and gave his you-know-who-I-mean look. Minolta's marketing coup was to associate Canon machines in consumers' minds with Klugman's mess: jammed paper, perhaps, or ink-blackened hands.

What happened: The Randall ads boosted sales of Minolta copiers, but they didn't hurt Canon's sales, so the company retained Klugman as their spokesman.

Survey result: 33% percent of respondents refuse to participate in surveys when asked to do so.

TOASTER FOODS

We wrote about how the toaster was invented back in BR #2—now here's the origin of America's two biggest-selling toaster foods.

EGGO WAFFLES

The *Eggo* name has probably been around longer than you think. It was coined in 1935, when three brothers—Frank, Tony, and Sam Dorsa—borrowed $35 to buy a waffle iron and started experimenting with waffle batter. When they got a batter they liked, they sold it to restaurants in Northern California. A fourth brother, George, suggested they call their product "Eggo" because "the batter has lots of eggs." In 1937, the company went public, and the brothers built a big waffle-batter factory in San Jose.

After World War II, when Americans began buying home freezers in record numbers, the Dorsas guessed there was a bigger market for frozen waffles than for waffle batter. So in 1950, they gambled and switched their entire production to ready-made waffles. Within a year, they were cranking out 10,000 an hour...and still couldn't keep up with demand. Kellogg's bought the company in 1968. Today, the brand controls an estimated 60% share of the $500 million frozen waffle industry.

POP-TARTS

The Pop-Tart story starts with dogfood, not cereal...and not with Kellogg's but with its rival, Post. According to Steve Hymon, in the *Chicago Tribune*:

> In 1957, Post's pet-food division came out with Gaines Burgers [which] were a novel concept because the dog food was semi-moist but didn't have to be refrigerated—a convenience many humans coincidentally sought in their breakfast food.
>
> In 1963, the Post research and development department, using some of the same technology that made Gaines Burgers possible, figured out a way to keep fruit filling moist while inhibiting the growth of spoilage-causing bacteria. The obvious application: a fruit-filled pastry that could be shipped and stored without having to be refrigerated.

On Feb. 16, 1964, Post unveiled its new product, Country Squares. The food industry oohed and aahed; the business press buzzed; grocers waited expectantly.

And waited.

Post blundered. It took so long to get its product to grocery stores that Kellogg's had had a chance to catch up. In just six months, Kellogg's created *and* test-marketed Pop-Tarts. People at Post knew they were sunk. Hymon goes on:

> The names given to the two products were one more indication of Kellogg's superior marketing savvy. Kellogg appreciated that kids were the primary target audience for Pop-Tarts because they had yet to establish breakfast habits of their own. Post seems to have been more confused. As awful a name as Country Squares seems in 1994, it was arguably worse in 1964, when the word "square" was widely used to mean "nerdy." When paired with "country," it seemed to describe a food for middle-age rubes from the sticks.

POPPING OFF

The original Pop-Tarts came in four flavors: Strawberry, Blueberry, Brown Sugar, and Apple-Currant (which Kellogg's quickly changed to Apple-Berry when it realized most consumers didn't know what currants were). Kellogg's put its marketing muscle behind the new product, blitzing kid's TV shows with commercials featuring Milton the Toaster. By 1967, they had both created and locked up the $45 million toaster pastry market. The brand maintained a 75% market share into the 1990s, with $285 million in sales in 1990...and nearly $500 million by 1993.

What happened to Country Squares? Post changed the name to Post Toast-Em Pop-Ups, but it was too late. Post finally gave up in the early 1970s and sold the marketing rights to someone else.

TOASTER FLOPS. *Not every toaster food works. Here are some other ideas that bit the big one...and the reasons why.*

• **Downyflake Toaster Eggs.** Too weird.

• **ReddiWip's Reddi Bacon.** Bacon fat dripped to the bottom of the toaster, creating a fire hazard.

• **Toaster Chicken Patties.** Same problem, with chicken fat.

• **Electric French Fries.** Stamped out in slab form, they "looked like a picket fence, tasted like a picket fence."

PRIMETIME PROVERBS

TV tidbits from the book Primetime
Proverbs, *by Jack Mingo and John Javna.*

ON DIVORCE

"Actress Robin Givens has
filed a libel suit against her es-
tranged husband Mike Tyson,
claiming he told a reporter she
was after his money...She's
asking $125 million."
—**NBC News**

"Did you ever notice that alimony is like keeping up payments on a car with four flats?"
—*Laugh-In*

ON CHILDBIRTH

"Home delivery is for newspa-
pers, not babies."
—**Oscar Madison,**
The Odd Couple

ON POLITICIANS

Rush: "Lincoln wasn't a
crook."
Wainwright: "We don't know
that. He never finished his
term."
—*Too Close for Comfort*

ON RACISM

"Bigotry started a long time
ago—nobody knows where.
Personally, I think the French
started it."
—**Johnny Fever,**
WKRP *in Cincinnati*

SUSPICIOUS ADVICE

"Never trust a woman. Even
the four-legged variety."
—*The Prisoner*

"My dad once gave me a few
words of wisdom which I have
always tried to live by. He said,
'Son, never throw a punch at a
redwood.' "
—**Thomas Magnum,**
Magnum P.I.

ON TV

"No wonder they call it a medium; it's so seldom rare or
well-done."
—**Mighty Mouse,**
*The New Adventures
of Mighty Mouse*

ON MONEY

"There's only one thing more
important than money, and
that's more money."
—**Pappy Maverick**
Maverick

"Money seems to have a rub-
berlike quality, because you
can bounce a check or stretch
a dollar. "
—**Mork,**
Mork and Mindy

No matter how cold it gets, gasoline won't freeze. Below −180 degrees F, it just turns gummy.

FAMOUS
FOR 15 MINUTES

Here it is again—our feature based on Andy Warhol's prophetic comment that "in the future, everyone will be famous for 15 minutes." Here's how a few people are using up their allotted quarter-hour.

THE STAR: Mr. Twister the Clown

THE HEADLINE: *Clown's Coins Create Controversy*

WHAT HAPPENED: Cory McDonald made his living as the balloon-sculpting Mr. Twister, performing at fairs and birthday parties. For six years, he also enjoyed wandering the streets of Santa Cruz, California, putting quarters in expired parking meters. One day in 1995, a frustrated meter maid handed him a citation; she'd found out that a local law prohibited "good samaritans" from feeding other people's meters. McDonald was outraged. A lawyer agreed to take his case "pro-Bozo," and together they waged a publicity campaign to embarrass the city and change the law.

THE AFTERMATH: It worked. Newspapers all over the U.S. picked up the story, and Mr. Twister became the symbolic victim of all bad laws and frivolous prosecutions in America. Anti-government editorials referred scathingly to the Santa Cruz city government. Finally, Santa Cruz city council members—eager to put the matter to rest—donned big red clown noses at a council meeting and repealed the ordinance. Mr. Twister expressed his appreciation by twisting balloon animals for them.

THE STAR: Lya Graf, a 20-year-old circus midget

THE HEADLINE: *Millionaire Mogul Meets Midget & Mellows*

WHAT HAPPENED: J. P. Morgan—one of the world's most feared robber barons—was in the Senate Caucus Room on June 1, 1933, waiting to testify before the Senate Banking and Currency Committee. Suddenly a publicity man for the Ringling Brothers Barnum & Bailey Circus popped a midget onto his lap. At that instant, a newspaper photographer who was in on the stunt snapped a picture. The whole room froze; Morgan was not known for his sense of humor…and didn't like physical contact. But to everyone's

---

Why a 7th-inning stretch instead of some other inning? 7 is considered a lucky number.

surprise, he smiled and chatted with her. The next day, the photo *and* Lya Graf were famous all over the world.

THE AFTERMATH: The photograph changed public perception of the robber barons. As John Brooks writes in *American Heritage* magazine:

> Morgan, and even Wall Street as a whole, profited adventitiously from the encounter. From that day forward until his death a decade later, he was in the public mind no longer a grasping devil whose greed and ruthlessness had helped bring the nation to near ruin, but rather a benign old dodderer. The change in attitude was instantaneous and Morgan took advantage of it.

Lya Graf wasn't so lucky. "She was shy and sensitive," writes Brooks, and though she could tolerate employment as an "ordinary circus freak," she couldn't stand being a "celebrity freak."

Two years later, hounded by fame, she left the United States and returned to her native Germany. She was half Jewish. In 1937 she was arrested as a "useless person" and in 1941 was shipped to Auschwitz, never to be heard from again.

THE STAR: Alvin Straight, a 73-year-old farmer

THE HEADLINE: *A Lawn Day's Journey: Laurens Man Mows Path to Fame*

WHAT HAPPENED: In the spring of 1994, Alvin Straight found out that his 80-year-old brother, Henry, had had a stroke. He hadn't seen Henry in seven years, and decided he'd better go see him "while I had the chance." The only problem: Alvin lived in Laurens, Iowa…and Henry lived 240 miles away in Mt. Zion, Wisconsin. Alvin didn't have a driver's license, didn't want anyone else to drive him, and wouldn't take public transportation. So he hitched a 10-foot trailer to his lawn tractor and started driving the back roads at 5 mph. It took him six weeks, and by the time he got to Mt. Zion, he was so sore "I could barely make it with two canes." CNN broadcast the story, and Alvin was an instant celebrity.

THE AFTERMATH: He was bombarded with offers to appear on talk shows—with Letterman, Leno, etc.—but he wouldn't go, because he refused to fly or take the train to either coast. He did sign a contract to make a TV movie of his life, but nothing ever came of it.

The term "rookie" comes from the Civil War slang "reckie," which was short for "recruit."

THE STAR: George Holliday, general manager of an L.A. plumbing company.

THE HEADLINE: *Camcorder Creates King Controversy*

WHAT HAPPENED: George Holliday gave his first wife a camcorder for Valentine's Day. He was playing with it on the evening of March 2, trying to figure out how it worked...so when sirens awoke him early the next morning, he instinctively grabbed for it. He pulled on some pants and stood shivering on his balcony, filming while some L.A. cops beat the hell out of a man named Rodney King. The next day, he took the tape to a local TV station and for $500, let them broadcast it. The broadcast was fed to CNN and in hours, the whole world knew about it. In a few days, Holliday was famous. Camera crews were at his door, and major news publications were interviewing him.

THE AFTERMATH: Holliday had lots of offers to cash in on his celebrity: a film company wanted to make *The George Holliday Life Story*, a producer talked about *The George Holliday TV Show*, a company wanted him to endorse a George Holliday "crimebuster" toy. All but a $39.95 video called *Shoot News and Make Money with Your Camcorder* fell through. He filed a $100 million lawsuit against the TV stations that had aired his film clip without his permission, but lost. By the time he met his second wife a few years later, says one report, "his notoriety had waned to the point where he had to tell her who he was."

THE STAR: Fred and Selena Payton, owners of a carpet and upholstery cleaning service in Rockville, Maryland

THE HEADLINE: *Selena and Fred are Giving It Up for Arsenio*

WHAT HAPPENED: In July 1993, Arsenio Hall—looking for a ratings boost for his TV show—announced that he would host one show at a viewer's house. He picked the Paytons. For some reason, this was national news—and the Paytons, now famous for 15 minutes...for being famous for 15 minutes...were interviewed by all the major news organizations.

THE AFTERMATH: The night went off without a hitch, as 1,200 people from the neighborhood hung out with the Paytons and watched Patti LaBelle and Bobcat Goldthwait entertain. Then the Paytons' 15 minutes were up. Hall's show went off the air soon afterward.

In 1789, the total U.S. federal government debt was $190,000.

A MUSICAL IS BORN

Some musicals are so famous that they are familiar even to people who never go to plays. Here are the origins of some favorites.

SHOWBOAT (1927)

Oscar Hammerstein, Jerome Kern, and producer Florenz Ziegfield were sick of the light, upbeat musicals that had made them famous. The wanted to do something with adult themes like alcoholism, interracial relationships, and marital troubles—even if no one came to see it. But they needn't have worried. Their adaptation of Edna Ferber's novel about life on a riverboat opened in 1927 to rave reviews and sold out so often that Ziegfield considered staging a second production in a nearby theater to handle the overflow. So far the show has had five Broadway revivals, more than any other play in history.

OKLAHOMA! (1943)

Based on a play called *Green Grow the Lilacs*, which had a limited run in the 1930-1931 Broadway season. A woman who'd helped produce it thought it would make a good musical and approached composer Richard Rodgers with the idea. He was interested, but his partner Lorenzo Hart—who'd become an unreliable alcoholic—wasn't. Rodgers's solution: he teamed up with lyricist Oscar Hammerstein...who hadn't had a hit in years and was considered a has-been. Together they wrote a musical called *Away We Go!* When it got to Broadway, it was renamed *Oklahoma!* and played to sellout crowds. It established Rodgers and Hammerstein as a team.

MAN OF LA MANCHA (1965)

In the late 1950s, a TV/film writer named Dale Wasserman went to Madrid to do research for a movie. The local press mistakenly reported that he was there to write a play about Don Quixote—which sparked his curiosity. Wasserman became so interested in Quixote and author Miguel Cervantes that he traveled all over Spain, retracing their steps. This, in turn, inspired him to write a TV drama called *I, Don Quixote*, which aired on CBS in 1959. He expanded it into *Man of La Mancha* in the early 1960s.

Julie Andrews didn't get to play Eliza in the film version of *My Fair Lady* because she wasn't

GREASE (1972)

Originally a five-hour rock 'n' roll musical written by two amateur actor-writers for a Chicago community theater. A producer bought the rights and had it trimmed by more than half before taking it to New York. Interesting sidelight: George Lucas's film, *American Graffiti*, is usually credited with starting the 1950s nostalgia boom, but this play opened off-Broadway on Feb. 14, 1972—a year before *American Graffiti* premiered. It ran for 3,388 performances, and the 1978 film version was the #1 box-office film of the year.

ANNIE (1977)

Lyricist Martin Charnin was browsing in a bookstore, doing some last-minute Christmas shopping, when he saw a book called *Arf: The Life and Hard Times of Little Orphan Annie*. He bought it for a friend and intended to wrap it and give it away. Instead, he stayed up that night reading it...and decided to turn it into a musical. Ironically, although the musical was a smash, the movie it inspired in 1982 was such a huge disaster that it even caused the *play's* ticket sales to plummet...and ultimately forced it to close in 1983.

CATS (1982)

When T. S. Eliot first wrote *Old Possum's Book of Practical Cats*, a children's book of verses, he only circulated it to his friends; it wasn't published until years later. The same thing happened when Andrew Lloyd Webber, a fan of the book, put some of the poems to music. At first, he only entertained friends with them. Eventually he decided to turn them into a short, one-act musical...then changed his mind and began working on a full-length performance. *Cats* is now the longest-running musical in Broadway history, earning more than $100 million since it opened.

LES MISERABLES (1987)

French playwright Alain Boubil got the idea after seeing *Jesus Christ Superstar* on Broadway: he figured that if pop-rock music could be used to tell the story of Jesus, why not tell the story of the French Revolution? Boubil wasn't sure how to do it...until he saw *Oliver!*, adapted from the Charles Dickens novel *Oliver Twist*. He decided to adapt a classic novel from the period...and settled on Victor Hugo's novel *Les Miserables*.

---

a "big enough star." So she signed as Mary Poppins...and won the Oscar for Best Actress.

INTO THE
MOUTHS OF BABES

In the late 1970s, Beech-Nut Baby Foods marketed "100% pure" apple juice that contained no apples at all. Were they trying to profit at the expense of our children...or were they the victims of unscrupulous business practices themselves?

B eech-Nut Foods, one of the oldest and most respected food labels in America, had fallen on hard times by the late 1970s. One by one, its most profitable divisions had been sold off, leaving only its baby food products—which had never turned a large profit.

• In 1979, after the Nestlé Company bought Beech-Nut, there was even greater pressure to make the baby food line profitable.

• Company executives had already been cutting costs wherever they could. To squeeze profits out of their apple products, for example, Beech-Nut bought its apple concentrate from Universal Juice, a wholesaler whose price was 20% below the market average.

WHAT HAPPENED

• Beech-Nut employees became suspicious of Universal almost immediately. In 1978, when Beech-Nut employees inspected Universal's plant in Queens, New York, they were "denied access" to the apple-concentrate processing facility. (In fact, there wasn't any.) Nonetheless, Beech-Nut continued buying from Universal Juice.

• By 1981, Beech-Nut's director of research, Jerome LiCari, had become concerned that the bargain concentrate might be tainted, so he suggested the company replace its wholesaler. When his bosses ignored him, he quit. Shortly after, however, the FDA began paying attention.

THE FDA

• In 1982, an FDA investigator found that despite Beech-Nut's claims of the product being "100% apple juice," it actually contained "beet sugar, malic acid, apple flavor, caramel color, corn syrup and cane sugar—but *no* apple juice" (*FDA Consumer*).

Cleopatra wasn't Egyptian; she was Greek. And she was the seventh queen by that name.

- Beech-Nut executives first claimed that they had no proof their product was not juice, then said that even if it were true, "Who were we hurting?"

- In 1986, the FDA indicted Beech-Nut, its suppliers, and its top executives for "conspiring to defraud the public by willingly distributing phony apple juice." There were more than 800 charges in all.

- According to *Financial World*: "In the end, the company pleaded guilty to 215 counts of introducing adulterated food" from 1981 to 1983, paid $2.5 million in fines, and lost 20% of their market because of bad publicity.

WAS THERE A CONSPIRACY?

Did Beech-Nut knowingly sell adulterated apple juice, then stonewall the FDA while the company dumped its inventory? Some facts to consider:

- When the FDA told Beech-Nut execs that their product was adulterated, instead of recalling it, they moved it out of their New York warehouse to avoid a New York state embargo, shipped much of it to the Caribbean to make it difficult to track, and dumped it on the market at "tremendous discounts."

- According to *Financial World*, Beech-Nut's president, Neils Hoyvald, explained in a letter to Nestlé: "If the recall had [occurred when the FDA first ordered it], over 700,000 cases in inventory would have been affected...due to our many delays, we were faced with having to destroy only 20,000 cases."

- An anonymous letter sent to the FDA in 1983 said Beech-Nut executives were laughing at federal authorities and stalling the FDA's investigation. It was signed "Johnny Appleseed."

FOOTNOTE

- Hoyvald's lawyer was Brendan Sullivan, who also defended Oliver North. Sullivan recommended that instead of sending Hoyvald to jail, he "be placed on probation and required to teach [ethics] to business students." Hearing of this, one professor quipped, "We may see CEOs deliberately polluting streams [or] using banned food additives, just so they can be convicted and sentenced to a job at Harvard." He added: "You can't overlook the fact that this Beech-Nut character and Ollie North have the same lawyer...I wouldn't be surprised if somebody started selling a Jollie Ollie Apple Juice that tastes like shad" (*Barron's*).

THE "ODD ELVIS" QUIZ

Elvis is one of the greatest rock singers of all time...as well as one of the most unusual people ever to walk the earth. Here's a little quiz based on some of the stranger recollections of his friends and associates. See if you are on the same wavelength as the King.

1. Elvis' friends learned not to show pain around him. Why not?

a) He hated weaklings.

b) He'd burst out crying if a friend was hurt, and wouldn't stop blubbering for hours.

c) He thought he had the power to "cure the sick." They'd have to sit there while he "laid hands" on them...then pretend he'd cured them.

2. The King was a big eater. Take breakfast, for example: Elvis usually ate a pound of bacon, six scrambled eggs, "a platter of butter-soaked biscuits with sausage," and pots of black coffee to wash it all down. Occasionally, though, Elvis experimented with new diets—like the time he developed an interest in vegetarianism. "Because the spiritual teachings say that you have to eat right," Elvis told friends over dinner one evening in 1973, "I'll be eating a lot of vegetables now, a lot of salads, and raw fruits. I'm telling the maids, and that's what they're going to make for me." How long did Elvis's vegetarian phase last?

a) Two hours.

b) Two days.

c) Two months.

3. Elvis liked TV, but he hated the show *The Streets of San Francisco.* "We made damn sure that *The Streets of San Francisco* was never on when Elvis was around," his bodyguard once said. "I promise you, Elvis was very likely to blow a television set out with his gun if it had come on the screen." It wasn't because the plots were dull, or because the acting was bad. What was the reason?

a) He didn't like the size of Karl Malden's nose.

b) He didn't like the sponsor.

c) He didn't like the character's name.

First president to wear long pants instead of breeches: James Madison (1809-1817).

4. Elvis hated dieting and exercise and often asked his doctor, George Nickopoulos, about other methods of losing weight. One night, "Dr. Nick" mentioned the possibility of an intestinal bypass or "shunt" that would cause food to pass through the King's body before it was completely digested. What was Elvis' reaction?
a) He said he wanted the operation that night.
b) He was so grossed out that he threw up.
c) He said he didn't want the operation himself, but wanted to watch Dr. Nick perform it on someone else "for scientific reasons."

5. In 1961, a friend of Elvis' on the Memphis police force died. What odd request did Elvis have?
a) He wanted to sing "Hound Dog" as they lowered the coffin into the grave.
b) He wanted to watch the mortician embalm his friend.
c) He wanted to prop his friend's body up in a police car and drive around Memphis with the sirens and lights on.

6. Elvis once met country singer Jimmy Dean. How did he greet him?
a) He pulled out a gun and stuck it up against his head.
b) He complained that he didn't look "anything like your cousin, *James* Dean."
c) He started running around, snorting and mooing.

7. Being asked to perform for the president in the White House is one of the biggest honors a musician can receive. Elvis was once asked to play at a party thrown by President Richard Nixon. It didn't work out because...
a) They insisted Elvis wear a business suit while he performed.
b) His manager snorted, "Elvis doesn't play for free."
c) Conservatives threatened to boycott the event if Elvis showed up.

8. Elvis is the only person we've ever heard of who actually died while reading in the bathroom. What was he reading?
a) A book about Nostradamus.
b) A book about the Shroud of Turin.
c) *Uncle John's Bathroom Reader*.

If you're an average American, you spend 4-6 hours/day watching TV.

FAMOUS LAST WORDS

It's never too early to get yours ready.

"Don't let it end like this. Tell them I said something."
—Pancho Villa

"I'd rather be fishing."
—Jimmy Gass, *murderer*

"O.K. I won't."
—Elvis Presley, *responding to his girlfriend's request that he not fall asleep in the bathroom*

"It's very beautiful over there."
—Thomas A. Edison

"Why not? Why not?"
—Timothy Leary

"Make my skin into drumheads for the Bohemian cause."
—John Ziska, *Czech rebel*

"I've never forgiven that smart-alecky reporter who named me 'Butterfingers'."
—Thomas Moran, *pickpocket*

"I'm tired of fighting. I guess this is going to get me."
—Harry Houdini

"Remember me to my friends, tell them I'm a hell of a mess."
—H. L. Mencken, *essayist*

"Monsieur, I beg your pardon."
—Marie Antoinette, *to her executioner, after stepping on his foot accidentally*

"Dying is a very dull affair. My advice to you is to have nothing whatever to do with it."
—*Author* Somerset Maugham

"But, but, Mister Colonel—"
—Benito Mussolini, *executed 1945*

"This isn't the worst. The worst is that they stole twenty-five years of my life."
—*Director* Erich von Stroheim's *last words to Hollywood*

"I'm not afraid to die, Honey …I know the Lord has his arms wrapped around this big fat sparrow."
—*Blues singer* Ethel Waters

"I am about to, or, I am going to die. Either expression is used."
—Dominique Bouhours, *grammarian*

"Never felt better."
—Douglas Fairbanks, Sr.

When asked what they feel most guilty about, 34% of Americans say "nothing in particular."

GROUCHO GETS ELECTED, ACT I

Here's a script from a recently rediscovered radio show featuring Groucho and Chico Marx. Close your ears and listen with your eyes as you enjoy an episode of Five Star Theater, performed on March 13, 1933.

SCENE: *The office of Beagle, Shyster & Beagle, Attorneys at Law. Miss Dimple, the receptionist, is typing. Judge Maxwell, a local politician, is waiting for Waldo T. Flywheel, attorney, to arrive. Ravelli(Chico Marx), Flywheel's assistant, is sleeping in the corner.*

The door opens.

MISS DIMPLE: Good morning, Mr. Flywheel.

GROUCHO: Can't you think of anything else to say? You say that to me every morning.

JUDGE: (Stepping forward) Oh, Mr. Flywheel, you remember me, Judge Maxwell. I've been planning for a long time to drop in and talk to you about the coming election.

GROUCHO (impatiently): I know. I know.

JUDGE: (Surprised): Really? How did you know?

GROUCHO: Why, you just told me.

JUDGE: Mr. Flywheel, my re-election is being bitterly fought by a group of crooked politicians.

Their leader is Big Boss Plunkett, who is going to be tried for bribery shortly after the election. He doesn't want me on the bench because he knows I can't be tampered with.

GROUCHO (indignantly): See here, Judge Maxwell. Did you come here to buy my vote?

JUDGE: Why, no, of course not.

GROUCHO: Then you're wasting my time...and my time is valuable. Do you realize that while you're here talking nonsense, I could be at my desk, sleeping?

JUDGE: You don't understand, Mr. Flywheel. I am here to enlist your support in my campaign.

RAVELLI (waking up): Attsa fine. I take two bottles.

JUDGE: Two bottles of what?

RAVELLI: Two bottles of campaign. (Laugh.) Attsa some joke!

JUDGE (Indignant): Gentlemen! From your attitude I can only conclude that you are in sympathy with Boss Plunkett and his crooked politics. I'm going. Good day.

First president to greet people with a handshake: Thomas Jefferson. Earlier presidents bowed.

Door slams.

GROUCHO: Ravelli, I'm ashamed of you. I saw you taking your hand out of Judge Maxwell's pocket.

RAVELLI: Well, I had to take it out sometime.

Knock, door opens.

MISS DIMPLE: Why, it's Boss Plunkett, the politician!

GROUCHO: Ravelli, take Plunkett's hat.

CHICO: You take it, boss. It won't fit me.

PLUNKETT: Flywheel, my pal. Joe Crookley tells me that if it hadn't been for the way you defended him in court, he would have gone to prison for 20 years. He says you're a pretty smart lawyer.

GROUCHO (Coyly): Oh! I don't take his flattery seriously. That Joe Crookley is just a silly old cutthroat.

PLUNKETT: Listen, Flywheel, I want to talk turkey to you.

GROUCHO (Whispering): I think you'd better talk English. I don't want Ravelli to understand.

PLUNKETT: Look here, I'm against Judge Maxwell. If you join our party, I'll see to it that you get the nomination for judge.

GROUCHO: Plunkett, I'm willing to accept the nomination, but I can't join your party.

PLUNKETT: Why not?

GROUCHO: Frankly, I haven't a thing to wear.

Does Groucho get the nomination? Find out in Act II, page 262.

BIG NUMBERS: A TRILLION

Trillions are the numbers we use to express the national debt. But few of us have a sense of how big they are. Tim Gutmann, a New Hampshire mathematician, came up with a way of getting proper perspective. He asks: "Where were you one trillion seconds ago?"

His answer: "One trillion seconds is over thirty one thousand six hundred and eighty-eight years. That's 31,688 years. Lots and lots longer than recorded history; indeed, writing was developed in Sumeria only 252 billion (not trillion) seconds ago. Humans were around, but they hadn't been for long. Lucy (*Australopithecus afarensis*—the oldest known human descendent) walked the earth around 110 trillion seconds ago."

Napoleon Bonaparte, a Frenchman, designed the flag of Italy.

OOPS!

Everyone's amused by tales of outrageous blunders—probably because it's comforting to know that someone's screwing up even worse than we are. So here's an ego-building page from the BRI Go ahead and feel superior for a few minutes.

LEFT OUT

In 1994, Susan Leury was commissioned to create a 9-foot, 800-lb. bronze statue of native son Babe Ruth for the new baseball stadium in Baltimore. "During the many months of modeling...Leury met countless experts and aficionados. Details were researched and debated. Did the Babe wear his belt buckle on the left or right? Was his hat cocked to the side or worn straight? No fact was too small to escape scrutiny. Except one.

"The bronze Babe, unveiled at the northern Eutaw Street entrance of Oriole Park, is leaning on a bat and clutching on his hip a right-handed fielder's glove. The real Babe was a lefty."

—from *Parade* magazine, 1/1/96

BOMBS AWAY!

"In 1994, the *Northwest Herald* of Crystal Lake, Illinois, ran a story about the controversy surrounding the Smithsonian Insitution's exhibit of the Enola Gay, the B-29 Superfortress that dropped the atomic bomb on Hiroshima in 1945.

"Apparently, the crack journalist who wrote the headline either failed to read the story, or had forgotten how World War II ended.

"The headline read: 'Atomic Bombers Criticize Enola Homosexual Exhibit.' 'It was a stupid thing on deadline,' the editor said. 'I'm not discussing it anymore.'"

—from the San Francisco *Chronicle*, 10/23/94

ASHES TO ASHES

"In 1990 the Wilkinsons, a family in Sussex, England received what they thought was a gift package of herbs from Australian relatives. They stirred the contents into a traditional Christmas pudding, ate half of it and put the remainder in the refrigerator.

"Soon thereafter, a member of the family relates, 'We heard from

Auntie Sheila that Uncle Eric had died, and had we received his ashes for burial in Britain.'

"Shocked, the Wilkinsons quickly summoned a vicar to bless, and bury, Uncle Eric's leftovers."

—from the *Wall Street Journal*, 12/18/90

A STIFF DRINK

"Coca-Cola is fixing an embarrassing typo in the word 'disk' in copyright information on about 2 million 12-packs of the drink.

"In the misprint, the 's' is replaced by a 'c.' The error appeared on boxes of Olympic promotional packages of Coca-Cola Classic distributed in the Atlanta area.

"Normally, the small type under the copyright information states that the 'red disk icon and contour bottle are trademarks of the Coca-Cola Co.' 'Everybody recognizes that it was an innocent mistake,' said a company spokesman, who wouldn't say how the error occurred. 'It's obviously a misprint.' "

—from wire service stories, 7/96

OOPS—WRONG AIRPORT

"Edward Valiz and Jose Gonzales were headed for the tiny Turlock, California airport, but when they emerged from their rented plane, they discovered instead that they'd landed at Castle Air Force Base…in the middle of a training exercise.

"Base officials said they had tried to warn off the plane, but never got any radio response.

"The pair were arrested when drug-sniffing police dogs found two pounds of methamphetamine, along with $1,300 in cash."

—from the *San Francisco Examiner*, 1994

WHICH PARTS?

"People calling an 800-number for Sears, Roebuck and Co. listed in the local phone directory were offered, instead, the chance to listen to 'the kinkiest group orgy line in America.'

"Apparently, a phone company clerk mistyped the number. 'I was amazed and shocked at first,' said one caller. 'After a few seconds, it seemed pretty funny. I mean, what a message to get when you're trying to reach a parts department.' "

—from wire service stories, 8/96

FABULOUS FLOPS

*Some consumer products are popular the moment they hit
the market, while others never get off the ground.
Their only legacy is a few bathroom laughs.*

Cheese-Filtered Cigarettes. In 1963, a Wisconsin businessman looking for new ways to use local cheese had a brainstorm: If smoke can be used to flavor cheese, why can't
cheese be used to flavor smokes? According to the *Wall Street Journal*, Univ. of Wisconsin chemists found that Parmesan and Roma-
no were the best filter cheeses, using "a combination of one-third
charcoal and two-thirds cheese." The cigarette industry didn't bite.

Grubbies Sneakers. You've heard of pre-washed jeans. In 1966,
B.F. Goodrich came up with a similar idea: "pre-tattered" sneakers.
You didn't have to wait months for your sneakers to look beat-up.
With Grubbies, all you added was the foot odor.

Indoor Archery. In the early '60s, bowling was one of America's
hottest sports. Hoping to "do for archery what automatic pin-
setters have done for bowling," a number of entrepreneurs opened
"archery lanes," with automatic arrow-returns. They expected to
have thousands around the United States by 1970.

Look of Buttermilk/Touch of Buttermilk Shampoo. A 1970s
"health product." Were you supposed to eat it or wash with it? Did
you *want* to wash with it? Rubbing dairy products into their hair
didn't exactly conjure up images of cleanliness in the minds of most
consumers. "Touch of Yogurt Shampoo" also flopped.

Plastic Snow. Before snowmaking machines, how did ski resorts
keep people skiing during dry spells? In the mid-'60s, plastics
seemed like the answer. One resort spread tons of styrofoam pellets
on their ski runs; they quickly blew away. Another company offered mats with nylon bristles, like Astroturf, and New Jersey's
Great Gorge ski area laid them out on its slopes. They worked
well...unless you fell down. "The bristles were needle-sharp and
everybody tore his pants," founder Jack Kurlander told reporters,
"There was blood, blood, blood. Boy were we embarrassed!"

FLUBBED HEADLINES

These are 100% honest-to-goodness headlines.
Can you figure out what they were trying to say?

Man Robs, Then Kills Himself

KHRUSHCHEV IS BURIED IN ENCYCLOPEDIA

Carter Plans Swell Deficit

LIVING TOGETHER LINKED TO DIVORCE

MAYOR SAYS D.C. IS SAFE EXCEPT FOR MURDERS

Town Okays Animal Rule

Deer Kill 130,000

BOYS CAUSE AS MANY PREGNANCIES AS GIRLS

Prostitutes Appeal to Pope

DEADLINE PASSES FOR STRIKING POLICE

Stiff Opposition Expected to Casketless Funeral Plan

DRUNK GETS NINE MONTHS IN VIOLIN CASE

Bar Trying to Help Alcoholic Lawyers

Criminal Groups Infiltrating Pot Farms

Teenage Prostitution Problem Is Mounting

Delegate sex switch advocated

DEAD EXPECTED TO RISE

LEGALIZED OUTHOUSES AIRED BY LEGISLLATURE

Lot of Women Distressing

"Dead" Woman Doesn't Recall What Happened

Blind workers eye better wages

SUN SUED IN PUERTO RICO BY CONSERVATION TRUST

Milk Drinkers Turn to Powder

U.S., China Near Pact on Wider Ties

TWO CONVICTS EVADE NOOSE; JURY HUNG

MRS. COLLINS BURNED AT DUMP

Hospitals Are Sued by 7 Foot Doctors

Farmer Bill Dies In House

JUMPING BEAN PRICES AFFECT POOR

LAWMEN FROM MEXICO BARBEQUE GUESTS

Columnist gets urologist in trouble with his peers

Antique Stripper to Demonstrate Wares at Store

Strange stat: More boys than girls are born during the day; more girls are born at night.

THE BIRTH OF RAMBO

Who created Rambo? If you said Sylvester Stallone, you're wrong—it was a mild-mannered Canadian college professor teaching at the University of Iowa.

Young David Morrell could not tolerate conflict of any kind. Whenever violence appeared on TV, he had to leave the room. Until his early teens, even news reports panicked him; he was convinced someone would suddenly announce that a new war had begun. As he got older, Morrell found that writing was a way to get over some of his fears.

AN IDEA IS BORN

In 1969, while studying American literature at Penn State University, Morrell saw a TV news program that sparked his imagination and changed his life. The first report of the evening showed soldiers sweating out a battle in Vietnam. The second was about National Guardsmen dodging rocks, bottles, and bullets trying to put down urban riots.

If a viewer turned the sound off, he mused, it would seem that both film clips were a part of the same story. That gave him an idea for a tale in which the Vietnam war literally came home to America. He imagined a disaffected Vietnam veteran returning, disturbed and embittered by his Vietnam experiences, wandering aimlesssly around the backroads of the country.

THE PLOT THICKENS

Another news story provided further inspiration. "In a Southwestern American town," Morrell recalled, "a group of hitchhiking hippies had been picked up by the local police, stripped, hosed, and shaved. I wondered what my character's reaction would be if he were subjected to the insults those hippies had received."

Morrell decided his character would probably go nuts. He began writing a novel about a longhaired Vietnam vet who's driven over the edge when he's arrested and abused by a small-town Kentucky sheriff.

The naked truth: People in nudist colonies play volleyball more often than any other sport.

The character still didn't have a name. But that changed one afternoon when—an hour after Morrell had read a poem by Arthur Rimbaud (pronounced "Rambo") for his French class—his wife returned from the supermarket with a type of apple she'd never heard of before...the Rambo.

Morrell rushed to his typewriter and typed: "His name was Rambo, and he was just some nothing kid, for all anybody knew, standing by the pump of a gas station on the outskirts of Madison, Kentucky."

FIRST BLOOD

It took years to complete *First Blood*. Morrell finally finished it in 1971, while he was a professor at the University of Iowa. Although the book was intended to be an antiwar novel, it was extremely violent. By the end of the book, the Kentucky town is destroyed, the sherriff is killed along with 200 National Guardsmen, and Rambo is executed by his former instructor, who blows the top of his head off with a shotgun.

That summer Morrell sent the manuscript to a literary agent. He was so unsure of how people would react to it—Was it too bloody? Too violent?—that he included his Ph.D. dissertation in the package, too. That way, he figured, the agent would still have something respectable to sell if publishers hated the novel.

He needn't have worried. *First Blood* was sold in three weeks... and it was a huge success. *Time* magazine put it at the top of its book review page, observing that it was the first in a new genre of fiction—"carnography," the violence equivalent of pornography.

Columbia Pictures snapped up the movie rights for $90,000 and then sat on it for a year. They then sold it to another studio...which passed it on to someone else, and so on. Over the next ten years, 18 different screenplays based on *First Blood* were developed. Nearly every Hollywood tough guy—Clint Eastwood, Paul Newman, Robert De Niro, Nick Nolte, and even George C. Scott—was considered for the lead role and rejected.

"The novel became a Hollywood legend," Morrell says. "How could so much money and so much talent be expended on an enterprise that somehow could not get off the page?"

For Part II of the Rambo story, turn to page 250.

Vultures fly without flapping their wings.

NOT WHAT THEY SEEM TO BE

We take a lot of things for granted, based on image. But things (and people) often aren't what we think they are. Here are some examples.

AMERICAN GOTHIC

Image: Grant Wood's famous painting of an old Indiana couple posing in front of their farmhouse is considered the definitive portrait of the straitlaced Midwestern farmer.

Actually: They aren't farmers...or a couple. Wood's sister, Nan, was the model for the woman; a dentist friend named Byron McKeeby posed as the man. And the "farmhouse" in the picture was once used as a bordello.

WILLIAM ENO

Image: Considered the "Father of Traffic Safety." According to David Wallechinsky in *Significa*, he "originated stop signs, one-way streets, taxi stands, pedestrian safety islands, and traffic rotaries."

Actually: He never learned to drive. He thought cars were a passing fad. And he preferred horses anyway.

THE CHRISTMAS SONG

Image: A classic of the Christmas season. With lyrics like "Chestnuts roasting on an open fire...Jack Frost nipping at your nose," it evokes the feeling of a cold December perfectly.

Actually: It was written during a summer heat wave in Los Angeles. According to one account: "Mel Torme and his lyricist... wrote it in less than an hour, while consuming cold drinks at the piano and putting ice to their foreheads."

THE BEACH BOYS

Image: The Kings of California Surfing. Led by Brian Wilson, who wrote and sang hits like "Surfin' Safari" and "Surfin' USA," they started a national surfing craze in the early 1960s.

Actually: Brian Wilson (and three other Beach Boys) never surfed. "I didn't really know anything about surfing at all," he admitted in

1995. In fact, says Stephen Gaines in his Beach Boy biography:

> Although the Beach Boys had sold an estimated 80 million records—20 million of them with surfing as a major theme—and Brian had splashed around in the water with his brothers for publicity photos, he had never mounted a surfboard....Indeed, photographing Brian in the surf was almost a cruel joke, because Brian had a deep, abiding fear of the water, and in his childlike manner he would warble in a thin voice, "The ocean *scares* me!"

Actually, the only Beach Boy who ever surfed was Brian's brother Dennis, the group's drummer, who drowned in 1983.

AIR JORDANS

Image: The first "air-cushioned" sneakers.

Actually: Nike tried air, and it didn't work—it leaked through the "airbag" material. They had to replace it with a gas that has larger molecules than air.

THE WEEKLY READER

Image: A benign weekly newspaper for elementary school kids.

Actually: Not so benign. In October 1994, the magazine ran an article "that discussed smokers' rights and the harm done to the tobacco industry by smoking restrictions. The article said nothing about smoking as a cause of lung cancer and heart disease." It turned out that the *Weekly Reader*'s owners were also the largest shareholders in RJR Nabisco, makers of Camel cigarettes.

THE "BLACK BOX"

Image: Whenever an airplane goes down, the first thing investigators say they're looking for is the "black box" that contains a recording of all conversations in the cockpit.

Actually: It's a yellow box.

KARL MARX

Image: Enemy of American capitalism.

Actually: Years *after* he had become famous as the author of the *Communist Manifesto*, he gratefully accepted a job as the London correspondent of the New York *Tribune*. His reason: His anticapitalist political writing hadn't earned him enough to live on.

THE GREENING OF AMERICA

*Here's a fad you've probably never heard of—chlorophyll. Does it
sound silly? Well, think of all the things popular today
that are going to be just as laughable in 40 years.*

THE GREEN STUFF

In the 1930s, Dr. Benjamin Gruskin found a way to make chlorophyll—the green stuff in plants that turns sunlight into chemical energy—soluble in water. This discovery interested scientists but didn't appear to have much practical use.

That didn't bother O'Neill Ryan, Jr. and Henry T. Stanton, two ad executives. They decided to get into the chlorophyll business and patented Gruskin's process. Then, they tried to get manufacturers to use chlorophyll in products as a breath freshener and odor-killer—even though they had no proof (or reason to believe) it worked as either.

A GREENER AMERICA?

Somehow, in 1950, Ryan and Stanton managed to talk Pepsodent into coming out with a chlorophyll-based toothpaste called Chlorodent. Backed by Pepsodent's advertising muscle, it sold so well that other toothpaste companies rushed their own versions to market. By mid-1951, 30% of all toothpastes sold in the United States contained chlorophyll.

Other companies began adding chlorophyll to *their* products. By the end of 1952, stores were filled with chlorophyll soaps, cigarettes, dog foods, mothballs, toilet paper, diapers, shoe insoles, even popcorn. Chlorophyll beer, men's shorts, and Hebrew National chlorophyll-treated salami were in the works.

The End: In 1953, the American Dental Association and the FDA announced that chlorophyll did not cure bad breath—or any other odor. As the New York State Medical Society put it, "chlorophyll has certainly...swept the nation clean, not of odors, but of money." The public got the message. In less than a year, sales of chlorophyll-based products plunged from $120 million to $10 million—and most of them were pulled from the market.

STRANGE LAWSUITS

These days, it seems that people sue each other over practically anything. Here are a few real-life examples of unusual legal battles.

THE PLAINTIFF: Robert Lee Brock, an inmate at the Indian Creek Correctional Center in Chesapeake, Virginia
THE DEFENDANT: Robert Lee Brock, an inmate at the Indian Creek Correctional Center in Chesapeake, Virginia
THE LAWSUIT: Brock (serving 23 years for grand larceny) sued himself "for getting drunk and violating his civil rights." In a handwritten brief, he said: "I partook of alcoholic beverages in 1993. As a result I caused myself to violate my religious beliefs. This was done by my going out and getting arrested." Since Brock is imprisoned and can't work, he asked the state of Virginia to pay him and his family $5 million.
THE VERDICT: The judge acknowledged Brock's "innovative approach to civil rights litigation," then dismissed it as "ludicrous."

THE PLAINTIFF: Gloria Quinan, owner of Banner Travel in Santa Rosa, California
THE DEFENDANT: Pacific Bell
THE LAWSUIT: Pac Bell made a slight error when they listed Quinan's travel agency in their 1988 "Smart" Yellow Pages. Her ad was supposed to say she specialized in "exotic" travel; they changed it to "erotic" travel. Quinan's business dropped off by more than 50 percent, and most of the calls she *did* get were "from people genuinely interested in erotic services." Pac Bell said they wouldn't charge Quinan for the ad. She preferred to sue for $10 million.
THE VERDICT: Settled quietly out of court.

THE PLAINTIFF: Thomas Zarcone, food truck operator
THE DEFENDANT: William M. Perry, a Suffolk County, New York, judge
THE LAWSUIT: On April 30, 1975, Judge Perry was presiding over night court in Hauppage, New York. He sent a deputy sheriff

---

Not-so-mobile society: 50% of Americans live within 50 miles of their birthplace.

out to buy coffee from Zarcone, who ran a food truck outside the courthouse. Fifteen minutes later, the deputy sheriff returned with three police officers. "He told me that Judge Perry wanted to see me about the coffee, because it was terrible," Zarcone recounted. "I said, 'You must be joking.'" They weren't. At the judge's orders, they handcuffed him and hauled him into the courthouse while bystanders gawked. "People were saying, 'Look, they're locking up the frankfurter man,'" Zarcone told a reporter. He was taken to Perry's chambers, where the judge screamed that his coffee was "garbage" and insisted it had been watered down. Zarcone sued the state.

THE VERDICT: Zarcone was awarded an unspecified amount for damages. Perry was removed from the bench for lying to the appellate court about the incident.

THE PLAINTIFF: Bob Glaser, a San Diego attorney
THE DEFENDANT: City of San Diego
THE LAWSUIT: In 1995, Glaser attended a Billy Joel / Elton John concert. He had to pee, and while he was in the men's room, women started using it because the lines for the women's room were so long. Glaser, "angered when a woman used a urinal in front of him," sued for $5.4 million for "embarrassment and emotional trauma."
THE VERDICT: Still pending.

THE PLAINTIFF: Rhonda Cook
THE DEFENDANTS: Des Moines Chrysler-Plymouth and Fred Owens, an ex-employee
THE LAWSUIT: In 1995, Cook stopped at the Iowa car dealership to look at a new Chrysler Concorde. Salesman Fred Owens convinced her to climb into the trunk "to check out its spaciousness." Then he slammed the trunk shut and bounced the car a few times. Cook claimed emotional distress and false imprisonment, and sued for unspecified damages. She pointed out that the sales manager had previously offered $100 to anyone who could get a customer to climb in the trunk.
THE VERDICT: Still pending.

Mel Brooks fought in the Battle of the Bulge in World War II.

MISS AMERICA, PART I: The Origin

There she is...on TV, in the newspapers, on cereal boxes. It's Miss America. You may think of it as an institution, but for all its pomp and pretension today, the Miss America Pageant started off as just a crass little money-making gimmick. See for yourself. This story may surprise you.

SUMMER'S TALE

H. Conrad Eckholm was the owner of Atlantic City's Monticello Hotel in the 1920s. The hotel made a lot of money during the summer, but business always dropped off drastically after the Labor Day weekend.

Eckholm figured that a festival of some sort, held at the end of September, might keep families at the beach a week or two longer. He pitched the idea to the Atlantic City Business Men's League, and they agreed to sponsor the "Fall Frolic" of 1920, which featured a masquerade ball and a "Rolling Chair Parade."

PUBLICITY STUNT

The Frolic was a success; the Business Men's League decided to sponsor a second one in 1921. This time, however, an Atlantic City newspaperman named Harry Finley suggested adding a new event to the schedule: a "popularity contest" for young women.

His idea was to have several Northeastern newspapers select young women to represent their cities. They'd be picked from photographs sent in by readers, and would compete against each other in Atlantic City to see who was the most popular of all.

Everyone would benefit from the contest: the newspapers would sell more papers, and Atlantic City hoteliers would get free publicity...which would draw paying customers to the boardwalk. So the Atlantic City Chamber of Commerce and the Hotelmen's Association got behind it. They agreed to add the event to the 1921 Fall Frolic.

CHOOSING A NAME

What would the popularity contest be called? At the first organizing committee meeting in 1921, someone suggested "Miss Ameri-

---

Future shock: 72% of Americans believe in heaven; 12% say they don't.

ca." But the rest of the committee thought that sounded weak. They insisted on "The Most Beautiful Bathing Beauty in America" instead. (Winning contestants did assume the title "Miss America" as early as 1925, but the pageant itself didn't officially take the name until 1941.)

JUST IN CASE

Perhaps to guarantee that at least some genuine beauties would show up, organizers divided the Beauty category into two groups. The "professional" division was open to "actresses, motion picture players, or professional swimmers"; the "amateur" division was composed of the newspaper nominees and any other nonprofessionals who wanted to enter.

The winners from each category would face off against one another for the grand prize, a mermaid statue "valued at $5,000"…but actually only worth about $50.

THE FIRST PAGEANT

No one remembers how many "professionals" competed that first year, but Miss America Pageant records show that newspapers from only eight cities—Atlantic City, Camden (NJ), Newark, Ocean City (NJ), Harrisburg (PA), Pittsburgh, Philadelphia, and Washington, D.C.—nominated contestants.

Of these, only seven actually competed for the title: Miss Atlantic City, citing a potentially unfair hometown advantage, dropped out of the competition and assumed the role of hostess. For the next 40 years—until the "Miss Atlantic City" contest was abolished in 1960—Miss Atlantic City hosted the Miss America Pageant, but did not actually compete.

LITTLE MISS WASHINGTON

One of the unintended consequences of letting *anyone* nominate a candidate for the newspaper competition was that some of the young ladies chosen didn't even know about the contest.

Margaret Gorman, a 15-year-old schoolgirl from Washington D.C., was playing marbles in the dirt with some friends when some reporters from the Washington *Herald* tracked her down and told her she'd just won the Miss Washington D.C. pageant.

Her parents had never heard of it and were a little apprehensive—but they weren't about to pass up a free trip to Atlantic City. They agreed to play along. The decision was a good one: Gorman won the amateur division and went on to beat Virginia Lee, winner of the professional division, for the bathing-beauty crown. She became the very first Miss America.

A GOLDMINE

With its eight contestants and $27,000 budget, the 1921 pageant was extremely modest by today's standards. Even so, an estimated 90,000 to 100,000 people turned out to see it, making it a huge success. It was just a swimsuit contest, not a polished TV ceremony draped in patriotism like today's pageants, but that didn't matter. What counted most was that it made money for Atlantic City merchants. As A. R. Riverol writes in *Live from Atlantic City: The History of the Miss America Pageant Before, After and in Spite of Television,*

> The pageant's original aim was not to promote pageantry, beauty, scholarship, or any other such lofty ideal. Its creation was to make money, a point that many aficionados still feel uncomfortable admitting. That the pageant provided a variety of events, diversions, and entertainment was a peripheral amenity to the organizer's aims—business and self-promotion.

"We brought people here by the thousands," Mayor Edward Bader observed dryly, "and if they wished to purchase anything, the merchants profited."

Not what you expected? That's just the beginning.
For part II of the Miss America story, turn to page 112.

*　　　*　　　*　　　*

RANDOM THOUGHT

"When I go to the beauty parlor, I always use the emergency entrance. Sometimes I just go for an estimate."

—*Phyllis Diller*

Phone survey: 61% of Americans like to hear music when put on hold; 22% prefer silence.

IS IT REALLY 2000?

On Dec. 31, 1999, we'll be getting ready to celebrate a new millennium ...or maybe expecting the end of the world. But according to this piece from The Bathroom Reader's Guide to the Year 2000, *it's all a mistake.*

A NEW BEGINNING

Prior to the 6th century, the European calendar was based on the years counted from the founding of Rome or A.U.C. (Anno Urbis Conditae—"the year of the founding of the city.")
• In 1288 A.U.C. (534 A.D.), a Ukrainian monk named Dionysius Exiguus decided that the Christian calendar ought to be based on Jesus' birth. Under the patronage of Pope John I, he set out to try to figure exactly when Jesus had been born.
• It was a near-impossible task: the date of Jesus' birth isn't mentioned anywhere in the Bible. Still, working from vague gospel accounts, official Roman records, and astrological charts, Dionysius eventually settled on 754 A.U.C. as Christ's birthday. He called it 1 A.D. (for Anno Domini, or the Year of the Lord).

IT ISN'T 2000

"Unfortunately, Dionysius Exiguus was wrong in his calculations," writes Isaac Asimov in *The March of the Millennia.*
• The proof is found in the New Testament, where it clearly states that King Herod was ruler of Judea at the time Jesus was born. Since Herod's death is firmly dated at 4 B.C., Jesus must have been born about then. (Some argue it may have been as early as 12 B.C.)
• "If we were really counting from the birth of Jesus, the year we call 2000 is really somewhere between 2004 and 2020, and the actual year of A.D. 2000 may already have passed," writes Asimov.

IT ISN'T THE MILLENNIUM

• Dionysius' decision to began his new calendar with year 1, instead of the year 0, meant that by the beginning of year 2 A.D., only one year had elapsed; by 10 A.D., only nine years had passed; and by 100 A.D., only 99 years had been completed.
• Extend this logic to the present day and you realize by the year 2000, only 1999 years will have elapsed. So it's the first day of the year 2001, not of 2000, that starts the next millennium.

It takes six months to build a Rolls Royce...and 13 hours to build a Toyota.

SEEDLESS FRUIT

In most cases, if there are no seeds, there is no fruit. Over time, however, several types of fruit that are good for eating have been found or created without pesky seeds inside. This piece is by Prof. David Sugar (no kidding!).

SEEDLESS WATERMELONS

The Seedless watermelon is not truly seedless—the seeds are so underdeveloped that they can be eaten while barely being noticed. It was developed by selecting watermelon strains in which the seeds matured much later than the flesh. So when the flesh is ripe for eating, the seeds still have a long way to go.

Where do seeds for planting seedless watermelon come from? When grown in parts of the world with very long, hot growing seasons, the seeds will finally mature. By that time, the flesh has deteriorated and is no longer good to eat.

SEEDLESS GRAPES

This is probably the best-known seedless fruit, especially the Thompson Seedless. In seedless grape varieties, the seed begins to form (which stimulates the grape berry's growth), but it stops developing while still very small, and becomes insignificant to the eater.

When grape seeds do develop, they produce hormones that stimulate the fruit and make it larger. So some seedless grape growers spray on a synthetic version of that hormone when the grapes are growing...to get those really big seedless grapes.

Making new seedless grape plants doesn't require seeds—pieces of grapevine cut in the winter will make new vines after rooting in moist soil.

SEEDLESS PEARS AND APPLES

Normally, apples and pears must have seeds. Each apple or pear has the capacity to develop 10 seeds, and needs at least one for the fruit to grow. However, a good load of seeds helps the fruit to become large and have a normal shape. An apple or pear with only one or two seeds may be misshapen—since the fruit grows more in the area near the seed than in other parts of the fruit.

Bathroom delight: Americans bought $25 billion worth of books in 1995.

But warm temperatures during flowering can sometimes overcome the need for seeds. For example, the Bartlett pear grown in Oregon and Washington generally needs seeds for fruit to form. In the warmer spring weather of California, on the other hand, Bartlett pears often grow without seeds. This is called "parthenocarpy" or "virgin fruit" (the Parthenon in Greece is the temple of virgins).

SEEDLESS "STONE" FRUITS

The "stone" fruits—peaches, nectarines, plums, apricots, cherries, and almonds—all have a single seed. While an occasional fruit may be found in which the seed did not fully develop, this type of fruit will usually fall off the tree if it doesn't have a seed inside.

By the way: you may be surprised to see almonds on this list of fruits. Actually, an almond tree is very much like a peach tree... except that in the almond, the *seed* grows large; the fleshy "fruit" part dries up and usually splits open before harvest.

☞　☞　☞　☞

NAME THAT YEAR

How do you pronounce "2001"? Thanks to Stanley Kubrick's film *2001: A Space Odyssey*, most people think of it as "Two Thousand and One."

That's no accident. Fred Ordway, who advised Kubrick on the film, recalls: "Stanley asked me if we should say 'two thousand and one' or 'twenty-oh-one.' And we decided that 'two thousand and one' sounded better." He adds: "We often wondered...whether [the film's title] would have an influence on the English language when we got into the 21st century."

It did. But William Safire, who writes a weekly column called "On Language" for the *New York Times*, opts for "twenty-oh-one." Safire explains: " 'Two thousand and one' may sound mysterious and futuristic today but by the time we get there, it will be a laborious mouth filler."

Apparently, Safire is in the minority. A poll conducted by the *Futurist* in 1993 showed that 62% of people surveyed favored "two thousand one," 18% preferred "two thousand and one," and only 10% approved of Safire's choice of "twenty-oh-one."

Chopsticks are known as "quick little fellows" in China.

OLYMPIC CHEATERS

Some people become famous at the Olympic games because they win a medal. Others become infamous because they don't play by the rules. Here's a look at the BRI's Olympic Hall of Shame.

ROMAN EMPEROR NERO
Year: 67 A.D.
Place: Olympia
What happened: Nero decided to compete in the chariot race. In the middle of the event, however, he fell off his chariot and was left behind in the dirt. He never completed the course.
Reaction: The Olympic judges, "under extreme pressure," declared him the winner anyway.

SPRIDON BELOKAS, Greek marathon runner
Year: 1896
Place: Athens, Greece (the first modern-day Olympics)
What happened: These Olympics were a matter of national pride for Greeks. So Belokas became a national hero when he won the bronze medal. But shortly after the games ended, he admitted "hitching a ride in a horse-drawn carriage" during the race.
Reaction: He was stripped of his medal and running shirt, and became a national disgrace overnight.

MEMBERS OF THE EAST GERMAN LUGE TEAM
Year: 1968
Place: Grenoble, France (Winter Games)
What happened: The East Germans placed first, second, and fourth in the luge competition. Then Olympic officials discovered that they'd "used a chemical to heat the runners of their toboggans to increase speed."
Reaction: They were disqualified and forfeited their medals. But the East German team never admitted guilt, blaming the incident on a "capitalist plot."

Most, if not all, polar bears are left-handed.

JOHN CARPENTER, American runner, 400-meter finals
Year: 1908
Place: London
What happened: Scottish champ Wyndham Halswelle, the fastest
qualifier and the person favored to win, was rounding the final
bend neck-and-neck with three U.S. runners when one of them—
Carpenter—shoved him sideways. John Taylor, another of the
Americans, "won" the race, but not before a British official broke
the tape and declared "no race."
Reaction: Carpenter was disqualified; Halswelle and the other two
American finalists were invited to re-run the race two days later,
"this time in lanes separated by strings." The Americans refused.
Halswelle re-ran the race alone and won the gold medal automati-
cally, the only person ever to win the gold in a "walkover."

**FRENCH OLYMPIC AUTHORITIES AND THE
FINNISH OLYMPIC COMMITTEE**
Year: 1924
Place: Paris
What happened: Finland's Paavo Nurmi was the world champion
long-distance runner. But for some reason, French officials didn't
want Nurmi to sweep the gold medals in the 1500-, 5000-, and
10,000-meter events. So they scheduled the 5000-meter final just
55 minutes after the 1500-meter final, hoping Nurmi would be too
tired to win the second race. Then Finnish officials arbitrarily
dropped Nurmi from the 10,000-meter race so Ville Ritola, Finland's second-best runner, would have a shot at a gold medal.
Reaction: Nurmi was furious, but there was nothing he could do
about it. He ran the 1500-meter event...and won in record time.
Then, less than an hour later, he ran the 5000 meter...and won
that in record time. Finally, according to legend, "as Ritola won the
10,000 meters by half a lap in world record time, Nurmi ran a lone
10,000 meters *outside* the stadium and beat Ritola's time."

☆　　☆　　☆　　☆

RANDOM THOUGHT: "It's strange that men should take up
crime when there are so many legal ways to be dishonest."

On some Caribbean islands, the oysters can climb trees.

IN ONLY 66 YEARS...

This comparison of the Wright brothers' first flight and that of Apollo 11, only 66 years apart, was supplied to Uncle John by NASA back in 1980. Uncle John recently found it among some old research papers, and immediately took it to the bathroom. It's a fascinating reminder of how fast things have changed.

WRIGHT BROTHERS		APOLLO 11
December 17, 1903	**Date**	July 16-24, 1969
Kitty Hawk, NC	**Place**	Cape Kennedy, FL; moon; Pacific Ocean
Less than $1,000 (including spare parts and round-trip rail tickets)	**Cost**	$355 million (Office of Manned Space Flight), or $375 million (Manned Spacecraft Center)
12 seconds	**Duration**	195 hours, 19 minutes, 35 seconds
15 feet	**Altitude**	242,000 statute miles (210,000 nautical miles)
120 feet	**Distance**	952,700 miles, 363 feet
3 pounds, 3 ounces	**Fuel Weight**	6.6 million pounds
Gasoline	**Fuel**	Liquid oxygen, liquid hydrogen, and kerosene
12 horsepower	**Power**	192,000,000 horsepower (7,600,000 pounds of thrust)
605 pounds	**Craft Weight**	6.4 million pounds
10 feet/second (31 mph)	**Speed**	35,000 feet/second
5	**Witnesses**	500,000,000 (est.)

The Wright brothers made four flights on December 17, 1903; the first was the shortest.

WRIGHT ON

Existential wisdom from comedian Steven Wright.

"Right now, I'm having amnesia and déjà vu at the same time. I think I've forgotten this before."

"I put tape on the mirrors in my house so I don't accidentally walk through into another dimension."

"A friend of mine once sent me a postcard with a picture of the entire planet Earth taken from outer space. On the back it said, 'Wish you were here.' "

"If you were going to shoot a mime, would you use a silencer?"

"I have the world's largest collection of seashells. I keep it on the beaches of the world. Perhaps you've seen it."

"I was cesarean-born. You really can't tell, although whenever I leave a house, I go out through a window."

"I locked my keys in the car the other day. But it was all right. I was still inside."

"I had amnesia once or twice."

"I have an existential map. It has 'you are here' written all over it."

"I'm writing a book. I've got the page numbers done, so now I just have to fill up the rest."

"If toast always lands butter side down, and cats always land on their feet, what happens if you strap toast on the back of a cat and drop it?"

"I walked into a restaurant. The sign said 'Breakfast Served—Any Time.' I ordered French toast…during the Renaissance."

"I like to reminisce with people I don't know. Granted, it takes longer."

"Cross-country skiing is great if you live in a small country."

"I used to work in a fire hydrant factory. You couldn't park anywhere near the place."

"I eat Swiss cheese, but I only nibble on it. I make the holes bigger."

Something's cooking: More than 10 million Easy-Bake Ovens have been sold since 1964.

FOOD QUESTIONS:
HOW DO THEY DO THAT?

The New York Times is famous for tackling important issues. Here's an excerpt from a NYT article proving the paper's focused on the things that really matter. It's "for those who contemplate not the state of the nation, but rather the status of their meal."

Why don't Cheerios sink?
"Cheerio dough is forced through a die that turns it into a long, pasta-like tube. The tube is then sliced and thrown into a pressure chamber that puffs up the pieces. The air gives them their buoyancy. 'It's kind of like an inner tube but it's not hollow,' said Kathryn Newton, General Foods' spokesperson. Because the cereal is firm-textured, it doesn't absorb milk quickly."

Who weaves Triscuits?
"Nabisco makes its Triscuits in much the same way it makes its shredded wheat. Wheat is slightly softened with water and steam so that it can go through a shredder and come out looking like 'fine spaghetti', according to a company spokesperson, Caroline Fee. For shredded wheat, the strands are piled up, all strands running in the same direction, and then put through a cutter that forms the biscuits. To make Triscuits, the wheat is piled first in one direction and then in another. 'They're not woven,' Fee says firmly."

How do they put the orange ice on a Creamsicle?
"The next time you look at a Creamsicle frozen pop, think 'suction evacuation'. To make them, Popsicle Industries pours an orange-flavored mix into a mold, which is then immersed in a very cold solution. The pop freezes from the outside in. 'Before the whole piece freezes, the inside is sucked out and the cavity is filled with ice cream,' said Paul Kadin, vice president of marketing."

How do they get pimentos into stuffed olives?
"Until 15 years ago, olives were stuffed with pimentos by hand. 'It used to be a tedious and very exacting job that was assigned to women because of their smaller hands,' said Joseph Perez,

---

Celebrated dropout: Mark Twain didn't even make it through elementary school.

purchasing director for Goya Foods. Now, a pin resembling a Phillips screwdriver is inserted at one end of the olive to force out the pit. "Pimentos that have been molded into a long sheet are cut into slivers and pushed by machine into the olives, at a rate of 1,500 a minute."

How do they get the pits put of prunes?

"A rubber cup holds the prune steady while a needle the size of a cigarette pushes out the pit. The cup design keeps the prune flesh from being pushed out with the pit," according to Harold Jackson, president of Sunsweet Growers Inc.

How do they get that perfect little "M" on M&Ms?

"M&M-Mars makes more than a hundred million M&Ms every day, but no outsiders are allowed to watch the process. 'That is one part that we do not show,' said Hans Fiuczynski, a company spokesman....But he compares the process to offset printing. 'Just imagine the individual M&Ms coming down in many lanes and running through the offset printing roll,' he says. 'It is a very gentle imprint.'

The printing roll normally contains only Ms, but on certain holidays it is filled with bunnies, chicks, and trees. "The challenge is to imprint it at high speed but to get 99 percent accuracy," Fiuczynski said. "No one is proofreading it."

How do they make chocolate-covered cherries?

"The process...seems to come straight from a home chemistry set. At Russell Stover Candies Inc. in Kansas City, Missouri, maraschino cherries are coated with a fondant mixture made of sugar, water, and Convertit, an enzyme that makes sugar molecules break down. When the fondant hardens, the cherry is dipped in chocolate. But over the next six to eight hours, the Convertit makes the sugar crystals disintegrate and become liquid again.

Tom Ward, the company's vice president, said Russell Stover makes 15.6 million chocolate-covered cherries a year, all by hand. Apparently, the candies are not as innocent as they look...Ward said they should not be taken in planes or driven up through the Rocky Mountains and then down again, because they will 'expand, contract and blow up.' "

Tsunamis travel as fast as jet planes.

GOOD NEWS FOR HITLER

*After William Randolph Hearst, America's most powerful newspaper
publisher, visited a German spa, he had new respect for Hitler.
Was there gold in the waters? Here's a piece from It's a
Conspiracy!, by the National Insecurity Council.*

In September 1934, William Randolph Hearst went to the world-
famous spa at Bad Nauheim to "take the waters." The Nazi government welcomed him. After a month of socializing with prominent Germans, Hearst was invited to meet the new chancellor,
Adolph Hitler. According to German newspapers, "Hearst was
charmed and converted by the Nazi leader."

The German newspaper may have been right. When he returned
to the United States, Hearst completely changed the editorial policy
of his 19 daily newspapers and began praising the Nazi regime. For
example, a September 1934 editorial signed by Hearst began:

> Hitler is enormously unpopular outside of Germany and enor-
> mously popular in Germany. This is not difficult to understand.
> Hitler restored character and courage. Hitler gave hope and
> confidence. He established order and utility of purpose....And
> the Germans love him for that. They regard him as a savior.

Was Hearst offering his praise for free, or was he paid?

SUSPICIOUS FACTS

As George Seldes reported in *Even the Gods Can't Change History:*
• Hearst's change in editorial policy came less than a month after
the Nazi Ministry of Propaganda first subscribed to his International
News Service (INS), a wire service that Hearst had created to compete against AP and UPI. INS was considered by journalists to be,
by far, the worst of the three services.
• Even so, the Nazis paid Hearst more than $400,000 a year for
their subsciption to INS, at a time when other customers were only
paying $50,000 to $70,000 for the same service. (The Nazis paid
only $40,000 for their subscription to AP.)
• Hitler appears to have gotten what he paid for. According to legal

papers filed in a lawsuit involving Hearst in the 1930s, "Promptly after the visit with Adolph Hitler and the making of... arrangements for furnishing INS material to Germany...William Randolph Hearst instructed all Hearst press correspondents in Germany, including those of INS, to report happenings in Germany only in a 'friendly' manner. All of such correspondents reporting happenings in Germany accurately and without friendliness, sympathy and bias for the actions of the then German government, were transferred elsewhere, discharged, or forced to resign."

• Week after week, Hearst papers ran pieces sympathetic to the Nazis. One article, which justified German rearmament to the American people, was written by Hitler's Minister of Aviation, Hermann Goering.

WAS IT A CONSPIRACY?

Was Hitler's payment a bribe to get Hearst to print pro-Nazi propaganda? The U.S. ambassador to Germany, William E. Dodd, thought so:

• According to Dodd, who was ambassador to Germany from 1933 to 1937, Hitler sent two of his chief propagandists to meet with Hearst at Bad Nauheim, to see how his image could be polished. When they found Hearst receptive, they set up a meeting and cut the deal.

• When Dodd found out about the arrangement, he "did not hesitate to tell the president that this was not a legitimate business deal; it was buying political support."

• Dodd noted that Hearst newspapers also began praising Italian dictator Mussolini after "Giannini, president of the Bank of America, had loaned Hearst some millions of dollars." Giannini was an avid Mussolini supporter.

• George Seldes wrote that in the 1940s, Hearst's deals with the two dictators were widely rumored in the industry, but he was so powerful that "of the 1,730 daily newspapers" Hearst *didn't* own, "not 1 percent ever said a word about the situation."

• Hearst, untouched by the scandal, continued to smear the patriotism of "socialists, liberals and other un-Americans" until the day he died. Ironically, no one seemed to question his motives.

George Washington and Abraham Lincoln were both descended from England's King Edward I.

BEHIND THE TITLE

*What does it take to come up with just the right book title? Here are a few
stories about famous titles that might give you an idea. For more of the
same, read* Now All We Need Is a Title, *by André Bernard.*

JAWS, by Peter Benchley

Benchley, a first-time author, struggled for months to come up
with a title for his book about a man-eating shark. He tried hundreds—from *The Shark* and *Great White* to *A Silence in the Water*.
His father, writer Nathaniel Benchley, suggested *What's That Nosh-
in' on My Laig?* Finally, Benchley's editor said the only *word* he
liked in any of the titles was "jaws." By then, Benchley didn't even
care anymore: "Nobody reads first novels anyway," he said.

CATCH-22, by Joseph Heller

In 1961, Simon & Schuster was all set to publish Heller's first novel
as *Catch-18*. Then another publisher protested that it was too similar to Leon Uris's new book, *Mila-18*—which they were about to release. Uris (who wrote *Exodus*) was a big name, Joseph Heller was
an unknown. Simon & Schuster gave in and changed the title.
Ironically, the phrase *Catch-22* has become part of the English language, and is arguably America's most famous modern book title.

BONFIRE OF THE VANITIES, by Tom Wolfe

During the 15th century, a monk named Savonarola inspired resi-
dents of Florence, Italy, to build a bonfire and burn all their worldly
possessions—their vanities. After two such fires were built, the citizens built a third—this one for Savonarola. Tom Wolfe came upon
the story during a trip to Italy. The idea of a bonfire for destroying
one's "vanities" intrigued him.

SEX AND THE SINGLE GIRL, by Helen Gurley Brown

Cosmopolitan editor Helen Gurley Brown wanted to "write a book
about sex being okay for single women." Her original title, *Sex for
the Single Girl*, was considered immoral; she didn't want readers to
think she was *promoting* sex after all. By changing one three-letter
word, the title became morally acceptable. The book was a huge
bestseller and helped create the "sexual revolution of the 1960s."

Gas guzzlers: 76% of U.S. commuters drive to work alone.

THE POSTMAN ALWAYS RINGS TWICE, by James M. Cain

Cain has given two different versions. He's said that while he was working on the manuscript, the mailman would ring the bell twice when delivering bills, once for personal letters. He's also said that the mailman would ring twice when delivering rejection letters from publishers. (On the day Alfred Knopf decided to publish the novel, the postman only rang once.) Cain named the novel as a memorial to his early failures.

A MOVEABLE FEAST, by Ernest Hemingway

Hemingway spent over 30 years writing this memoir about his life as a struggling writer in Paris. He died before it was published, and still hadn't come up with a satisfactory title (rejects: *The Paris Nobody Knows*; *To Write It Truly*). Finally, Hemingway's widow thought of a letter he'd written a decade earlier: "If you are lucky enough to have lived in Paris as a young man," he wrote, "then wherever you go for the rest of your life, it stays with you, for Paris is a moveable feast."

THE MALTESE FALCON, by Dashiell Hammett

Hammett had this title before he had written the book. But his publisher, Alfred Knopf, tried to talk him out of it. "Whenever people can't pronounce a title or an author's name," he said, "they are…too shy to go into a bookstore and try." The word Knopf objected to? *Falcon.* Hammett stuck to his guns, and the title is a part of American pop culture.

CAT ON A HOT TIN ROOF, by Tennessee Williams

Williams created the character of Brick in a short story called "Three Players of a Summer Game." Later, he turned the story into a play, adding Brick's wife—Maggie the Cat. That reminded him of something his father always used to say: 'Edwina, you're making me as nervous as a cat on a hot tin roof!' "

WHO'S AFRAID OF VIRGINIA WOOLF?, by Edward Albee

Albee found the phrase scrawled on a mirror in a Greenwich Village bar.

When he didn't wear a pocketwatch, George Washington used a small sundial to tell the time.

MARILYN'S SECRETS

*Marilyn Monroe's life has been examined and re-examined so often,
you may feel there's nothing you don't know about her...but thanks
to the diligence of BRI member Jack Mingo, we're able to
bring some interesting little-known facts to light.*

H er mother was a film-negative cutter in Hollywood. Her father could have been any of several men her mother was sleeping with at the time, but later in life Marilyn Monroe convinced herself that Clark Gable was her biological father.

• Two weeks after her birth, she was placed with a religious foster family that taught her that going to movies was a sin.

• Her closest playmate was a stray dog she adopted. Just after her seventh birthday, a neighbor killed him with a shotgun. That same day, her mother suddenly appeared and took her back.

• Still working as a film cutter, her mom used movie houses as a form of day care, knowing her daughter would stay cool and safe while she worked. The devout seven-year-old spent hours praying that her shockingly amoral mother wouldn't be condemned to hell.

• When Monroe was 10, her mother was committed to a mental institution. She went to live with an aunt, who dyed young Marilyn's hair platinum blonde and bought her only white clothes.

• As a child, she vowed she would never get married. She was going to become a schoolteacher and have lots of dogs, instead.

• She quit high school at 16 to marry a 21-year-old. She took a job spraying varnish on fabric for airplanes, but soon became a model. Her agent said she was "too plump" and "smiled too high on her face," but two years later she had appeared on 33 magazine covers.

• As a young adult, she spent her small income on acting classes and rent. She filled the gaps by providing quick in-car sex in exchange for restaurant meals, and began getting movie parts by sleeping with movie executives.

• Monroe's beauty wasn't all natural. Her hairline was heightened by electrolysis, her teeth were bleached, and an overbite was corrected. A plastic surgeon removed a lump of cartilage from the tip of her nose and inserted a crescent-shaped silicone implant into her jaw to give it a softer line.

PRIMETIME PROVERBS

Television wisdom from the book Primetime Proverbs, *compiled by Jack Mingo and John Javna.*

ON AMERICA
"You know what makes this country great? You don't have to be witty or clever, as long as you can hire someone who is."
—Ted Baxter,
The Mary Tyler Moore Show

"There's about three great moments in a man's life: when he buys a house, and a car, and a new color TV. That's what America is all about."
—Archie Bunker,
All in the Family

ON ARTISTS
"Artists are always ready to sacrifice for art—if the price is right."
—Gomez Addams,
The Addams Family

ON TELEVISION
"This show is ridiculous. I can't recommend this to children. I couldn't even recommend it to a Marine. Parents, you should be ashamed to let your children watch this show. Let 'em read a book, go out and play, watch the fruit ripen. Anything but this."
—Dick Loudon,
Newhart

ON EMPLOYEES
"Nobody has ever stood up to me the way you did. I find you bold, forceful, a man of conviction—three qualities I *despise* in an employee."
—Mr. Wainwright III,
Too Close for Comfort

ON WINNING
"As my Great Aunt Maude always said, 'If you can't win the game, the next best thing is to upset the chessboard.'"
—Artemus Gordon,
The Wild, Wild West

Jane Hathaway: "Chief, haven't you ever heard of the saying, 'It's not whether you win or lose, it's how you play the game'?"
Mr. Drysdale: "Yes, I've heard it. And I consider it one of the most ridiculous statements ever made."
—*The Beverly Hillbillies*

"There's nothing to winning, really. That is, if you happen to be blessed with a keen eye, an agile mind, and no scruples whatsoever."
—Alfred Hitchcock,
Alfred Hitchcock Presents

Armadillos can get leprosy.

FAMILIAR PHRASES

Here are the origins of some everyday phrases.

H IGHTAIL IT
Meaning: Leave quickly.
Origin: Dates back to the Old West. Cowboys on the Great Plains noticed that wild horses jerked their tails very high just before galloping off. Soon anyone who left quickly was said to have "hightailed it."

RED HERRING

Meaning: Distraction; diversionary tactic.

Origin: Comes from hunting. When herring is smoked, it changes from silvery gray to brownish red and gives off a strong smell. Hunters use red herrings to train dogs to follow a scent…and, by dragging a red herring across the trail, they can also throw a dog *off* a scent.

STUFFED SHIRT

Meaning: Braggart or pompous person.

Origin: In the days before mannequins, clothing shops displayed shirts in their windows by stuffing them with tissue paper or rags. The shirt looked broad-chested, like a strong man, but was really light and flimsy.

RIGHT-HAND MAN

Meaning: Important assistant.

Origin: In 17th-century cavalries, the soldier at the far right of a line of troops had a position of special responsibility or command.

AT THE DROP OF A HAT

Meaning: Quickly; without delay.

Origin: The term dates back to the days when races, prizefights, and other sporting events were literally started with the wave or the drop of a hat.

The average American female will have 3.3 pregnancies in her lifetime.

WIENERS ON WHEELS

Here's a BRI inside look at the Oscar Mayer Wienermobile,
perhaps the most popular pop-culture icon on four wheels.

THE EVOLUTION OF THE WIENERMOBILE

In the beginning, there was the "Weiner Wagon," a horse-drawn cart that the Oscar Mayer Company sent to Chicago-area butcher shops to promote its products. A German band rode on the back, oom-pahing for crowds wherever the wagon stopped.

Modern thinking. In the mid-1920s, Oscar's nephew, Charlie, joined the company right out of college. He came up with the idea of hiring a midget to dress up in a chef's uniform and make appearances with the band. Dubbed "Little Oscar, the world's smallest chef," the midget sang, plugged Oscar Mayer products, and gave away prizes at each stop.

Rolling along. In the 1930s, there was a nationwide craze for vehicles in the shape of products. There were milk bottle-mobiles, vacuum cleaner-mobiles, cheese-mobiles, and so on. Mayer's nephew decided to create a special vehicle for Little Oscar. He paid the General Body Company of Chicago $5,000 to convert an old car into a 13-foot, open-cockpit hot dog—the first "Wienermobile." It rolled off the assembly line in 1936.

Wieners everywhere. Putting the world's smallest chef behind the wheel of the World's Largest Wiener, as Oscar Mayer called it, generated plenty of publicity. In fact, it was such a good promotional gimmick that by the 1940s the company had an entire fleet of Wienermobiles. Every time they opened a new meat-packing plant, they commissioned a new Wienermobile to go with it. The vehicles were on the road continuously from 1936 to 1977, stopping only during World War II gasoline rationing.

Dead dog. By the mid-1970s, it looked like the Wienermobile's days were running out. Oscar Mayer wanted to move away from its regional meat plant promotions toward nationwide TV advertising campaigns...and who knows, maybe it thought the dogs-on-wheels

According to Oscar Mayer, the 1995 Wienermobile is 55 hot dogs long and 25 hot dogs high,

were getting too dorky. So, in 1977, the entire wienie fleet was put up on blocks.

On a roll. The giant wieners might have stayed there forever. But in 1986, the company decided to commemorate the 50th anniversary of the original Wienermobile. As Wienermobile manager Russ Whitacre explains, "We brought the last working one out of storage and put it on the road, driven by two college students for the summer. We got a great deal of response…a lot of nostalgia. Boomers said it was a piece of their lives." When thousands of fans wrote to Oscar Mayer about the vehicles, company officials decided they had something worth preserving, and ordered a brand-new fleet of six to be built. They hit the road in 1988.

LAMBORWIENIE

The pre-1980s Wienermobiles had been pretty spartan as sausages go, but the 1988 models were genuine Wienerbagos, complete with microwave ovens, refrigerators, CB radios, cellular phones, and stereo systems capable of belting out 21 different renditions of the Oscar Mayer Wiener song, including country, rap, and rock 'n' roll versions. Even the car's exhaust system was improved—in addition to ordinary automobile fumes, the Wienermobiles give off a "fondly familiar hot dog scent" during appearances.

The car's V6 engine has a top speed of 110 mph. But the only person known to have driven the car that fast was Al Unser Jr., who took one of the wienies for a spin at the Indianapolis Motor Speedway. Oscar Mayer hotdoggers (the company's name for Wienerdog drivers) are pretty much stuck driving at the legal speed limit. As Whitacre explains, "Because of the vehicle's visibility, we hear about it if someone drives a Wienermobile in an unsafe manner."

WIENERMOBILE 2000

By 1994, the new Wienermobiles had logged an average of 200,000 miles apiece on American highways and byways, so Oscar Mayer hired California auto designer Harry Bradley—creator of the original Mattel Hot Wheels—to design a Wienermobile for the 21st century. Among his improvements: He extended the wienie theme to the *inside* of the vehicle, giving it a hot dog dashboard and glove box, a condiment control panel, and relish-colored captain's chairs for the driver and passengers. Estimated total cost of each vehicle: $150,000.

WIENERMOBILE FACTS

• Nine different men played Little Oscar; the last one retired in 1971. Why wasn't he replaced? Oscar Mayer is mum on the subject. Our theory: As times changed, dressing midgets up as chefs could be considered "bad taste."

• What happens to old Wienermobiles? Most are sent to Canada, Mexico, and other countries where Oscar Mayer has affiliates, but at least one is always kept on hand as a "loaner wiener" in case any of the new ones break down.

• Which is harder to get into: Harvard Law School, or the driver's seat of the Wienermobile? Hint: Every year, more than 1,000 recent college graduates apply for the coveted position of "hotdogger"; only 12 get the nod. Oscar Mayer says "outgoing personalities and impressive academic credentials" are key qualities for the job.

• Once you're hired on as a hot dogger, you have to put in a week of on-the-dog training at Hot Dog High, the company's Wienerdog training facility. "The curriculum takes about seven days," hotdogger Brian Spillane explains, "including one day to learn how to drive the 'Dog,' just so no one gets in a pickle when they miss a turn."

• Mastery of hot dog puns is another must. "Go ahead and grill us," Dan Duff, another hotdogger, challenges. "In this job, we're trained to cut the mustard. It's a job to relish...and that's no bologna."

• Wienermobiles log an average of 1,000 miles per week visiting baseball games, children's hospitals, grocery stores, etc. Even so, there have been very few traffic accidents involving the Wienermobile—although there was at least one accident involving a Wienermobile fan. As one hotdogger admits: "One guy saw the Weinermobile, and laughed so hard, his false teeth fell out—right into the big air vents on the buns. We never did find them. He really sank his teeth into our buns."

Clothes horses: 9% of Americans buy their pets clothing on birthdays and holidays.

THE FIRST PHONE BOOKS

Today, the phone directory is the most widely used book in America. Practically every household has at least one. Here's how they got started.

THE FIRST WHITE PAGES

The first personal phone directory was issued in 1878—just two years after Alexander Graham Bell invented the telephone—by Boston's Telephone Dispatch Company. It was different from today's White Pages in two major respects:

1. It was only one page long, because only 97 Bostonians owned telephones in 1878.

2. It didn't list any phone numbers. Why not? There weren't any. Direct dial hadn't been invented; you just picked up the receiver and turned a hand crank that rang a bell alerting the operator. When she came on the line, you told her who you wanted to talk to. That was it.

THE FIRST YELLOW PAGES

The first business directories were actually printed on white paper. The R.R. Donnelley Company, a Chicago printing firm, was already publishing listings of local companies with their addresses. When phones came along in 1877, Donnelley just noted which businesses had them.

The first *Bell* Telephone business directory followed almost immediately in 1878; like the first personal directories, it was only one page long. Businesses were divided into seven listings: Physicians; Dentists; Stores; Factories, etc.; Meat and Fish Markets; Miscellaneous; and Hack [horses for hire] and Boarding Stables.

The number of phone customers grew exponentially over the next decade, and as directories got larger, printing costs soared. In the late 1880s, telephone companies around the country began selling advertising space in their directories to defray expenses. Today

Approximately 56,000 courier pigeons "fought" in World War II.

the ads actually *make* money—a lot of it—for phone companies: U.S. businesses bought more than $10 billion worth of yellow-page ads in 1995.

THE COSMIC QUESTION

Of course, we still haven't answered the *real* question: why are yellow pages yellow? Well, research conducted by Bell Laboratories has shown that black ink on dark yellow paper is the second-most visible paper-and-ink combination—after black ink on white paper. But nobody knew that in 1881, when the first yellow pages were printed.

Here's what happened: The Wyoming Telephone and Telegraph Co. hired a printer in Cheyenne to print its first business directory. But he didn't have enough white paper to complete the job. So, rather than lose the phone company's business altogether, he used the stock he had on hand—yellow paper.

Like the first personal directories, the first "yellow pages" were actually a yellow *page*—a single sheet that contained only 100 business listings, under such headings as Boots, American Indian Jewelry, and Soda Water Companies. Most of the telephone numbers on it were just one, two, or three digits long.

✠   ✠   ✠

PHONE PRANKS

In April 1996, some hackers tapped into the main number that directs callers to New York City's 76 police precincts and replaced the standard recording with the following message:

> You have reached the New York City Police Department. For any real emergencies, dial 911. Anyone else—we're a little busy right now eating some donuts and having coffee. (In the background, the *New York Post* reported, a second voice could be heard saying "A *big* cup of coffee. And masturbating.")

The recording ended, "You can just hold the line. We'll get back to you. We're a little slow, if you know what I mean. Thank you."

There are 635,013,559,599 possible hands in a game of bridge.

THE BIRTH OF "THE SIMPSONS"

It may be the most popular prime-time cartoon in history. But how did such an outrageous show make it onto the air in the first place? Read on.

OFF THE WALL
In the mid-1980s, producer James L. Brooks was hired to develop a comedy series called "The Tracey Ullman Show" for the fledgling Fox TV network. Ullman was immensely popular in England…but Brooks wasn't sure her humor would play well in the United States. He figured that inserting short cartoon segments between her comedy sketches might help keep the show interesting to American audiences.

Brooks was a fan of counterculture cartoonist Matt Groening (pronounced *Graining*), whose weekly cartoon strip *Life in Hell* runs in *The Village Voice* and more than 200 other "alternative" newspapers. He had a *Life in Hell* poster in his office, and one day he remarked to an assistant, "We should get this guy and have him animate for us."

LOST IN SPACE
So Fox officials approached Groening about animating *Life in Hell* and making its characters—two humans named Akbar and Jeff and three rabbits named Binky, Sheba, and Bongo—part of the show. At first, Groening agreed. Then he ran into a problem: "Fox told me outright, 'We must own the characters and the marketing rights.' The studio was still getting over the fact that a few years ago it gave George Lucas all the licensing rights to *Star Wars*."

Groening was making a pretty good living licensing the *Life in Hell* characters for calendars, mugs, T-shirts, etc., and didn't want to give it up. But rather than walk away from Fox's offer, he came up with another idea. He dashed off a short story based on his real-life family—Homer and Marge Groening (his parents); Lisa and Maggie (his sisters); and an autobiographical character named Bart (an anagram of the word "brat"). He proposed using them instead of the *Life in Hell* characters. Fox agreed to give it a try.

A NEW FAMILY

As Groening developed these characters for TV, they began to lose their resemblance to his real family. (His father, for example, isn't bald, and his mother no longer wears "big hair.") He changed their last name to the all-American sounding "Simpson," and fashioned their lives after old sitcom characters. "I used to spend hours transfixed in front of a TV set watching family situation comedies," he told the *San Francisco Chronicle* in 1990. "It's no accident that the Simpsons live in Springfield—that's the town in 'Father Knows Best.' " Later, he added: "What is 'The Simpsons' but a hallucination of the sitcom? And that has to be the ultimate American nightmare."

The original sketches were only 15 to 20 seconds long, so Bart was the only well-developed character. "He was like what would have happened if 'Leave It to Beaver's' Eddie Haskell got his own show," Groening says. "He was a deviant." Homer—his voice, at least—was a Walter Matthau impersonation, Lisa was supposed to be a "female Bart," and Marge and Maggie weren't much more than backdrops for the other characters.

BUST AND BOOM

The "Tracey Ullman Show" debuted in 1987. It was a critical success, but ratings were terrible. Despite this, "The Simpsons" attracted a huge cult following, and Fox responded by increasing the length of the sketches from 20 to 90 seconds. Then they introduced a line of Simpsons T-shirts, posters, and other items to cash in on the fad.

But the biggest boost to the Simpsons' popularity came from a candy bar company. The makers of Butterfinger and Baby Ruth licensed the Simpson characters for their candy bar ads—which aired on network TV. So kids who'd never heard of "The Tracey Ullman Show" (or Fox, for that matter) finally got a glimpse of Bart and his family. Their popularity grew.

ON THEIR OWN

In 1988, Fox decided to spin "The Simpsons" off into their own show. It was scheduled to premiere in September 1989. But when the initial 13 episodes came back from Korea, where they were being animated, Groening discovered that the director had added a few unauthorized "jokes" of his own. In one episode, for example, when the Simpsons are watching a TV show called "The Happy Little Elves Meet the Curious Bear Cubs," the animators inserted a scene in which a bear cub rips off the head of an elf and drinks its blood.

"Not exactly a minor addition," Groening told *The New York Times* in 1990. "When we watched it, we sat in the dark for about two minutes in silence. Then we ran for the door. I thought my career in animation had sunk to the bottom of the sea. Had that gotten on the air, there would be no show today." The director and animators were fired, and the show was postponed until January 1990 while new animators fixed the episodes.

SHOWTIME

"The Simpsons" as we know it today finally made it onto TV on January 13, 1990. It earned the second-highest ratings in its time slot—pretty impressive when you consider that Fox didn't have as many affiliates around the country as ABC, CBS, or NBC. ("The Tracey Ullman Show" went off the air five months later.) "The Simpsons" went on to become Fox's highest-rated show. In March 1990, it placed 20th in the weekly Nielsen ratings, and in June went all the way to #3. It has, without question, played a key role in establishing Fox as a viable fourth network.

SOUR GRAPES

In 1992, Tracey Ullman filed suit against Fox for $2.25 million, arguing that since "The Simpsons" got their start on her show ("I breast-fed those little devils," she told a reporter), she was entitled to a share of the merchandising profits. In court, however, she admitted that she did not create "The Simpsons," write any of the shows, or take part in any of the merchandising. She lost the case.

ᴄᴈ   ᴄᴈ   ᴄᴈ

"The creativity of the way people respond to the show is fantastic. You should see the fan mail. Kids send in their pictures of Bart beating up other cartoon characters."

— *Matt Groening*

Henry Ford was Charles Lindbergh's first passenger in the Spirit of St. Louis.

FAMOUS INDIAN IMPOSTORS

It's common for North Americans to romanticize the traditions of Native Americans, so it shouldn't be surprising that the "Indian way" is fertile ground for hoaxes and impostors. Here are two notable examples.

GREY OWL

In the 1930s, Grey Owl was one of the most famous naturalists in the world. "He is no stuffed Indian," *The New York Times* reported at the time. "He is real and honest."

Who He Said He Was: Grey Owl claimed to be the son of a Scottish man and his Apache wife. At the age of 15, his story went, he went to live with the Ojibway tribe near Ontario, Canada. They named him Wa-Sha-Quon-Asin, which translates as "He-Who-Flies-by-Night" (an appropriate name), or "Grey Owl." They also taught him how to trap beavers...but when his traps killed a mother beaver and left its young as orphans, he decided to stop killing animals and start protecting them.

The Canadian government was impressed. They made a film about his work and gave him a job as a conservationist in their national parks. His fame grew; he wrote two bestselling books (in 1931 and 1935) and toured England twice, speaking in packed lecture halls to more than 250,000 people. He was even invited to meet with King George...whom he greeted as an equal, extending his hand and saying, "I come in peace, brother."

Who He Really Was: A few days after He-Who-Flies-by-Night died in 1938, an Ontario newspaper discovered that he was actually Archibald Stansfeld Belamey, an Englishman who'd moved to Canada at the age of 18. Once there, he quickly acquired four wives, several children, a police record, and a reputation for public drunkenness. He abandoned them all for the fantasy world of a half-Indian beaver lover.

What Happened: Belamey is still held in high esteem. As *History Today* reported in 1994, "Grey Owl has never been forgotten. His books remain in print. His cabins in the National Parks where he worked have been restored, and some of his canoe routes have been mapped for park visitors."

LITTLE TREE

In 1976, Delacorte Press published *The Education of Little Tree*, by Forrest Carter. The book became a #1 bestseller on the *New York Times* nonfiction list. More than a million copies were in print by the late 1980s, and in 1991 the American Bookseller's Association voted it the book "they most enjoyed selling."

Who He Said He Was: Carter said *The Education of Little Tree* was an autobiographical account of the way his Cherokee grandmother and her Scottish husband taught him how to weave baskets, make moccasins, hunt wild game, and live off the land.

Who He Really Was: In 1991, an historian was researching a biography of segregationist Alabama governor George Wallace when he discovered Forrest Carter's true identity. Incredibly, he was really Asa Carter, a violent white supremacist and former speechwriter for Wallace. As the historian wrote in *The New York Times*:

> Between 1946 and 1973, [Asa] Carter carved out a violent career in Southern politics as a Ku Klux Klan terrorist, right-wing radio announcer, home-grown American fascist and anti-Semite....He even organized a paramilitary unit of about 100 men that he called the Original Ku Klux Klan of the Confederacy.

In time, Carter became too bigoted even for the Wallace campaign. So he ran against Wallace for governor in 1970 (he got 15,000 votes out of more than 1 million cast). Then he dropped out of sight, moved to Texas, and began writing novels as Forrest Carter (after Nathan Bedford *Forrest*, the Confederate general who founded the Ku Klux Klan). His two most successful novels were *Gone to Texas*, which Clint Eastwood made into the film *The Outlaw Josey Wales*, and *The Education of Little Tree*. Carter died in 1979...and his true identity remained a secret until 1991.

What Happened: *The New York Times Book Review* moved *The Education of Little Tree* from its nonfiction list to its fiction list. Carter's books are still in print, and sales remain strong.

SPEAK OF THE DEVIL

Here are some random bits of information about the Devil.

T**HE DEVIL YOU SAY**
- The Devil as we think of him—with the horns, pitchfork, etc.—dates back to the 10th and 11th centuries; his popular image was not taken from the Bible. According to the New Testament, the devil takes the form of a lion, a wolf, a dragon, and a serpent. Early Christians sometimes thought of him as a three-headed dog.

So where does the Devil we know come from?
- His beard (goatee), horns, hooves, hairy legs, pointy ears, etc. were borrowed from the goat. Scholars cite two reasons:

1. "The domestic goat was renowned for the size of its phallus," writes historian J. C. J. Metford, and, according to legend, "tempted saints by whispering in their ears lewd details of the sexual pleasures they had relinquished."

2. One of the ways the Church discouraged interest in other religions was by literally "demonizing" gods that competed with theirs. So a lot of the imagery is derived from pagan sources: the goatlike features also come from Pan, the Greek god of shepherds, fertility, and nature.

- His red skin is the color of blood and fire.

- His three-pronged fork, or *triton*, was borrowed from Poseidon, the nasty-tempered Greek god of the sea and of earthquakes, whose main symbol was a three-pronged spear.

DEVOLUTION
- Modern mythology paints the Devil as the kind of all-powerful, evil being who possesses little girls in *The Exorcist* or tries to destroy the world in *The Omen* But that hasn't always been the case.

- During the Middle Ages in parts of Europe, he was seen as more of a mean-spirited, clumsy, dimwitted lout with a fondness for pranks—like Bluto in the *Popeye* cartoons—that the wise and the holy could easily outsmart. "There was nothing grand about their Satan," historian Charles Mackay writes in his book *Extraordinary Popular Delusions and the Madness of Crowds*.

Mary Stuart became Queen of Scotland when she was six days old.

On the contrary, he was a low, mean devil, whom it was easy to circumvent, and fine fun to play tricks with....It was believed that he endeavored to trip people up by laying his long invisible tail in their way, and giving it a sudden whisk when their legs were over it; that he used to get drunk, and swear like a trooper, and be mischievous. ...Some of the saints spat in his face, to his very great annoyance; others chopped off pieces of his tail, which, however, always grew on again.

• Of course, some countries were extremely serious about Satan. Historians estimate that from 1450 to 1750, more than 200,000 alleged witches were executed in Europe and America for "dealing with the Devil."

DEVIL'S FOOD

• How did devil's food cake get its name? One theory: The stuff was so tasty that people assumed that the inventors had to sell their soul to the Devil to get the recipe.

• You've probably eaten pumpernickel bread before...but did you know the word *Pumpernickel* means "Devil's fart" in German? Apparently, when German bakers invented the bread centuries ago, it was awful. The 1756 book *A Grand Tour of Germany* described it as bread "of the very coarsest kind, ill-baked and as black as coal, for they never sift their flour." Locals joked that it was so difficult to digest that even the Devil himself got gas when he ate it.

• In some countries, the Devil is nicknamed "the good man," "the old gentleman," and even "the great fellow." Why? Tradition had it that if you "spoke of the Devil," he would appear. So people didn't.

SATAN ON TRIAL

In 1971, a man named Gerald Mayo filed suit against Satan in the U.S. District Court in Pennsylvania, alleging that "Satan has on numerous occasions caused plaintiff misery and unwarranted threats, against the will of plaintiff, that Satan has placed deliberate obstacles in his path and has caused plaintiff's downfall. Plaintiff alleges that by reason of these acts Satan has deprived him of his constitutional rights."

The case, "Gerald Mayo v. Satan and His Staff," was thrown out of court after Mayo failed to provide the U.S. marshall with instructions on how to serve Satan's subpoena, and could not prove that Satan lived within the jurisdiction of the District Court.

THE CREATION OF FRANKENSTEIN

You might assume that the flat-headed, bolts-in-the-neck monster we all know was taken directly from Mary Shelley's original novel. Nope. It was created specifically for the movies. Here's the story of how the world's most famous monster was born.

FIRST FRIGHT

History books credit Thomas Alva Edison with inventing the lightbulb, the phonograph, the movie camera, and many other things. But one invention they usually leave off his resume is the horror movie. His Edison Film Company invented it in 1910, when they put Mary Shelley's 1818 novel *Frankenstein* on film for the first time.

Edison's *Frankenstein* was barely 16 minutes long and was only loosely based on the original. The filmmakers thought the book was too graphic, so they eliminated "all the…repulsive situations and concentrated on the mystic and psychological problems found in this weird tale."

CREATIONISM

But one scene in Shelley's book wasn't graphic *enough* for Edison executives: the "creation scene" in which Dr. Frankenstein brings the monster to life. Shelley devoted only two sentences to it:

> I collected the instruments of life around me, that I might infuse a spark of being into the lifeless thing that lay at my feet. It was already one in the morning; the rain pattered dismally against the panes, and my candle was nearly burnt out, when, by the glimmer of the half-extinguished light, I saw the dull yellow eye of the creature open; it breathed hard, and a convulsive motion agitated its limbs.

That was all Shelley wrote. So the folks at Edison used their imagination and decided to make a "cauldron of blazing chemicals" the source of the monster's life. Edison's monster looked nothing like the Frankenstein we know now. It was a white-faced hunchback with matted hair and a hairy chest.

ON THE ROAD

Following the success of Edison's *Frankenstein*, other studios filmed their own versions of the story. The first full-length Frankenstein film, called *Life Without a Soul*, hit the silver screen in 1916, and an Italian film called *Il Mostro di Frankenstein* followed in 1920.

But the Frankenstein monster might never have become a Hollywood icon if it hadn't been for Hamilton Deane, an English actor who ran (and starred in) a traveling *Dracula* show during the 1920s. Tired of performing *Dracula* night after night, Deane began looking for material he could use as an alternate. He settled on *Frankenstein*.

In 1927 he asked a member of the *Dracula* troupe, Peggy Webling, to adapt *Frankenstein* into a play. Like the folks at Edison, she got creative with the story. For example:

• Webling saw the monster—whom Mary Shelley called *Adam*—as an alter ego of Dr. Victor Frankenstein. She became the first person ever to refer to both the man *and* the monster as Frankenstein. To make the connection obvious, she dressed the characters in identical clothing throughout the play.

• She changed the ending. In the novel, Dr. Frankenstein pursues the monster to the Arctic circle, where the monster strangles him, jumps onto an ice floe, and drifts off to a sure death. The scene made good reading, but it was boring on stage. So Webling had the monster jump off a cliff instead.

Unfortunately, Hamilton Deane, who played the monster, wasn't much of an athlete. As troupe member Ivan Butler recalled years later, the new ending was "very tame indeed, because of Deane's tentative jump." So Webling wrote a more exciting ending. "The final version was quite a bloodthirsty affair," Butler recalled, "with the monster apparently tearing his maker's throat out before being destroyed by lightning. Old Deanie revelled in it."

CLASSIC FRANKENSTEIN

Universal Pictures bought the screen rights to Deane's *Dracula* and cast Bela Lugosi in the starring role. Even before the film was released in 1931, studio executives knew it would be a hit. So they commissioned a *Frankenstein* film, too. They bought the rights to Webling's play, then hired fresh screen writers to craft a brand-new script.

A WHALE OF A TALE

First, Universal hired director James Whale to work on the film. Whale had just finished work on *Hell's Angels* and *Journey's End*, two films about World War I, and Universal officials were so impressed with them that they offered Whale his pick of any of the dozens of film projects they had in the works. He chose *Frankenstein*. Why? As he later recalled:

> Of thirty available stories, *Frankenstein* was the strongest meat and gave me a chance to dabble in the macabre. I thought it would be amusing to try and make what everybody knows is a physical impossibility seem believable....Also, it offered fine pictorial chances, had two grand characterizations, and had a subject matter that might go anywhere, and that is part of the fun of making pictures.

And besides, Whale was sick of working on war movies.

BEG, BORROW, AND STEAL

Once again, writers changed Shelley's story. Universal's screenwriters followed the novel only loosely, adding and deleting details as they saw fit. They also appropriated ideas from other films:

• An early draft of the script said the lab should be filled with electrical gadgets that were "something suggestive of the laboratory in *Metropolis*," a 1926 German film about a mad scientist.

• Dr. Frankenstein's lab was moved from the top floor of his house to an old watchtower. This idea was taken from *The Magician*, a 1926 film in which a student of the occult finds "the secret of the creation of human life...in an ancient sorcerer's tower."

• *The Magician* was also an inspiration for the creation scene. As in *Frankenstein*, lightning bolts that strike the tower create life.

• Both *Metropolis* and *The Magician* provided ideas for the character of Igor, Dr. Frankenstein's assistant. In both films, the mad scientist has a dwarf for an assistant. Whale's scriptwriters changed him from a dwarf to a hunchback.

- Universal scriptwriters moved the final scene to an abandoned windmill, where angry peasants trap Dr. Frankenstein and the monster inside and burn it to the ground. Why was a windmill chosen? Scriptwriter Robert Florey remembers, "I was living in a [Hollywood] apartment above a Van de Kamp bakery," which had a windmill as its company symbol. The sight of the company's "windmill rotating inspired me to place the final scene in an old mill."

- In Mary Shelley's *Frankenstein*, the monster is extremely articulate and drones on for entire chapters without stopping. But movie audiences were still getting used to the idea of *people* talking (and screaming) in movies, let alone monsters—so the scriptwriters decided to make the Frankenstein monster a mute. Throughout the film, all he does is grunt.

CREATING THE MONSTER

Whale cast an actor named Colin Clive to play Dr. Frankenstein and selected a woman named Mae Clarke to play Dr. Frankenstein's fiance. (Bette Davis was also considered for the part.)

Casting the monster turned out to be more difficult. Bela Lugosi, probably Universal's first choice for the part, filmed a full-dress screen test. But because the *Frankenstein* makeup hadn't yet been finalized, the makeup department gave Lugosi a big, fat head "about four times normal size," and "polished, clay-like skin."

Nobody knows if Lugosi's performance was any good; the screen test was lost shortly after it was filmed. But it didn't really matter—Lugosi figured the nonspeaking role was beneath him and worried that his fans wouldn't recognize him under all that makeup. The role went to someone else, someone who was almost completely unknown in Hollywood.

For Part II of the Frankenstein story, turn to page 277.

★   ★   ★

BLACKENSTEIN

In 1972, a "blaxploitation" version of Frankenstein was released—*Blackenstein*. The plot: Dr. Stein experiments on a black Vietnam vet. Something goes awry…and a "crazed monster with a square Afro" is created. A planned sequel, *Blackenstein Meets the White Werewolf*, was never made.

WARHOLISMS

Don't let the blank look fool you. Andy Warhol had insight.

"If a person isn't generally considered beautiful, they can still be a success if they have a few jokes in their pockets. And a lot of pockets."

"The most beautiful thing in Tokyo is McDonald's. The most beautiful thing in Stockholm is McDonald's. Peking and Moscow don't have anything beautiful yet."

"Good B.O. means good box office. You can smell it from a mile away."

"If the lines on your hands are wrinkles, it means your hands worry a lot."

"When I look around today, the biggest anachronism I see is pregnancy. I just can't believe that people are still pregnant."

"After you pay somebody back, you never run into them anymore. But before that, they're everywhere."

"In the '60s, everybody got interested in everybody. In the '70s, everybody started dropping everybody."

"They say that time changes things, but actually you have to change them yourself."

"People look the most kissable when they're not wearing makeup. Marilyn's lips weren't kissable, but they were **very** photographable."

"Changing your tastes to what other people don't want is your only hope of getting anything."

"Even beauties can be unattractive. If you catch a beauty in the wrong light at the right time, forget it."

"If people want to spend their whole lives creaming and tweezing and brushing and gluing, that's really okay too, because it gives them something to do."

"I really do live for the future, because when I'm eating a box of candy, I can't wait to taste the last piece."

"The best time for me is when I don't have any problems that I can't buy my way out of."

Medical Alert for Vince Lombardi: "Telesphobia" is the name given to "the fear of being last."

LUCKY FINDS

*Ever found something valuable? It's a great feeling. Here's
a look at a few people who found really valuable stuff...
and got to keep it. You should be so lucky.*

FLEA MARKET TREASURE

The Find: A copy of the Declaration of Independence, printed on the evening of July 4, 1776

Where It Was Found: Inside a picture frame

The Story: In 1989, an unidentified "middle-aged financial analyst from Philadelphia" paid $4 for a painting at a flea market. He didn't even like the painting, but liked the frame, so he took the picture apart...and when he did, a copy of the Declaration of Independence fell out. "It was folded up, about the size of a business envelope," says David Redden of Sotheby's Auction House. "He thought it might be an early 19th-century printing and worth keeping as a curiosity."

A few years later, the man showed the print to a friend, who suspected it might be valuable and encouraged him to look into it. He did, and learned that only hours after finishing work on the Declaration in 1776, the Continental Congress had delivered the hand-written draft to a printer with orders to send

> copies of the Declaration...to the several Assemblies, Conventions & Committees...and the Commanding Officers of the Continental troops, that it be proclaimed in each of the United States & at the head of the Army.

This was one of those original copies. No one is sure how many were printed that night; today only 24 survive, and most are in poor condition. But the one in the picture frame was in mint condition, having spent the better part of two centuries undisturbed. In 1991, it sold at auction for $2.4 million.

UNCLAIMED MERCHANDISE

The Find: More than 20,000 previously unreleased recordings by Bob Dylan, Elvis Presley, Johnny Cash, Roy Orbison, Frank Sinatra, Louis Armstrong, and other music stars.

Mussolini dodged the Italian draft.

Where It Was Found: At a Nashville warehouse sale

The Story: In 1990, Douglas and Brenda Cole went to an auction in Nashville. On a whim, they paid $50 for the contents of a storage locker that a recording engineer had abandoned. Among the contents: boxes of used recording tapes that Nashville's Columbia Studios had apparently sold the engineer between 1953 and 1971 as scrap. "They were considered waste material, waste tape," an attorney explains. After listening to a few of them, the Coles realized they had something special, but they couldn't get Columbia Records interested. So, in 1992, they sold the tapes for $6,000 to Clark Enslin, owner of a small New Jersey–based record label.

Enslin contacted Sony Records (Columbia's parent company) about the tapes—and they filed suit against him, claiming he'd acquired the tapes illegally. The case was in court for three years and ended in a mixed verdict. Sony won commercial control over the 30% of the tapes recorded by artists who were signed with Columbia at the time the recordings were made; Enslin kept control of the remaining 70%—including songs by Presley, Sinatra, Williams, Armstrong, Orbison, and Jerry Lee Lewis. Actual estimated value of the tapes: $100 million. "It's very exciting," Enslin says. "It's hard to describe what it's like, knowing I have the best collection of recorded music in the world."

TREASURE IN THE TRASH

The Find: The $200,000 grand prize–winning cup in a Wendy's Restaurant fast food contest

Where It Was Found: In the garbage

The Story: In 1995, Craig Randall, a 23-year-old trash collector in Peabody, Massachusetts, noticed a Wendy's contest cup sitting in some garbage he was collecting. "I won a chicken sandwich the week before," he told reporters, "and I figured, hey, I'd get some fries to go with it." Instead, when he peeled off the sticker he saw: "Congratulations. You have won $200,000 towards a new home." The fact that he *found* the cup didn't matter; Wendy's gave him the money anyway. "I have no idea where it came from," he said. "It was just sitting there."

Q: Who invented the talking doll? A: Thomas Edison, in 1888.

I'M GAME

You've played them. You've loved them.
Now here's a look at where they came from.

THE GAME OF LIFE

In 1860, young Milton Bradley's lithography company was in trouble; sales of his bestselling product, pictures of a clean-shaven Abraham Lincoln, had fallen off drastically when Lincoln grew a beard. Desperate, he printed up a board game called "The Checkered Game of Life." Players who landed on "Idleness" were told to "Go to disgrace"; the "Bravery" square led to "Honor"; and so on. It was perfect for the puritanical Victorian era, and sold so well that Bradley became America's first game mogul.

In 1960, the Milton Bradley Company came out with the 100th-anniversary "Game of Life." It became the second bestselling game of all time (after Monopoly).

PARCHEESI

In the late 1800s, a manufacturer approached Sam Loyd, one of America's premier game designers, with a problem: His company had a surplus of cardboard squares. Could Loyd devise some sort of game that would use the squares, so his company could get rid of them?

Borrowing from a centuries-old Indian game called *pachisi*, Loyd created a "new" game he called Parcheesi. It didn't take him very long. In fact, it was so easy that he only charged the manufacturer $10 for his services. Within a few years, the game became one of the most popular in the United States—but that $10 was the only money Loyd ever got for it.

TWISTER

In the early 1960s, Reynolds Guyer worked at his family's sales-promotion company designing packages and displays. He also created premiums—the gifts people get for sending in boxtops and proofs-of-purchase.

One day in 1965, the 29-year-old Guyer and his crew started work on a premium for a shoe polish company. "One idea," he says, "was to have kids standing on this mat with squares that told them where to put their feet....but I thought, this is bigger than just a premium."

He expanded the mat to 4' x 6' and turned it into a game. "I got the secretaries and the designers and everyone together to play. You know, in 1965 no one ever touched. It really broke all the rules of propriety having people stand so close together."

At first it was a flop. No one knew what to make of a game where people were the main playing pieces. But when Johnny Carson and Eva Gabor played it on the "Tonight Show" in 1966, America got the point. Overnight, it became a runaway hit.

TRIVIAL PURSUIT

In December 1979, Scott Abbott, a sports editor with the *Canadian Press*, and Chris Haney, a photographer with the *Montreal Gazette*, sat down to play Scrabble. Then they realized their game was missing four pieces. Haney went out to buy a new game...and was astonished that he had to cough up $16 for it. Abbott suggested that they invent their own game. They tossed around some ideas until they came up with the magic word "trivia."

"I was the sports buff," Abbott remembers, "and Chris was the movie and entertainment buff. We sat down...and started doodling a game board. The whole thing was done in about 45 minutes."

They offered $1,000 shares in the game to friends and co-workers, but hardly anyone was interested. "I heard people call them small-time shysters," one colleague remembers. As Haney puts it, "Of course, it was no, no, no, and they all came to us later, and of course we said no, no, no." Abbott and Haney eventually raised the money to produce 20,000 games...and managed to sell them all, mostly in Canada. Still, according to Matthew Costello in *The World's Greatest Games*:

> Trivial Pursuit might have stayed just a moderate success if the daughter of the Canadian distributor for Selchow & Righter (ironically, the maker of Scrabble) hadn't discovered "this terrific new game." She told her father, and Selchow & Righter bought the rights to it. With their marketing push, North America was besieged by Trivial Pursuit.

Since then, more than 60 million sets—over *$1 billion* worth of the games—have been sold in 33 countries and in 19 languages around the world.

WOULD YOU BELIEVE?

According to Webster's Dictionary, *a cynic is "one who believes that human conduct is wholly motivated by self-interest." Does that describe you? Find out by taking this handy-dandy, 100% all-true quiz.*
(Answers on page 318.)

POLITICS

1. Presidential security advisor Oliver North testified in 1987 that information leaked by Congress had "seriously compromised intelligence activities" during an incident involving Egyptian terrorists. Actually...
a) North made the incident up.
b) North was the one who'd leaked the information.
c) Since Oliver North never lies, everyone believed him.

GOOD CAUSES

2. As a spokesperson for AIDS awareness, pop singer Madonna advised Americans that using condoms is "the best way to say I love you." However in her own life, she explained...
a) She never uses condoms. .
b) She doesn't trust most condoms, so she has them custom-made.
c) When she *really* loves someone, she says, "The hell with the condom."

3. Candy Lightner founded Mothers Against Drunk Driving (MADD) in 1980 when her daughter was killed by a drunk driver. In 1994, she took a job as...
a) A paid lobbiest for a liquor industry trade group.
b) A nightclub comedian doing a "drunk" act.
c) An advisor to Seagram's.

EDUCATION

4. In May 1996, an 18-year-old crusader for sexual abstinence named Danyale Andersen was in the news. After spending more than 100 hours preaching abstinence to younger students in her high school and appearing before the school board in her hometown to support an "abstinence-only health curriculum," she...
a) Posed for Playboy.
b) Became a nun
c) Had a baby out of wedlock.

Ancient Egyptian tombs are decorated with pictures of watermelons.

SPORTS

5. Japan's Yasuhiro Yamashita overcame a torn leg muscle to win a gold medal in judo at the 1984 Olympics. His opponent, Mohamed Ali Rashwan of Egypt, told reporters he hadn't attacked Yamashita's leg because "I would not want to win this way." For his sportsmanship, he received the 1985 Fair Play Trophy. Actually...
a) The first thing Rashwan did was attack Yamashita's leg.
b) Japanese businessmen had bribed Rashwan to lose.
c) He only found out the leg was injured *after* the match was over.

6. The National Football League presents itself as an advocate of "family values." So when David Williams, a lineman for the Houston Oilers, missed a game to be with his wife during the birth of their son, the Oilers' front office...
a) Gave him a special award.
b) Gave him two weeks of paternity leave.
c) Docked him a week's pay.

FINANCES

7. Benjamin Franklin, America's "apostle of thrift," coined phrases like "A penny saved is a penny earned." Historians now say that Franklin's own bank account...
a) Was with a Mafia bank.
b) Was perpetually overdrawn.
c) Had the lowest interest rate in the Colonies.

8. The IRS says it's every American's duty to keep good, accurate financial records. But a 1994 audit showed that...
a) No one understands what they're talking about.
b) Even the IRS's records are a mess.
c) Only about 47% of Americans keep any records at all.

THE NEWS MEDIA

9. *The New York Times'* well-known slogan is "All the News That's Fit to Print." But when the *Times* summarized the Supreme Court's decisions in 1973, it omitted one. Why?
a) It was a paternity suit brought against their publisher, Arthur Ochs Sulzberger.
b) It involved obscene grafitti, and they refused to print the four-letter words involved.
c) It was a libel suit against a major news organization, and they didn't want to publicize it.

THE GREAT CRISWELL

This is excerpted from a book called The
Bathroom Reader's Guide to the Year 2000.

BACKGROUND

Although he's best known for his cameo appearance in the worst movie of all time—*Plan Nine from Outer Space*—Jeron Criswell was also a famous (or infamous) psychic. In 1968 he wrote *Criswell Predicts—From Now to the Year 2000*, which has become a classic of millennial weirdness.

Criswell claims his predictions have an 86% accuracy rate. "Over the next thirty years," he tells readers, "you may keep your own score as to their accuracy. After that, it will not matter."

But in case you have the urge to take him seriously, you should know that Criswell also predicted the following events on these specific days:

- Fidel Castro is assassinated on August 9, 1970
- Earthquake destroys San Francisco on April 7, 1975
- Women in Missouri will lose their hair on February 11, 1983
- Meteor destroys London on October 18, 1988
- Denver is destroyed on June 9, 1989
- The First Interplanetary Convention is held on March 10, 1990

MORE PREDICTIONS

Here are a few more of Criswell's bizarre predictions:

Aphrodisiac Spray

"I predict that our own United States will, in the future, be swept by the popular clouds of an Aphrodisian fragrance. It will be invented by a scientist who is searching for an improved antiseptic spray. Instead he will invent a spray that is almost odorless but when breathed stimulates the most basic sexual erotic areas.

"This aroma will fill every man and woman who inhales it with uncontrollable passion...I predict that the sex urge will advance rapidly, and many men will flagrantly expose themselves in public...I predict a wealthy San Francisco attorney will announce his

---

Heavy thought: The average adult male has 40 lbs. of bone and 65 lbs. of muscle in his body.

marriage to his mother and a Hollywood producer will openly declare his daughter is going to bear his child, and a young man in Arkansas will ask to be legally wed to his pet cat."

Birth Control

"I predict that birth control will no longer be a major problem in the United States. Placed in the water system of the country, in every city, regardless of size, will be chemicals which will act as contraceptives on the entire populace. In addition to this, the electricity that comes into each home will have certain ionic particles that cause contraception."

The Destruction of Denver

"I predict that a large city in Colorado will be the victim of a strange and terrible pressure from outer space, which will cause all solids to turn into a jelly-like mass."

Men Become Cannibals

"I predict an outburst of cannibalism that will terrorize the population of one of the industrial cities in the state of Pennsylvania—Pittsburgh!...I predict that over one thousand flesh-mad and blood-crazed men will wander through the streets suddenly attacking unsuspecting victims."

The End

"The world as we know it will cease to exist...on August 18, 1999.

"A study of all the prophets—Nostradamus, St. Odile, Mother Shipton, the Bible—indicates that we will cease to exist before the year 2000! Not one of these prophets even took the trouble to predict beyond the year 2000! And if you and I meet each other on the street that fateful day, August 18, 1999, and we chat about what we will do on the morrow, we will open our mouths to speak and no words will come out, for we have no future...you and I will suddenly run out of time! Who knows but what future generation from some other planet will dig down through seven layers of rubble and find us some 2,000 years hence, and crowd around a museum glass containing a fragment of a Coke bottle, a bent hairpin and a parched copy of our Bible which managed to escape destruction! They will wonder what on earth was meant by the words 'Ford' or 'Hollywood'... and what in heaven's name was a *Criswell*."

CAB CALLOWAY'S JIVE DICTIONARY

In the '30s and '40s, Cab Calloway and his band were famous for tunes like "Minnie the Moocher" and "St. James Infirmary." But he was also known as a "hep-cat," identified with outrageous zoot suits and jive talk. His guide on how to talk like a hipster was published in the 1940s. It was unearthed by BRI member Gordon Javna.

APPLE: The big town, the main stem

BARBEQUE: The girlfriend, a beauty

BARRELHOUSE: Free and easy

BATTLE: Crone, hag

BEAT IT OUT: Play it hot

BEAT UP THE CHOPS: To talk

BEEF: To say, to state

BLIP: Something very good

BLOW THE TOP: To be overcome with emotion or delight

BUDDY GHEE: Fellow

BUST YOUR CONK: Apply yourself diligently, break your neck

CLAMBAKE: Every man for himself

COOLING: Laying off, not working

CORNY: Old-fashioned, stale

CUBBY: Room, flat, home

CUPS: Sleep

CUT RATE: Low, cheap person

DICTY: High-class, nifty, smart

DIME NOTE: $10 bill

DRAPE: Suit of clothes, dress

DRY GOODS: Dress, costume

DUKE: Hand, mitt

FALL OUT: To be overcome with emotion

FAUST: An ugly girl

FEWS AND TWO: Money or cash in small quantity

FRAME: The body

FROMPY: A frompy queen is a battle or faust

FRUITING: Fickle, fooling around with no particular object

GATE: A male person

GLIMS: The eyes

GOT YOUR BOOTS ON: You know what it is all about, you are wise

GOT YOUR GLASSES ON: You are ritzy or snooty, you fail to recognize your friends

GUTBUCKET: Low-down music

Game maker Nintendo sold its *one billionth* video game in October 1995.

HARD: Fine, good

HEP CAT: A guy who knows all the answers, understands jive

HOME-COOKING: Something very nice

ICKY: A stupid person, not hip

IN THE GROOVE: Perfect

JACK: Name for all male friends

JEFF: A pest, a bore

JELLY: Anything free, on the house

JITTER BUG: A swing fan

KILL ME: Show me a good time, send me

KILLER-DILLER: A great thrill

LAY YOUR RACKET: To jive, to sell an idea

LEAD SHEET: A coat

LILLY WHITES: Bed sheets

MAIN IN GRAY: The postman

MAIN ON THE HITCH: Husband

MAIN QUEEN: Favorite girl friend, sweetheart

MESS: Something good

METER: Quarter, twenty-five cents

MEZZ: Anything supreme, genuine

MITT POUNDING: Applause

MOUSE: Pocket

MURDER: Something excellent or terrific

NEIGHO POPS: Nothing doing, pal

OFF THE COB: Corny, out of date

OFF TIME JIVE: A sorry excuse, saying the wrong thing

PIGEON: A young girl

PINK: A white person

POPS: Salutation for all males

POUNDERS: Policemen

QUEEN: A beautiful girl

RUG CUTTER: A very good dancer

SALTY: Angry or ill-tempered

SEND: To arouse the emotions (joyful)

SET OF SEVEN BRIGHTS: One week

SHARP: Neat, smart, tricky

SLIDE YOUR JIB: Talk freely

SOLID: Great, swell, okay

SQUARE: An un-hip person

STAND ONE UP: To assume one is cut-rate

TAKE IT SLOW: Be careful

TOGGED TO THE BRICKS: Dressed to kill

TRILLY: To leave, to depart

TRUCK: To go somewhere

WHIPPED UP: Worn out, exhausted

WRONG RIFF: Saying or doing the wrong thing

Poll results: 2% of Americans "always" tip a waiter/waitress; 70% say it "depends on service."

WHO CRACKED THE LIBERTY BELL?

What do you know about the Liberty Bell? This piece, adapted from
American Heritage magazine, might fill in a few details.
Thanks to John Dollison for sending it along.

THE FIRST CRACK

T • "In 1751, the Assembly of the Province of Pennsylvania wanted a...bell for the newly completed belfry of their State House in Philadelphia. They ordered one from the Whitechapel Bell Foundry in London [and] it arrived at Philadelphia in the late summer of 1752. To everyone's surprise and dismay it promptly cracked...'as it was hung up to try the sound.' "

• "To save a round-trip to England, two local foundrymen—John Pass and John Stow—were engaged to recast the bell....They made a mold from the original bell to preserve the design, melted down the metal...and recast. The bell that resulted, however, was judged to have poor tone, and they tried again."

• "When Pass and Stow's second attempt came out...it was deemed acceptable if not altogether satisfactory, and was hung in the State House belfry." Why did it become known as the Liberty Bell? Probably because of the inscription on its crown:

PROCLAIM LIBERTY THROUGHOUT ALL THE LAND UNTO
ALL THE INHABITANTS THEREOF LEVITICUS. XXV VSX.

THE SECOND & THIRD CRACKS

• It's commonly assumed that the Liberty Bell cracked a second time when people enthusiastically rang it to celebrate the signing of the Declaration of Independence in 1776. Actually, it broke in 1835—"either in July while tolling for Chief Justice John Marshall's death, or on Washington's Birthday, when a group of small boys pulled too energetically on the rope."

• The latter is more likely. In 1911, Emmanuel Rauch, one of the boys, was interviewed, and he insisted that it was he and his friends who had cracked the bell. He pointed out that during Marshall's funeral "the bell's clapper would have been muffled and unlikely to cause damage."

The founding fathers' name for the American Revolution was "The War with Britain."

• Eleven years later, in 1846, the bell cracked again. "An attempt was made to put the great bell in ringing order by drilling out the edges of the crack to prevent their rubbing together. This worked about as well as the dentistry…of the period.…When the bell was rung on Feb. 23 [Washington's Birthday], the crack suddenly split open farther. Since then the only sound heard from the bell has been a disappointing *thunk* created by tapping it gently with a small mallet on occasions like the invasion of Normandy in 1944."

WHY DID IT CRACK?

"But why did the bell crack in the first place? This…question has recently been [studied] by a professional metallurgist, Dr. Alan R. Rosenfield, an expert on metal fracture.…In general, he points out, 'bells are necessarily made out of brittle metal, and they often break. Even Big Ben is slightly cracked.' " Specifically, he notes:

1. "Pass and Stow were not skillful enough to produce a bell with a uniformly smooth surface: there are numerous pockmarks and some seams." On top of that, it contains too much tin and "many nonmetallic impurities, globs of lead, and small voids. Any of these irregularities…could have started the fatal crack."

2. "The Liberty Bell had a rough time during the Revolution. When the British approached Philadelphia in 1777, it was loaded on a wagon and jolted over bad roads to Allentown for safekeeping until 1778. It [was] dropped at least once en route, which may have produced an incipient, microscopic crack."

3. "Any big bell is subject to metal fatigue—the gradual deterioration of part of the bell under a repeated number of strikings." The Liberty Bell could have developed "a fatigue crack some time in its first 50 or 60 years of existence. This would not have impaired the tone of the bell until the crack reached a critical size and then fractured rapidly and catastrophically, as apparently it did in 1835."

POSTSCRIPT: "Could the Liberty Bell be melted down and recast so that it could ring again? Certainly, our expert says; and in fact the Whitechapel Bell Foundry, still in business in London, offered to do just that in 1943. The offer was politely turned down by the federal government. The crack, it would seem, has become as sacred as the bell itself."

An adult giraffe's tongue is 17 inches long.

TRUE CONFESSIONS

A little bathroom pastime: Match the intimate revelation with the celebrity who said it. Inspired by Jon Winokur's book of quotes, True Confessions.

1. "Brain the size of a pea, I've got."

2. "I never wanted to be famous; I only wanted to be great."

3. "I learned the way a monkey learns—by watching its parents."

4. "If only I had a little humility, I would be perfect."

5. "The only reason they come to see me is that I know life is great—and they know I know it."

6. "It costs a lot of money to look this cheap."

7. "I guess I look like a rock quarry that someone has dynamited."

8. "Sometimes, at the end of the day when I'm smiling and shaking hands, I want to kick them."

9. "I left high school a virgin."

10. "I never had a date in high school or in college."

11. "I'm not smart enough to lie."

12. "I'm at the age where food has taken the place of sex in my life. In fact, I've just had a mirror put over my kitchen table."

13. "I pretended to be somebody I wanted to be until I finally became that person. Or he became me."

14. "Sitting on the toilet peeing—that's where I have my most contemplative moments."

A. Tom Selleck

B. Cary Grant

C. Sally Jesse Raphael

D. Charles Bronson

E. Richard Nixon

F. Ronald Reagan

G. Madonna

H. Ray Charles

I. Princess Diana

J. Clark Gable

K. Dolly Parton

L. Prince Charles

M. Ted Turner

N. Rodney Dangerfield

ANSWERS 1-I, 2-H, 3-J, 4-M, 5-J, 6-K, 7-D, 8-E, 9-A, 10-C, 11-F, 12-N, 13-B, 14-G

Maine is the only U.S. state with a one-syllable name.

THE REMOTE CONTROL

Over 400 million TV remote controls are currently in use in the United States. Here's the story of their creation.

THE FIRST TV REMOTE

• Commander Eugene MacDonald, Jr., president of the Zenith Radio Co., hated TV commercials. He figured other Americans did too, so he told his researchers to create a system that would mute all ads by remote control.

• Zenith wasn't the only one working on this idea. In 1953, another company introduced a TV remote control that operated with radio waves. Unfortunately, the waves traveled through walls and down the street, and tended to operate *neighbors'* TV sets as well.

TRY, TRY AGAIN

• In 1953 and 1954, Zenith developed two remote-control systems, both of which flopped:

1. The "Lazy Bones" connected to the TV with a long cable. It worked, but among other problems, it kept tripping people.

2. The more advanced "Flashamatic" used four photo cells, one in each corner of the TV cabinet. Each cell controlled one function—volume, channels, etc. All a viewer had to do was aim a flashlight at the right cell. Unfortunately, first-generation couch potatoes couldn't remember which cell did what…and direct sunlight operated all of them at once.

• In 1955, Robert Adler, a Zenith acoustics expert, developed a remote system using high-frequency sound. The device contained an aluminum rod that rang when hit by a hammer. Called the Space Command 200, it debuted in 1956. Retail price: $399.95. Unfortunately, any noise produced by small pieces of metal, such as jingling keys or dog chains, produced tones similar to the remote's, so channels changed and sets turned on and off unpredictably.

• By 1962, the kinks in the Space Command were worked out. Bulky vacuum tubes were replaced with transistors, making the remote smaller and cheaper. But Adler's development of ultrasound remained *the* technique for all remote controls until the early 1980s, when new semiconductors make infrared remote controls capable of transmitting digital codes.

Q: How did Levi's 501 jeans get their name?   A: The original version had 501 copper rivets.

FAMILIAR PHRASES

More origins of everyday phrases.

START WITH A CLEAN SLATE

Meaning: Make a fresh start.

Origin: From the days when tavern keepers used slate blackboards to keep track of money owed by customers. When a person paid off a debt, their name was erased, and they literally got to "start with a clean slate."

HARP ON SOMETHING

Meaning: Dwell obsessively on the same topic.

Origin: The modern expression is a shortened version of the old phrase, "harping on one string," which meant playing the same note of a harp over and over.

BAIL OUT

Meanings: (1) Remove water from a ship; (2) pay to get someone out of jail; and (3) jump out of a plane in an emergency.

Origin: The expression and all of its meanings come from a time when English sailors used buckets known as *beyles* to remove unwanted water from their ships.

BIGWIG

Meaning: Important person.

Origin: Judges and lawyers have worn wigs in British courts since the 18th century. Lawyers wear short wigs, but the judge wears a long wig, sometimes down to his shoulders. That makes the judge —the most important person in the room—literally a "bigwig," because he wears the biggest wig.

CANARY / CANARY ISLANDS / CANARY YELLOW

Meanings: Species of bird; islands near Africa; a shade of yellow.

Origin: When ancient Romans first set foot on an archipelago off the coast of West Africa, they quickly discovered that the islands were crawling with wild dogs. They named the islands *Canariae Insulae*, "Dog Islands." In time, they became known as the "Canary

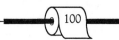

Islands" and the small gray and green finches that lived there became known as "canaries." When selective breeding resulted in a bright yellow variety of the bird, the color itself became known as "canary yellow."

THROW INTO STITCHES
Meaning: Make someone laugh hard.
Origin: This stitch has nothing to do with sewing: it comes from *stice*, an Old English word that means "to sting." When you throw someone into stitches, you make them laugh so hard that it hurts.

TURN A BLIND EYE
Meaning: Deliberately overlook something.
Origin: Goes back to the British admiral Lord Nelson, who was blind in one eye. In 1801, Nelson was second-in-command during a naval attack on Copenhagen. The commanding admiral signaled an order to cease fire. Rather than obey it, Nelson held his telescope up to his blind eye, turned toward the admiral's ship, and told a subordinate, "I don't see anything." The attack continued, and the Danish eventually surrendered.

EAT HUMBLE PIE
Meaning: Admit you're wrong; humiliate yourself.
Origin: In the Middle Ages, when the lord of a manor returned from deer hunting, he and his noble guests dined on *venison* (deer meat), considered the finest part of the deer. His servants and other commoners ate a pie made from the *umbles*—the heart, liver, entrails, and other undesirable parts. Originally, "umbles" and "humble" were unrelated words. But eating the pie was such a humble act that when the word *umble* disappeared, *humble* took its place in this expression.

FORK IT OVER
Meaning: Surrender something.
Origin: Centuries ago, most of the farmland in England was owned by great lords. Farmers were supposed to pay the lords their rent with silver coins. When the farmers had no coins, landlords took wagons into the fields and demanded that the farmers use pitchforks to "fork over some" of the crop instead.

CELEBRITY MUMMIES

Here are a few contemporary mummies of note.

JOHN WILKES BOOTH (aka John St. Helen)
After he shot Lincoln, Booth was a fugitive for 12 days. The government said that federal troops tracked him down and shot him in a Virginia tobacco barn. Then, to prevent his gravesite from becoming a Confederate shrine, they quickly buried him in an unmarked grave at the Washington Arsenal. But this made people suspicious. Why so fast—were they hiding something? Was the man they buried really Booth...or had the assassin escaped?

Over the years, more than 40 people made deathbed "confessions" claiming they were Booth. One of these was John St. Helen. In 1877, thinking he was about to die, St. Helen confessed to a man named Finis L. Bates that he was Lincoln's assassin.

St. Helen actually survived and lived until 1903. When he finally died, Bates had St. Helen's body mummified and moved to his basement, where it was stored for the next 20 years. Then, when Bates died in 1923, his wife sold the mummy. It ended up in the hands of carnival operators who exhibited it as Booth until the mid-1970s. It then disappeared, and hasn't been seen since.

ELMER J. MCCURDY
In 1976, an episode of TV's "The Six Million Dollar Man" was filmed at the Nu-Pike amusement park in Long Beach, California. There was a dummy hanging from a fake gallows in the fun house; when a technician tried to move it out of the way, its arm came off at the elbow...exposing human bones. It was a mummy, not a dummy!

The film crew was horrified. The mummy's face had been painted and shellacked so many times that the amusement park owners thought it was made of *wax*. But who was the mummy? And how did it wind up in the park?

The L.A. County coroner had one clue: the mummy's mouth was stuffed with carnival ticket stubs. They were traced to Oklahoma, and, working with Oklahoma historians, the coroner finally identified the body as Elmer J. McCurdy, a long-forgotten bandit.

According to a 1993 *Wall Street Journal* article:

> Eighty years ago, [McCurdy] robbed the wrong train and rode off
> with $45 and a load of whiskey. When the posse caught him two
> days later, the whiskey was gone and he was having a nice nap. Ac-
> cording to local legend, he decided to shoot it out anyway. That was
> another mistake. An...undertaker in Pawhuska, OK, mummified his
> body and put it on display for 5¢ a view until 1916, when two men
> posing as Mr. McCurdy's brothers claimed the corpse. They were
> actually carnival promoters. For decades, the unfortunate Mr.
> McCurdy crisscrossed the country as a sideshow attraction.

The town of Guthrie, Oklahoma, paid for McCurdy's trip back to
the state and gave him a Christian burial. His grave (which has
been sealed in concrete to ensure that it is his *final* resting place)
is now the town's biggest tourist attraction.

EVA "EVITA" PERON

Juan Peron was the president of Argentina from 1948 to 1954. His
wife, Eva, a former actress and a crusader for the poor, was extremely popular. When she died of cancer in 1952 at age 33, Peron had
her mummified and put on public display. The procedure took
about a year and cost $100,000.

Peron fell from power while his wife was still lying in state, and
went into exile in Spain before he could arrange her burial. Evita
was put in storage in Buenos Aires. Then her body disappeared.

It turned out that anti-Peronists—making sure the body was never again used as a pro-Peron political symbol—had stolen the coffin, sealed it in a packing crate, and eventually buried it in a Milan
cemetary. In 1971—19 years later—a sympathetic Spanish intelligence officer told Peron where his wife was buried. Peron had her
exhumed and brought to Spain. When the ex-dictator pried open
the coffin, his wife was so well preserved that he cried out, "She is
not dead, she is only sleeping!"

Rather than bury his Evita again, Peron kept her around the
house; he and his third wife, Isabel, propped her up in the dining-
room and ate in her presence every evening, even when they entertained guests. The arrangement lasted until 1973, when Peron returned to power in Argentina and left his beloved mummy in
Spain. Later, Evita was brought across the Atlantic and was buried
in Argentina.

If you want to hardboil an ostrich egg, bring along something to do. It takes up to four hours.

GROUCHO SEZ...

A few choice words from the master, Groucho Marx.

"I've had a perfectly wonderful evening. But this wasn't it."

"I was married by a judge. I should have asked for the jury."

"Remember men, we're fighting for this woman's honor—which is probably more than she ever did."

"If I held you any closer, I'd be on the other side of you."

"Those are my principles. If you don't like them I have others."

"From the moment I picked up your book until I laid it down, I was convulsing with laughter. Someday I intend to read it."

"The husband who wants a perfect marriage should learn how to keep his mouth shut and his checkbook open."

"Oh, are you from Wales? Do you know a fellow named Jonah? He used to live in Wales for a while."

"Blood's not thicker than money."

"He may look like an idiot and talk like an idiot, but don't let that fool you. He really is an idiot."

"The secret of success is honesty and fair dealing. If you can fake those, you've got it made."

"Well, Art is Art, isn't it? Still, on the other hand, water is water! And East is East and West is West and if you take cranberries and stew them with applesauce they taste more like prunes than rhubarb does.... Now you tell me what *you* know."

"I've been around so long I can remember Doris Day before she was a virgin."

"Outside of a dog, a book is a man's best friend. Inside of a dog it's too hard to read."

"Who are you going to believe, me or your own eyes?"

"Well, I hardly know where to begin. I hardly know when to stop, either; just give me a few drinks and see for yourself."

SILENT PARTNERS

Everyone knows that Hollywood is a world of fiction and fantasy; even so, it's hard to believe that people who appear to like one another on TV and in film sometimes loathe each other in real life. Some examples:

FRED AND ETHEL MERTZ ("I LOVE LUCY")

How we remember them: Fred and Ethel (William Frawley and Vivian Vance) were like everybody's next-door neighbors. Both were frumpy and grumpy, but underneath, they had an abiding love for one another...at least in front of the cameras.

How they really were: Frawley and Vance could barely stand each other from the moment they began working on the show... and things got worse from there: Vance, who was 25 years Frawley's junior (39 to his 64), hated the idea that viewers believed she could be married to someone so old. "He should be playing my *father*, not my husband," she routinely complained. Another thorn in her side: there was a clause in her contract that allowed the show to dump her if Frawley died or became too ill to work.

Frawley wasn't any happier: his nicknames for Vance were "Old Fat Ass" and "that old sack of doorknobs," and he was famous for frequently asking Desi, "Where did you dig up that bitch?"

Silent treatment: Things came to a head near the end of the "I Love Lucy" run, when Desi Arnaz approached Vance about spinning off the Fred and Ethel characters into their own show.

As Vance later recounted,

> I loathed Bill Frawley, and the feeling was mutual....There was no way I could do a series with him on our own, so when Desi asked me, I refused. I still wouldn't budge when he offered me a bonus of $50,000 just to do a pilot. When Bill found out, he was furious, not because he wanted to work with me any more than I did with him, but because he stood to earn a lot more money than he did on "Lucy." He never spoke to me again except when work required it.

A few years after "I Love Lucy" ended, someone asked Frawley if he'd kept in touch with Vance. "I don't know where she is now and she doesn't know where I am," he replied, "and that's exactly the way I like it."

Why are all the continents wider in the north than in the south? Nobody knows.

ABBOTT AND COSTELLO

How we remember them: The quintessential buddy comedy team of the 1930s, 1940s, and 1950s. Sure, they fought onstage, but that was part of their act…and it never seemed to get in the way of their warm friendship.

How they really were: According to Penny Stallings in *Forbidden Channels*, Abbott and Costello's relationship deteriorated toward the end of their careers. Abbott was one of showbiz's greatest straight men, but Costello came to believe that he'd "carried" Abbott for years. Mel Blanc, who worked on Abbott and Costello's TV show in the 1950s, recalled, "They hated each other. Especially Costello. Even at the end he was still trying to get other straight men, but he could just never find one as good."

Silent treatment: The pair frequently hosted "The Colgate Comedy Hour," but Costello stormed off the set after an argument one day and never returned. Instead, he became a frequent guest on a competing show hosted by Steve Allen. Abbott was so upset by the split that he fell ill and had to check into a hospital. The relationship remained troubled from then on: Costello later sued Abbott for $222,000 in unpaid royalties, but he dropped dead of a heart attack in 1959 before the suit was resolved.

SONNY AND CHER

How we remember them: The ultimate hippie power couple of the 1960s and early 1970s, Sonny and Cher were a beacon of stability at a time when people were questioning the merits of traditional relationships. In their songs, on their show, and in their marriage—or so we thought—Sonny and Cher proved that two people didn't have to be square to be devoted to one another.

How they really were: Not long after they hit superstardom with their variety TV show, Sonny and Cher's private life began to crumble. In November 1972, Sonny says, Cher announced she was having an affair with their guitarist. Sonny was devastated, but within a few months, he realized their marriage was over for good…at least behind the scenes. Public perception was another story, as Bono recounts in his autobiography *And the Beat Goes On.*

How about you? 37% of U.S. coffee drinkers use milk & sugar; 21% drink it black.

Despite their differences, he and Cher decided to stay together for the sake of their bank accounts:

> I told Cher that she had to realize that we were involved in a business, a highly profitable business, and though the marriage was gone and the love lost, it was silly to give up the tremendous sums of money we were making. I'd come to terms with the reality of our situation. I accepted it...and I was OK with her pursuing whatever personal life she wanted. I'd do the same. But Sonny and Cher were names too valuable to simply walk away from. She agreed.

Silent treatment: For the last year of their marriage and their variety show, Sonny and Cher lived a lie: pretending to be happily married, they set up separate households in different parts of their 54-room mansion, Sonny with his lover in one corner and Cher with hers in another. The charade lasted until February 1974, when Cher moved out and filed for divorce on grounds of "involuntary servitude." They've been taking potshots at each other in the media ever since.

"Cher wants to run like a racehorse, but she can't find a track," Bono laments in his autobiography. "I used to be the jockey, but Cher quite nicely shoved the saddle up my ass."

SISKEL AND EBERT

How we think of them: The best film critics on TV. "The fat one" (Ebert) and "the other guy" (Siskel) seem to get along pretty well despite their different opinions about movies.

How they really are: As *Time* magazine reported in 1987, "The two have little in common outside the TV studio....They rarely socialize...Nor are their fights confined to the TV cameras. In the middle of an interview, for example, Ebert will complain that Siskel won't let him plug his books on TV. And Siskel will deride his partner for his "megalomania." "He thinks the world revolves around him," Siskel sneers to the reporter. Are they just kidding? No one knows.

Silent treatment: Siskel and Ebert don't even sit together during their film screenings. Siskel sits at the rear of the screening room, and Ebert sits closer to the front, *Time* reports, "usually munching from a box of Good & Plenty."

"Hansel" means "Johnny" in German.

I SCREAM, YOU SCREAM

We've uncovered a lot of food origins in the Bathroom Readers, but until now, we never got around to one of the best foods of all.

ICE AGES

Which is oldest—ice cream, sherbet, or snow cones?

As far as anyone can tell, snow cones are the oldest: they date back at least as far as Roman emperor Nero (37 A.D. to 68 A.D.), who had snow brought down from mountaintops to cool his wine cellars. On hot days he'd mix some of the extra snow with honey, juices, and fruit pulps, and eat it as a snack.

Sherbet—which has more fruit and less milk or cream than ice cream—came next. In the late 13th century, Marco Polo brought a recipe for sherbet from China to Italy. Only a few people knew about it. "Recipes [for sherbet] were secrets, closely guarded by chefs to the wealthy," explains Charles Panati in *Extraordinary Origins of Everyday Things.*

Historians estimate that sometime in the 16th century one of these chefs—no one knows who—increased the milk content in the recipe and reduced or eliminated the fruit entirely...inventing ice cream in the process.

RICH DESSERT

Iced dessert remained an exclusive, upper-class treat for over a century. "With refrigeration a costly ordeal of storing winter ice in underground vaults for summer use," Panati says, "only the wealthy tasted iced desserts." Then, in 1670, a Sicilian named Francesco Procopio dei Coltelli opened Paris's first coffeehouse, Cafe Procope. It was the first business ever to make ice cream available to the general public.

This inspired other coffeehouses around Europe to do the same. By the mid-17th century, ice cream could be found in most of the continent's major cities...and by the end of the century, people were addicted to it. Beethoven wrote from Vienna in 1794: "It is very warm here....As winter is mild, ice is rare. The Viennese are afraid that it will soon be impossible to have any ice cream."

The average U.S. farm has 467 acres of land; the average Japanese farm has 3 acres.

ICE CREAM IN AMERICA

Meanwhile, ice cream had gotten a foothold in the New World. It was first brought over in 1690, and by 1777 it was being advertised in New York newspapers. Ice cream was popular with many of the Founding Fathers, including Alexander Hamilton, George Washington (who ran up a $200 ice cream tab with one New York merchant in the summer of 1790), and Thomas Jefferson (who had his own 18-step recipe for ice cream and is believed to be the first president to serve it at a state dinner). First Lady Dolly Madison's ice cream parties helped make ice cream fashionable among the new republic's upper crust.

CRANKING IT OUT

By the 1790s, ice cream was becoming more readily available in the United States, but it was still a rare treat due to the scarcity and high price of ice—and the difficulty in making it. Most ice cream was made using the "pot freezer" method: the ingredients sat in a pot that, in turn, sat in a larger pan of salt and ice. The whole thing had to be shaken up and down by one person, while another vigorously stirred the mixture.

Over the next 50 years, two developments made ice cream an American staple:

1. In the early 1800s, "ice harvesting" of frozen northern rivers in winter months, combined with insulated icehouses that sprang up all over the country, made ice—and therefore ice cream—cheap for the first time. By 1810, ice cream was being sold by street vendors in nearly every major city in the United States.

2. In 1846, Nancy Johnson created the world's first hand-cranked ice cream freezer. With this invention, ice cream was both affordable *and* easy to make for the first time. By 1850, it was so common that *Godey's Lady's Book* could comment: "A party without it would be like a breakfast without bread."

WE ALL SCREAM

By 1900, electricity and mechanical refrigeration had given rise to a huge domestic ice cream industry. And it had become so closely identified with American culture that the people in charge of Ellis Island, determined to serve a "truly American dish" to arriving immigrants, served them ice cream at every meal.

End to end, the number of Crayola crayons made in a year would circle the globe 4-1/2 times.

WEIRD BAR SPORTS

Here's a look at some of the more unusual ways that bar owners have tried to keep customers busy and entertained while they drink.

DWARF TOSSING
How It's Played: A dwarf dresses up in body padding, a crash helmet, and a harness. Then contestants hurl him across the room into a pile of mattresses. The "winner" is the person who throws the dwarf the farthest. In some contests, dwarfs have been thrown as much as 30 feet. Why do the dwarfs do it? They can make as much as $2,000 a night.

History: Invented at a Queensland, Australia, bar in 1985. It later produced an offshoot—dwarf bowling: "A helmeted dwarf is strapped to a skateboard or mechanic's creeper and rolled headfirst into bowling pins, which are made of plastic."

In 1987, a few American bars tried out this "sport," and it was a commercial success. But the bad publicity—combined with lobbying by groups like Little People of America—killed it.

THE HUMAN (BAR)FLY

How It's Played: Wearing a velcro suit, bar patrons sprint down a runway, leap on a small trampoline, and hurl themselves onto a wall covered with velcro hooks. First prize goes to the person whose feet stick highest on the wall. Getting off the wall can be fun, too. "One of our rules is that the men peel off the women, and the women peel off the men," says a bar owner. "Sometimes it takes three women to peel off one guy."

History: Inspired by David Letterman, who performed the stunt on his show in 1984. The Cri Bar and Grill in New Zealand began holding "human fly" contests in 1991, and other New Zealand bars followed suit. *Sports Illustrated* covered it in 1991; it quickly spread to the United States, where it flourished for a few years.

SUMO SUIT WRESTLING

How It's Played: Participants don 43-pound rubberized vinyl and nylon suits that make them look like 400-pound sumo wrestlers—

Most frequently used words in the English language: the, of, and, to, a, in, that, is, I, for, and as.

complete with the traditional Japanese sumo "diaper" and a crash helmet with a sumo wig glued on the outside. Then they slam into each other on a big padded mat. (Not to be confused with human cockfighting, in which—no kidding—people dress up in padded chicken costumes and peck, bump, and scratch each other.)

History: Englishman Peter Herzig invented the suits after seeing sumo wrestlers in a Miller Beer commercial. Miller then bought hundreds of the suits and began promoting the "sport" in nightclubs in the early 1990s.

HUMAN BOWLING

How It's Played: Like real bowling, you have to knock down as many pins as you can…but in this sport, the pins are five feet tall and made of canvas and styrofoam; the bowler is strapped *inside* a huge metal-frame bowling ball. A partner rolls them down the 30-foot lane toward the pins. "Just because you're in the ball doesn't mean you have no obligations to the team," says Lori Fosdick, a regular bowler. "I've seen some pretty maneuvers—but I've also seen people who seemed to be going straight and rolled right around the pin."

History: Creator Thomas Bell got the idea in the early 1990s after watching some gerbils running on an exercise wheel. He figured humans might enjoy doing the same thing. "Bowling has always been a competitive sport," he says straight-faced. "We're just taking it to a more competitive level."

GERBIL RACING

How It's Played: Eight gerbils race in a portable race track that's set up on the wall behind the bar. Betting is not allowed, but customers who pick the winning gerbil win free drinks.

History: Invented in 1992 by a bar in Alberta, Canada, with the blessings of the Canadian SPCA. "My gerbils live to the age of two, unlike wild gerbils, which have a lifespan of only eight months," says Morley Amon, owner of the Alberta track. "They aren't running against their will. They run just to see what's on the other side."

BRAND NAMES

*Here's another look at brand names you
know and where they come from.*

Q-TIPS. In the early 1920s, the owner of the Gerstenzang Infant Novelty Company noticed that his wife cleaned their daughter's ears by wrapping cotton around a toothpick. Inspired, he built a machine that made "ready-to-use cotton swabs." At first he called the product Baby Gays. In 1926, they became Q-Tips ("Q for Quality") Baby Gays...and finally just Q-Tips.

ZIPPO LIGHTERS. Introduced as a revolutionary windproof lighter in 1932 and named after another revolutionary invention of the time—the zipper.

MAYBELLINE. In 1915, Mabel Williams created an eye makeup for herself out of black pigment and petroleum jelly. Her brother decided to sell it in his mail-order catalog as Lash-Brow-Ine. It sold extremely well, and in 1920 he changed the name to Maybelline, as a gesture to her.

SARAN WRAP. In 1933, Dow researchers discovered a plastic called *monomeric vinylidene chloride.* They called it VC Plastic. In 1940, a salesman suggested they rename it Saran (the name of a tree in India). Dow liked the new name because it had only five letters and had no negative connotations. During World War II, Saran was used in everything from belts to subway seats. In 1948, it was marketed to housewives as a plastic film called Saran Wrap.

MAX FACTOR. In the early days of the movie industry, Max Factor devised a new makeup that made actors look natural on film. It established his reputation as Hollywood's premier cosmetics authority, which gave him cachet with the general public.

RAY-BANS. Originally called "Anti-Glare goggles" in 1936. Bausch & Lomb, the manufacturer, decided "anti-glare" would be too hard to protect as a trademark, so the glasses—designed to "inhibit ultraviolet and infrared rays"—were re-christened Ray-Bans.

MISS AMERICA, PART II:
The Early Years

Here's more of the history of the Miss America Pageant. (Part I is on page 49.) One aspect we find fascinating: The same "traditionalists" who call Miss America their own and fight to preserve it whenever it's threatened today were its biggest enemies in the 1920s and 1930s. It goes to show how transient some notions of "decency" and "morality" can be.

RAKING IN THE DOUGH

The 1921 Fall Frolic was such a moneymaker that the Atlantic City government increased its contribution from $1,000 to $12,500 the following year. The number of participating newspapers also increased in 1922, from 8 to 57 (this time the entire country was represented). As the pageant grew, so did the crowds that thronged to see it. In 1922, 250,000 people visited Atlantic City during the pageant; 300,000 came the following year.

To maximize the time (and money) that tourists spent in Atlantic City, organizers spread the events out over three days in 1922, and then to five days in 1924 and afterward. As A. R. Riverol writes in *Live from Atlantic City:*

> The ingenuity in the pageant was that it was structured to keep the people at the resort happily spending their money. Most events were scheduled either on separate days or on the same day but hours apart....To enjoy all of the offerings of the *Miss America* pageant, the day tripper would either have to wait for hours or travel to Atlantic City the next day. The answer? Stay overnight.

A MAJOR SETBACK

But as the Atlantic City festivities grew in popularity, they also attracted increasing opposition. Even in the "Roaring '20s," bathing suit contests were as controversial as wet T-shirt contests are today. Women's groups and civic and religious organizations condemned the pageant for being indecent, for exploiting women for money, and for corrupting the youthful contestants.

On top of the general criticism, there were also a number of "scandals" that muddied the pageant's reputation. In 1923, for example, Miss Brooklyn and Miss Boston turned out to be married; Miss Alaska was not only married, but also a resident of New York City—not Alaska.

As the '20s wore on, hotel owners began to lose faith in the pageant as a moneymaker. Frank Deford writes in *There She Is:*

> They became convinced that the pageant, for all its notice, was starting to give Atlantic City a bad name, and cost the hotels respectable cash-and-carry patrons.

HARD TIMES

Finally in 1928, after years of negative publicity and vehement opposition from conservative groups, the Atlantic City hotel operators decided to shut Miss America down, stating that it had degenerated into a "worn out and useless...cheap exploitation of physical beauty."

From the very beginning critics had charged that the pageant lured "bad" women to the boardwalk and turned innocent young girls into hussies; now the organizers believed it themselves. The Hotelmen's Association declared:

> There has been an epidemic recently of women who seek personal aggrandizement and publicity by participating in various stunts throughout the world, and the hotelmen feel that in recent years that type of woman has been attracted to the Pageant in ever-increasing numbers....Many of the girls who come here turn out bad later and though it may happen in other cities, it reflects on Atlantic City.

SECOND TRY—THE 1933 PAGEANT

"Miss America" seemed to be dead and buried. But memories of the big bucks the pageant had brought in lingered on...and in 1933, in the middle of the Great Depression, a handful of organizers decided to bring it back to life.

The Hotelmen's Association and the Chamber of Commerce refused to support it, and the newspapers—who'd sponsored earlier beauty contests—declined to participate. So the pageant had to turn to carnivals, amusement parks, theaters, and other seedy businesses to find beauty queens to compete in the 1933 event.

There were so many problems during Pageant Week that the 1933 contest became, arguably, the biggest disaster in Miss America history. For example:

- Miss West Virginia had to drop out because of stomach pains after she ate lobster with her ice cream.
- Miss New York State collapsed onstage from an abscessed tooth.
- Miss Oklahoma was rushed to the hospital for an emergency appendectomy.
- Miss Arkansas was revealed to be married.
- Misses Iowa, Illinois, and Idaho were disqualified because they actually resided in neither Iowa, Illinois, nor Idaho.

The 1933 crown ultimately went to Miss Connecticut, 15-year-old Marian Bergeron, but her shining moment was tarnished. "The crown was so big it came right down over my eyes, and it made me look retarded," she recalled years later. The crown was stolen the day after and was never recovered.

IF AT FIRST YOU DON'T SUCCEED...

The 1933 pageant was such a loser that until the mid-'50s, organizers of the Miss America pageants never recognized it as an "official" pageant...or acknowledged Bergeron as a genuine Miss America.

Nonetheless, in 1935, "respectable" members of Atlantic City society decided to hold another one. Why? They were probably motivated by competition. In 1934 an "American Queen of Beauty" was crowned in Madison Square Garden. And a year later, a "Miss America" was named at the San Diego County Fair. These contests were even sleazier than their Atlantic City predecessor. According to *There She Is*, the San Diego crown was conferred upon the winner by "the two gentlemen who ran the midget and nudist concessions at the fairs." And the San Diego Miss America didn't get a cash prize, a college scholarship, or anything like that. Instead, she won "the 'right' to pose in the buff for two years."

Rather than let a good thing get away—and perhaps also to keep the Miss America name from sinking deeper into the muck, if such a thing were possible—Atlantic City decided to give the pageant one more chance in 1935.

Stay tuned—there's more on page 151.

Ben and Jerry's Ice Cream gives its ice cream waste to Vermont farmers, who use

1995: THE YEAR OF THE TOILET

This article on film history, by movie critic Mick LaSalle,
appeared in the S.F. Chronicle on Dec. 24, 1995.

Hollywood went into the toilet in 1995. On that, most critics agree. But the fact that this was quite specifically true—that a disproportionate number of scenes took place in bathrooms, dealing with bathroom concerns, has been strangely overlooked.

Face it: The bedroom has been exhausted for shock effect. The bathroom is virgin territory. And it's open season out there.

[In 1995] there were bathroom Peeping Toms (*Homage*), women's-room gang fights (*Only the Brave*), men's-room fistfights (*Shallow Grave*), and casual conversations unimpeded by the fact that one of the participants was sitting on the throne (*The Brothers McMullen*). And the bathroom became the "in" place to get murdered (*GoldenEye*, *Fair Game*, *Copycat*).

What made these and other scenes unique is not that they took place in bathrooms but that they strained to be unblinking and explicit about why the characters were there.

This is new. Until recently, using the bathroom was the one thing you never saw characters doing. In fact, for 30 years the Production Code forbade showing a toilet on screen. But today, were *Psycho* being made, the shower scene would be preceded by an interlude of the heroine rather humbly and nonchalantly making use of the facilities.

The factors that combined to make 1995 the Year of the Toilet are difficult to pinpoint. But the beginnings of the trend can be traced to 1991 and the British film *Twenty-One*. That film concluded with the protagonist (Patsy Kensit) addressing the audience as she sat on the bowl

Since then, American films have shown an increase in bathroom activity. *Mac*, *Deep Cover*, *Jimmy Hollywood*, and, especially, *Dumb and Dumber* all depicted characters heeding the call of nature. Yet even the most astute observer of popular culture could not have anticipated 1995's cinematic run to the john.

"The bathroom is a space very much tied up with ritual and convention," says Jason Drucker, who teaches at De Paul University in

Chicago and works in the field of semiotics (the study of signs). "For example, when I go up to a urinal, I don't have a conversation with the people standing next to me. The question is how are these movies transforming the conventional perspective?"

Turns out, movies are using bathrooms in deliberately unconventional ways. Most people, for example, shut the door—unlike Elisabeth Shue in *Leaving Las Vegas*. And, despite what you see in movies (and on TV shows such as "NYPD Blue"), men usually do not stand next to each other at the urinal talking up a storm. They stand as far apart as possible. They shut up. And they concentrate.

We've always had powder-room scenes," says Dr. Joyce Brothers, "women repairing their makeup, having catty chats. Now we're seeing men that way, unguarded, bonding, gossiping about business."

Yet the more effective men's-room scenes of 1995 tapped into a sense of vulnerability. In *High Risk*, the Jet Li action film from Hong Kong, when two men get alongside another man at a urinal, it's an invasion of space that signals menace, not camaraderie.

Using the bathroom as a place of danger and intimidation has plenty of precedents, and not just in *Jurassic Park* and *Pulp Fiction*. "There's a folklore tradition of people being assaulted by spirits in outhouses," says University of California at Berkeley professor Carol Clover, author of *Men, Women and Chainsaws*. "It dates back to the Middle Ages."

The bathroom took on other functions as well in 1995. "A bathroom scene can be used to tell audiences that people are comfortable with each other—as a kind of shortcutting," Brothers says. "People will be married years before they will leave the door open."

In *My Life and Times with Antoni Artaud*, the lovers were so familiar that the woman didn't even bother with the bathroom. She squatted on the sink.

According to Barbara Dixon of the Motion Picture Association of America, which assigns ratings to films, the MPAA has "no special policy" with regard to the bathroom.

The Year of the Toilet might be an anomaly, some unexplainable thing that happened to be in the air, as it were. Then again, maybe not. It's clear we've come a long way from the soft-focus close-ups of 50 years ago. The last decades have shown a move from the unreal and glamorous to the down and dirty. As an extension of that trend, 1995 may be the watershed —or water closet—year.

George Washington was named after King George of England.

THE ORIGINS OF HALLOWEEN

Why do we dress up on Halloween? Here's the story from an old favorite,
Charles Panati's Extraordinary Origins of Everyday Things.

GHOSTBUSTERS
Even in ancient times, Halloween was a festival for dressing up as witches, goblins, and ghosts, as well as for lighting bonfires and playing devilish pranks. What has changed over the centuries are the reasons for doing these things. Now they are done for fun—and by children; in the past, they were done in deathly earnest—and by adults.

Named "All Hallows Eve," the festival was first celebrated by the ancient Celts in Ireland in the fifth century B.C. On the night of October 31, then the official end of summer, Celtic households extinguished the fires on their hearths to deliberately make their homes cold and undesirable to disembodied spirits. They then gathered outside the village, where a Druid priest kindled a huge bonfire to simultaneously honor the sun god for the past summer's harvest and to frighten away furtive spirits.

THAT'S THE SPIRIT

The Celts believed that on October 31, all persons who had died in the previous year assembled to choose the body of the person or animal they would inhabit for the next 12 months, before they could pass peacefully into the afterlife. To frighten roving souls, Celtic family members dressed as demons, hobgoblins, and witches. They paraded first inside, then outside, the fireless house, in as noisy and destructive a manner as possible. Finally, they clamored along the street to the bonfire outside town. A villager, deemed by appearance or mannerism to be already possessed, could be sacrificed in the fire as a lesson to other spirits contemplating human possession.

The Romans adopted Celtic Hallows Eve practices, but in 61 A.D. they outlawed human sacrifice, substituting the Egyptian custom of effigies ([they] buried scores of statuettes with a pharaoh in place of his living attendants).... In time, as belief in spirit possession waned, the dire portents of many Halloween practices lightened to ritualized amusement.

The average office worker spends 50 minutes a day looking for lost files and other items.

Irish immigrants fleeing their country's potato famine in the 1840s brought to America with them the Halloween customs of costume and mischief. The favorite pranks played by New England Irish youths on "mischief night" were overturning outhouses and unhinging front gates.

THE JACK-O-LANTERN

The Irish also brought with them a custom that New England agriculture forced them to modify. The ancient Celts had begun the tradition of a sort of jack-o'-lantern, a large turnip hollowed out and carved with a demon's face and lighted from inside with a candle. Immigrants found few turnips in their new land but numerous fields of pumpkins. Whereas the Pilgrims had made the edible part of the pumpkin a hallmark of Thanksgiving, the Irish made the outer shell synonymous with Halloween.

It was also the Irish who originated the term jack-o'-lantern, taken from Irish folklore. As the legend goes, a man named Jack, notorious for drunken and niggardly ways, tricked the devil into climbing up a tree. Quickly carving a cross into the tree's trunk, Jack trapped Satan until he swore he'd never again tempt Jack to sin.

Upon his death, Jack found himself barred from the comforts of heaven for his repeated sinning, and also refused entrance to the heat of hell from an unforgiving Satan. Condemned to wander in frigid darkness until Judgment Day, he implored the devil for burning embers to light his way....Satan...allotted Jack a single coal that would last an agonizingly short time. Putting the ember into a turnip he had chewed hollow, he formed Jack's lantern.

TRICK OR TREAT

The most widely accepted theory on the origins of trick-or-treating traces the practice to the ninth-century European custom of "souling." On All Soul's Day, Christians walked from village to village begging for square biscuits with currants, called "soul cakes." The beggars promised to offer up prayers for the dead relatives of the donors, the number of prayers to be proportional to the donors' generosity. The quantity of prayers a dead person amassed was significant in a practical way, for limbo was the penitential layover stop on the journey to heaven, and sufficient prayer, even by an anonymous individual, greatly shortened the stay.

Q: Why do helium-filled balloons float?   A: Helium is seven times lighter than air.

DUMB CRIMINALS

*Many Americans are worried about the growing threat of crime. Well,
the good news is that there are plenty of crooks who are their own
worst enemies. Here are a few true-life examples.*

TAKE ALL YOU WANT

"SEATTLE — Police got an early morning call from the owners of a motor home parked on a Seattle street. When officers arrived, they found sewage and what looked like vomit on the ground. Nearby, they found a man curled up ill next to the car.

"The man admitted he had been trying to siphon gas and had plugged his hose into the motor home's sewage tank by mistake. The motor home's owner declined to press charges, calling it the 'best laugh he's ever had.' "

—The Eugene *Register-Guard*, Aug. 6, 1991
(Submitted by BRI member Karen Roth, Eugene, Oregon)

DOG YUMMIES

"SPRING VALLEY, Calif. — Thieves broke into a commercial meat freezer in Spring Valley and are not being pursued as a high priority. The freezer is located equidistant between two buildings. The thieves undoubtedly thought the freezer belonged to a restaurant and that they were stealing frozen steaks for resale; in reality, it belongs to the restaurant's next-door neighbor, the Paradise Valley Road Pet Hospital, which reported nine euthanized dogs missing."

—*News of the Weird, March, 1996*

MAKING TRACKS

"SPOKANE, Wash. — Police had little difficulty catching up with a woman who robbed the Five Mile branch of the Washington Trust Bank last Saturday. The woman, who walked into the bank and showed the teller what appeared to be the handle of a gun, was given an undetermined amount of cash. She then walked out of the bank, got into a waiting cab and left. Police traced the taxi and got the woman's address. She was arrested without incident.

—Wire service story, March 8, 1996

A watermelon is 92% water; a raw apple is 84% water.

EYE DID IT

"EL CERRITO, Calif. — Robbery suspect Aaron Lavell Harris has given new meaning to the word *eyewitness*. Police searching the scene of an aborted armed robbery last week found one clue—a glass eye with Harris's name stenciled on it. Apparently, it popped out when Harris jumped from a second-story window to escape."
—San Francisco *Chronicle*, March 24, 1993

BALED OUT

"LANCASTER, Calif. — An inmate who fled prison by hiding in a garbage truck found himself trapped in a compacted bale of trash on Thursday. The prisoner thought he could escape the minimum-security prison by hiding in a trash bin. But the bin was collected by a truck that crushes garbage into a bale about one-fifth the size of the original load. The bale and prisoner were dumped at a land-fill. He was discovered by the operator of a tractor breaking up garbage. He is listed in fair condition with broken bones."
—The *Oregonian*, Jan 14, 1996

THANKS FOR THE RIDE

"OSLO, Norway — Thomas Braendvik was walking to the local police station to report the theft of his bicycle, when a kind bicyclist headed his way offered him a lift. Braendvik accepted, and took a seat on the luggage rack.

" 'I thought the bike looked suspiciously like mine, so I asked if he minded me trying my key in the lock,' Braendvik told a reporter. The key fit, proving that the bike belonged to Braendvik. A policeman happened to have been watching the whole episode. He arrested the thief on the spot."
—Associated Press, July 7, 1996

WRONG BAR

"CHICAGO — Two would-be robbers could not have picked a worse place than Z's Sports Tap for their holdup attempt. Much to their chagrin, there was a retirement party going on…for a police officer. There were more than 100 cops in the bar. They quickly subdued the robbers and called on-duty police. 'That's what makes this job interesting,' said a police spokesman. 'Dumb people.' "
—Wire service reports, December 21, 1995

According to our resident astronomer, 41% of the moon is not visible from earth at any time.

WILL ROGERS SAID...

A tiny piece of the rich legacy left by America's national humorist in the 1920s and early 1930s. (He died in 1935.)

"Even if you are on the right track, you'll get run over if you just sit there."

"If stupidity got us into this mess, why can't it get us out?"

"We can't all be heroes... because someone has to sit on the curb and clap as they go by."

"Alexander Hamilton started the U.S. Treasury with nothing—and that was the closest our country has ever been to being even."

"There's no trick to being a humorist when you have the whole government working for you."

"I belong to no organized party. I am a Democrat."

"You can't say civilizations don't advance...In every war they kill you a new way."

"The man with the best job in the country is the Vice-President. All he has to do is get up every morning and say, 'How is the president?' "

"Diplomacy is the art of saying 'Nice doggie' until you can find a rock."

"Nothing you can't spell will ever work."

"If you make any money, the government shoves you in the creek once a year with it in your pockets. All that don't get wet you can keep."

"Liberty don't work as good in practice as it does in speeches."

"I see we are starting to pay attention to our neighbors in the south. We could never understand why Mexico wasn't just crazy about us; for we have always had their good will, and oil and minerals, at heart."

"Half our life is spent trying to find something to do with the time we have rushed through life trying to save."

"I never expected to see the day when girls would get sunburned in the places they do today."

A female mackerel lays 500,000 eggs at a time.

CELEBRITY SUPERSTITIONS

They're only human, after all.

Luciano Pavarotti: "I won't sing a note or act a word until I find a bent nail onstage. It's like a good-luck charm for me. If I can't spot my nail onstage, I search the wings."

Larry Bird (basketball player): Always makes sure to rub his hands on his sneakers before a game, to give him "a better feel" for the ball.

Lena Horne (singer): Thinks peanut shells in her dressing room bring bad luck.

Winston Churchill: Thought it was unlucky to travel on Fridays. Tried to arrange his schedule so he could "stay put" on that day.

Tony Curtis (actor): Wears only slip-on shoes. Thinks laces are unlucky.

Cornelius Vanderbilt (America's richest man in the 1860s): Had the legs of his bed placed in dishes of salt, to ward off attacks from evil spirits.

Drew Barrymore (actor): Says "peas indicate good luck."

Jim Kelly (Buffalo Bills quarterback): Vomits for good luck before each game. He's been doing it since high school.

Queen Elizabeth II: Insists on making a token payment for scissors used to cut ribbons at official openings. (It's bad luck to accept scissors as a gift and return nothing.)

Babe Ruth: Always stepped on first base when he came in from his right field position.

Zsa Zsa Gabor: Thinks it's bad luck to have goldfish in the house.

Wayne Gretzky (the NHL's all-time leading scorer): Puts baby powder on his stick before every game, and tucks only one side of his jersey into his pants.

Joan Rivers: "I knock on wood so often I have splinters in all ten knuckles."

Princess Diana: Had a lock of hair sewn into her wedding dress. (For luck?)

Great name: In some parts of England, garbage collectors are known as "swill solicitors."

FAMILY REUNIONS

You know how strange it seems when you find out you have an unexpected connection to someone. But what if the person were closely related to you? These stories are almost too weird for words, but they're all true. Inspired by an article sent by BRI member Joann McCracken in Boston.

WHO: James Austin and Yvette Richardson / Brother and sister

SEPARATION: When Yvette was three years old and James was seven months old, their father and mother separated. The father took James; the mother took Yvette. That was the last time the siblings saw or heard of each other.

TOGETHER AGAIN: James went to school in Philadelphia and got a job at the main post office. He worked the 4 p.m. shift, along with 4,100 other people. One day, he was talking to his shop steward, Barrie Bowens, about his life. As the *Boston Globe* reported:

> Austin told her that his father died young and that he never knew his mother. Bowens asked his mother's name and realized it was the name of Richardson's mother, too.
>
> For two years, James and Yvette had worked side by side, shooting the breeze but never prying into each other's personal life....Now they discovered they were brother and sister.

They were stunned. "Working in the same department side by side," the 34-year-old Richardson said, shaking her head. "The same place, the same time, every day. What are the odds of that?"

WHO: John Garcia and Nueng Garcia / Father and son

SEPARATION: During the late 1960s, John Garcia was stationed in Thailand with the Air Force. He lived with a woman named Pratom Semon, and in 1969, they had a son. Three months later, Garcia was shipped back to the States; he wanted to take Semon, but she refused to go. For two years, Garcia regularly wrote and sent checks to support his son. Then Semon started seeing another man and told Garcia to end his correspondence. Garcia lost touch with his son. Although he tried to find him, even sending

---

The typical U.S. 18-year-old has spent 11,000 hours in school and 18,000 hours watching TV.

letters to the Thai government requesting an address, he was unsuccessful. He reluctantly gave up.

TOGETHER AGAIN: In 1996, John (who lived in Pueblo, Colorado) was driving through Colorado Springs when he decided to stop at a gas station. He filled up and bought two lottery tickets, then handed the clerk a check for $18. According to news reports, when the clerk saw the name on the check, the conversation went like this: "Are you John Garcia?" "Yes." "Were you ever in the Air Force?" "Yes." "Were you ever in Thailand?" "Yes." "Did you ever have a son?"

"With that question," writes the *San Francisco Chronicle*, "the two stared at each other and realized at the same moment that they were the father and son who had been separated 27 years ago and half a world away." Nueng's mother, it turned out, had married an American and moved to Colorado in 1971.

Incredibly, the elder Garcia had never been to that gas station before and wasn't even particularly low on fuel. "I don't even know why I stopped for gas," he admitted on "Good Morning America." "I started thinking—this couldn't be. I was totally shocked."

WHO: Tim Henderson and Mark Knight / Half-brothers

SEPARATION: When Mark Knight was a year old, his parents divorced. His father remarried and had a son named Tim. His mother remarried, too, and Mark took his stepfather's last name. The brothers met once, when Mark was five and Tim three, but the families fought and never saw each other again.

TOGETHER AGAIN: In February 1996, Henderson had to travel from Newcastle, England, to London. He couldn't afford the train fare, so he called the Freewheelers Lift Share Agency, which matches hitchhikers and drivers. They have 16,000 names on file. The name they gave him was Mark Knight.

According to a report in the *Guardian*: "As they drove, they started talking about friends and relatives. 'There was a moment of complete silence as we both stared at each other in disbelief,' said Mr. Henderson. 'Then one of us said, "You must be my brother." It was pretty mind-blowing. I always knew I had a half-brother but never thought we would meet.'"

A FOOD IS BORN

*These foods are such a big part of our lives that sometimes it's
hard to believe they weren't always around. Here's
a brief history of how they got to your house.*

HEINEKEN BEER. In the 1860s, a young Dutch man
named Gerard Adriaan Heineken wanted to start his own
business. He didn't have any money...but his mother did.
Heineken knew she hated the way drunks wandered the streets of
Amsterdam on Sunday mornings after all-night Saturday binges.
So he suggested that if she helped him start a brewery, local men
might drink *beer* all night instead of hard liquor, and public drunkenness might decrease. It was a pretty strange sales pitch...but it
worked. Today, Heineken N.V. is the largest beer producer in Europe, and the second largest in the world.

MIRACLE WHIP. Early in the Great Depression, prepared mayonnaise went from a household staple to an expensive luxury item
that few could afford. Kraft began researching ways to make an in-
expensive substitute and eventually came up with something made
of oil, egg yolks, cooked starch paste, and seasonings. It had less oil
than regular mayonnaise, so it was cheaper to produce...but was
also harder to make. Kraft invented a new mixer they called the
"miracle whip" to give the product its creamy consistency. Then
they named the product after the machine.

INSTANT COFFEE. In the early 1930s, Brazilian coffee harvests
were so huge that the worldwide price of coffee nearly collapsed. In
desperation, the Brazilian Coffee Institute started looking for new
ways to use the coffee beans. They approached the Nestle Company with the idea for "coffee cubes," which would convert quickly
into coffee when immersed in water.

Nestle took on the project...then gave up. But Max Morgenthal-
er, a company researcher, continued on his own time, using coffee
he bought himself. In 1937, he finally found a way to turn coffee
into powder without destroying its flavor. Nestle awarded him a
gold medal and a percentage of the profits. They marketed the "in-

---

Good news? In 1960, 3% of U.S. lawyers were women. In 1991, the number was up to 20%.

stant" coffee under the brand name Nescafe, leaving it in powdered form (rather than cubes) so consumers could make their brew as strong as they wanted. It was issued to American GIs as part of their daily rations during World War II, and soldiers brought their taste for it home when the war was over.

BEN & JERRY'S ICE CREAM. In the late 1970s, Bennett Cohen and Jerry Greenfield, friends since high school, moved to Vermont to start a business. They weren't sure what kind of business, except that it would involve food. "We were both big into eating," Jerry says. Their first idea was bagels, but they gave that up when they learned that bagel-making equipment costs at least $40,000. So they paid $5 for a five-day ice cream–making correspondence course, rented an old gas station in Burlington, and began turning out ice cream by hand. Today, Ben & Jerry's ice cream is sold all over the world, and their factory in Waterbury is Vermont's leading tourist attraction.

CRISCO. You've probably seen "hydrogenated vegetable oil" on ingredients lists of cookies or crackers. It means that hydrogen was added to the oil to harden it. Crisco was the first food product to use this process: In the early 1900s, Proctor & Gamble experimented with hydrogenation to "harden" liquid cottonseed oil so it could be used as a substitute for lard. After they came up with a "creamy shortening" they could sell, they held an employee contest to name the new product. "Cryst" was rejected for religious reasons; "Krispo" was nixed because it was already trademarked. In the end, the company combined the two to get "Crisco," an acronym for "crystallized cottonseed oil."

ICED TEA. "While tea drinking is a nearly 5,000-year-old pleasure that began in China," Maureen Sajbel writes in the *Los Angeles Times*, "Sipping iced tea is a fairly recent American invention. The story goes that on a hot, humid day at the St. Louis World's Fair, a discouraged vendor wasn't having much success in selling Indian hot tea. With a scratch of the head and a burst of American inventiveness, he added ice. Within hours, fair-goers were drinking glass after glass of the thirst-quenching iced drink."

MYTH AMERICA

*Here are a few more stories about America
that we've been taught are true...*

THE MYTH: Jackie Robinson broke baseball's color barrier in 1947 when he joined the Brooklyn Dodgers.

THE TRUTH: Robinson was *not* the first black man to play major league baseball; in fact, he came along more than 60 *years* after Moses "Fleet" Walker, a catcher who played 42 games for the Toledo Mudhens of the American Association in 1884. Walker's brother joined him later in the season, but only played five games. When the season ended, both Walkers were gone. Apparently, a country with dozens of Jim Crow laws still on the books wasn't ready to integrate their national pastime just yet.

THE MYTH: Machine Gun Kelly coined the expression "G-men" (for government men). In 1933, the story goes, FBI agents surrounded him on a Tennessee farm. Rather than shoot his way out, Kelly threw up his hands and shouted to the government agents, "Don't shoot, G-men, don't shoot!"

BACKGROUND. FBI director J. Edgar Hoover recounted the tale in a 1946 issue of the *Tennessee Law Review.*

THE TRUTH: Hoover made it up to generate publicity for the Bureau and to give his agents a nickname. The FBI wasn't even responsible for capturing Kelly; he was actually caught by a posse of lawmen led by W. J. Raney, a Memphis police officer. And, according to contemporary accounts, what Kelly really said was, "Okay, boys, I've been waiting for you all night."

THE MYTH: The *Spirit of '76,* the famous painting showing a flag-carrier, a drummer, and a man playing a fife (flute), was inspired by an actual scene in the Revolutionary War.

THE TRUTH: It started off as a *Civil War* painting. Archibald Willard, a Civil War veteran himself, first painted a cartoonish version, depicting three imaginary war recruits parading around "in

Americans will eat 90 acres worth of pizza today.

lighthearted fashion." It wasn't until a friend talked him into painting a more somber version that he added the revolutionary themes and gave the painting its now-famous name.

THE MYTH: George Washington was a great military tactician.

THE TRUTH. "So notorious was his reputation for losing battles ineptly," writes Michael Korda in *Success*, "that John Adams called him 'an old muttonhead' and Jefferson commented, with great delicacy, that Washington was 'not a great tactician.'"

> As a young officer, he once constructed a fort at Great Meadows, Pennsylvania, on a swampy creek bottom, hemmed in on all three sides by wooded hills. This position for a fortress was so ludicrous that the French, in this case Washington's enemies, captured him immediately, and generously released him with the advice to take up some other line of work.
>
> Giving up fortifications, Washington then...became the personal aide to Lt. General Edward Braddock, whom Washington persuaded to divide the forces in the siege of Fort Duquesne. The result? Braddock lost the battle, his army, and his life.

After taking over the command of the Continental army,

> Washington proceeded through 1775 and 1776 to retreat from Long island to Brooklyn Heights, from Brooklyn Heights to Kips Bay, from Kips Bay to Washington Heights, from Washington Heights to White Plains, and from there across the Hudson into New Jersey. ...It can be truly said that...Washington beat the British by retreating faster than they could advance.

THE MYTH: Geronimo was the name of a famous Apache chief.

THE TRUTH: His name was actually Govathlay, which doesn't sound anything like Geronimo. Mexican settlers, who couldn't pronounce Govathlay, referred to the chief as "Jerome," or "Geronimo" in Spanish. And there's nothing in the historical record to suggest that Govathlay ever shouted "Geronimo!" as he jumped from a cliff into a river to escape the U.S. Cavalry. That scene was invented for a 1940 movie, which probably led directly to the legend. (World War II paratroopers *did*, however, frequently shout "Geronimo!" when they jumped out of planes.)

The average woman shaves 412 inches of skin on her body; the average man, 48.

DR. STRANGELOVE

Dr. Strangelove is considered one of the best satires of the Cold War era...if not one of the funniest movies ever made. Here are some little-known, behind-the-scenes details.

BUT SERIOUSLY, FOLKS

In the late 1950s, a 28-year-old film maker named Stanley Kubrick began reading up on the U.S.-Soviet arms race. He subscribed to *Aviation Week* and the *Bulletin of the Atomic Scientists*, and over the next six years read more than 70 books on the subject. As he read, he became fascinated by what he called "people's virtually listless acquiescence in the possibility—in fact, the increasing probability—of nuclear war."

One of the books Kubrick read was *Red Alert,* a novel about a paranoid U.S. military general who goes insane and launches an unprovoked nuclear attack on the Soviet Union. The book, by former Royal Air Force officer Peter George, was so intriguing that Kubrick bought the film rights and hired George to help him write a screenplay from the book.

BLACK HUMOR

The screenplay was supposed to be serious...but Kubrick's dark sense of humor kept intruding. Finally, he stopped fighting it and placed a phone call to satirist Terry Southern. Kubrick hadn't actually met Southern, but he'd read one of his books—*The Magic Christian.* A few years earlier, Peter Sellers had bought 100 copies of it and sent it to his friends...including Kubrick. Southern recalls Kubrick telling him on the phone that

> he had thought of the story as a "straightforward melodrama" until ...he "woke up and realized that nuclear war was too outrageous, too fantastic to be treated in any conventional manner." He said that he could only see it now as "some kind of hideous joke." He told me he had read a book of mine which contained, as he put it, "certain indications" that I might be able to help him with the script.

So Southern became a co-writer on the world's first black comedy about nuclear war.

A SELLERS' MARKET

That wasn't Sellers's only behind-the-scenes contribution. For some reason, the corporate geniuses at Columbia Pictures decided that the movie *Lolita*, which Kubrick had directed in 1962, had succeeded because of "the gimmick of Peter Sellers playing several roles." So before *Strangelove* even had a title, they agreed to give Kubrick the green light for it…as long as it "would star Peter Sellers in at least four major roles."

Kubrick made that promise…but it turned out to be impossible to fulfill. Sellers did play *three* parts in the film brilliantly: Dr. Strangelove, President Merkin Muffley, and Group Captain Lionel Mandrake. Unfortunately, at the last minute, he was injured and had to give up the role of Major T. J. "King" Kong. Southern remembers:

> Kubrick's response was an extraordinary tribute to Sellers as an actor: "We can't replace him with another actor, we've got to get an authentic character from life, someone whose acting career is secondary—a real-life cowboy."…He asked for my opinion and I immediately suggested big Dan ("Hoss Cartwright") Blocker…of the TV show *Bonanza*….
>
> [Kubrick] made arrangements for a script to be delivered to Blocker that afternoon, but a cabled response from Blocker's agent arrived in quick order: "Thanks a lot, but the material is too pinko for Dan. Or anyone else we know for that matter."
>
> As I recall, this was the first hint that this sort of political interpretation of our work-in-progress might exist.

It was only then that Slim Pickens, a former rodeo clown, was hired for the part. (Ironically, Pickens was more conservative than Blocker, even supporting presidential candidate George Wallace.)

MIXED REVIEWS

As the film progressed, Kubrick had a growing uneasiness about the reception that awaited it. At one point, Mo Rothman, the executive producer assigned by Columbia Pictures, called with the message that "New York does *not* see anything funny about the end of the world!" Ultimately, many critics agreed. When it premiered in January 1964, Bosley Crowther wrote in *The New York Times*:

Dr. Strangelove...is beyond any question the most shattering sick joke I've ever come across....I am troubled by the feeling, which runs all through the film, of discredit and even contempt for our whole defense establishment, up to and even including the hypothetical Commander in Chief....Somehow, to me it isn't funny. It is malefic and sick.

Columbia was spooked and distanced itself from the film. "Even when *Strangelove* received the infrequent good review," Southern wrote, "the studio dismissed the critic as a pinko nutcase." At one point, Columbia's publicity department called the film "a zany novelty flick which does not reflect the views of the corporation in any way." But of course, when the Library of Congress listed *Strangelove* as one of the "50 greatest American films of all time," former Columbia execs were "in prominent attendance."

THE LOST SCENE

Something to look for: In many of the scenes filmed in the Pentagon war room, a long table filled with cakes, pies, and other desserts can be seen off to one side. The table isn't there by accident—Kubrick originally intended to end the movie with a pie fight. He even filmed the scene, as set director Ken Adams remembers:

It was a very brilliant sequence with a *Hellzapoppin* kind of craziness. Undoubtedly one of the most extraordinary custard pie battles ever filmed. The characters were hanging from chandeliers and throwing pies which ended up by covering the maps of the General Staff.... The sequence ended with the President of the United States and the Soviet ambassador sitting on what was left of the pies and building 'pie castles' like children on a beach.

But Kubrick removed the scene. Why? He forgot to tell the actors to play it straight. As the scene progressed, it was obvious that they were having a great time—which didn't fit with the rest of the film. Unfortunately, there was no time or money left to reshoot it.

FINAL THOUGHT

"Confront a man in his office with a nuclear alarm, and you have a documentary. If the news reaches him in his living room, you have a drama. If it catches him in the lavatory, the result is comedy."

— *Stanley Kubrick*

LANGUAGE OF LOVE

They say that it's international, but a good vocabulary can help. Here are some forgotten Victorian words that might come in handy.

THE GOOD:

Ravary: A fit of passion

Babies-in-the-eyes: The reflection of oneself in a loved one's pupils

Lavolt: A lively dance

Frike: Lusty, bawdy

Enterbathe: To bathe together, literally, to mix tears

Fairhead: A beauty

Amoret: A loving look, glance

Smick: To kiss

Fardry: To paint the face with white make-up for cosmetic benefit

Greade: A woman's bosom

Loveship: Act of love-making

Bridelope: Wedding

Frim: Fleshy, vigorous

Halch: To embrace tightly

Fucus: A kind of rouge made from lichen

Half-marrow: A husband or wife

Modesty-piece: A lace cloth that covers a woman's chest

Muskin: A term of endearment for a woman; sweetheart

THE BAD:

Curtain-sermon: A lecture given by a wife at bedtime

Grandgore: Infectious disease

Acharne: To thirst for blood

Chichevache: A thin, ugly face

Gandermooner: A man who chases other women during the first month after his wife has given birth

Clarty-paps: A slovenly, dirty wife

Delumbate: To sexually maim

Mormals: Inflamed sores

Winchester goose: A sexually transmitted disease

Fulyear: A man who dishonors women

Rush ring: To "wed" without a ring; to convince a woman that a false marriage was legal

Bespawled: Covered with spittle and saliva

Flesh-shambles: A dirty, ill-reputed brothel

Lib: To castrate

Stewed prune: Madam in a brothel

Longest word in Shakespeare's plays: "honorificabilitudinitatibus" (*Love's Labour's Lost*)

HONESTLY, ABE

A few random thoughts from our 16th president, Abraham Lincoln.

"It's better to be silent and thought a fool than speak and remove all doubt."

"People are just about as happy as they make up their minds to be."

"Whatever you are, be a good one."

"If I were two-faced, would I be wearing this one?"

"How many legs does a dog have if you call the tail a leg? Four. Calling a tail a leg doesn't make it a leg."

"If both factions, or neither, shall abuse you, you will probably be right. Beware of being assailed by one, and praised by the other."

"If you intend to go to work, there is no better place than right where you are."

"A woman is the only thing that I am afraid of that I know will not hurt me."

"The severest justice may not always be the best policy."

"Things may come to those who wait, but only the things left by those who hustle."

"The loss of enemies does not compensate for the loss of friends."

"If this country cannot be saved without giving up that principle [equality]....I would rather be assassinated on this spot than surrender it."

"A fellow once came to me to ask for an appointment as a minister abroad. Finding he could not get that, he came down to some more modest position.... When he saw he could not get that, he asked me for an old pair of trousers. It is sometimes well to be humble."

"It is said an Eastern monarch once charged his wise men to invent him a sentence...which should be true and appropriate in all times and situations. They presented him the words: 'And this, too, shall pass away.'"

"A universal feeling, whether well- or ill-founded, cannot be safely disregarded."

TAKE ME OUT TO THE BORU GAME

This is a page for baseball fans.

The Japanese have adopted baseball as their national game. They've also taken a number of American baseball terms and made them Japanese. Here are some of the words, written phonetically. Some are easy, some confusing. See if you can tell what they mean. Answers are at the bottom of the page.

1. Batta
2. Boru
3. Kochi
4. Besuboru
5. Besu-ryne
6. Chenji appu
7. De Gemu
8. Era
9. Herumetto
10. Mitto
11. Maneja
12. Suisaido sukuiizu
13. Homuran
14. Auto
15. Fain Puray
16. Kyatcha
17. Pasu boh-ru
18. Sukoa bodo
19. Batta bokkusu
20. Kuriin hitto
21. Foku boru
22. Wairudo pitchi
23. Banto
24. Pitchingu sutaffu
25. Furu kaunto
26. Puray boru!
27. Senta
28. Gurobu
29. Fauru
30. Pinchi ranna
31. Hitto endu ran
32. Battingu sutansu
33. Foa boru
34. Daburu Hedda
35. "Gettsu"
36. Katto ofu puray

ANSWERS: 1. Batter; 2. Ball; 3. Coach; 4. Baseball; 5. Baseline; 6. Change-up; 7. Day game; 8. Error; 9. Helmet; 10. Mitt; 11. Manager; 12. Suicide squeeze; 13. Home run; 14. Out; 15. Fine play; 16. Catcher; 17. Passed ball; 18. Score board; 19. Batting box; 20. Clean hit; 21. Fork ball; 22. Wild pitch; 23. Bunt; 24. Pitching staff; 25. Full count; 26. Play ball!; 27. Center field or center fielder; 28. Glove; 29. Foul ball; 30. Pinch runner; 31. Hit-and-run; 32. Batting stance; 33. Four balls (a walk); 34. Double-header; 35. "Get two" (double-play); 36. Cutoff play

In 1995, world population was almost 6 billion; about 1/3 of the people are under age 15.

KILLING MASS TRANSIT

"Some people say that the people of Los Angeles chose the automobile over the trains, chose paved highways over palm trees, chose smog over clean air—all for the freedom and mobility associated with automobile travel. In fact, the people of L.A. had no say in the matter." —Russell Mokhiber

Before the Second World War, nearly every major city in the U.S. had a network of low-polluting public transportation—streetcars, electric trains, or trolleys. Los Angeles, for example, had the largest electric train system in the world. It linked the 56 towns of greater L.A. and carried 80 million passengers a year.

Many public transit systems around the country were owned by electric companies. They had been built in the years before most homes were wired for electricity, to increase sales of electric power.

But in the mid-1930s, Congress began breaking up the utility monopolies. In 1935, it passed antitrust laws that forced them to sell their mass-transit holdings.

MOTOR POOLS

• These mass-transit companies were put up for sale at a time when the nation's automakers, mired in the Great Depression, were looking for ways to increase sales.

• "The [auto] industry was in a vulnerable position," writes Russell Mokhiber in his book *Corporate Crime and Violence*. "It was not clear that the four-wheeled buggy would become the transportation method of choice for a nation in the midst of its worst economic depression...[but] the industry knew that without efficient rail systems, city-dwellers around the country would be forced to find alternative means of transportation. So General Motors, determined to sell more cars and buses, decided to destroy the rail systems."

GM GOES TO WORK

• In 1932, GM formed a holding company called United Cities Motor Transit. Through UCMT, the automaker bought three mass- transit companies in Ohio and Michigan, converted them to buses, then sold them back to local companies with the stipulation that they buy only GM buses in the future. GM had hoped to use these "showcase" bus lines to persuade other companies to make the switch, but there was little interest.

• When GM tried to use the same technique in Portland, Oregon, it ran into trouble. The American Transit Assn. publicly exposed GM's plan and censured it. GM was forced to dismantle UCMT.

• That didn't stop GM however. In fact, it then decided to skip the small companies and wipe out New York's trolley system— America's largest. To protect itself from criticism, GM worked with an existing bus company, the Omnibus Corporation, rather than setting up its own. It took only 18 months to dismantle New York's massive public transportation system.

THE SECOND STAGE

• GM was now ready to take on the rest of the country. Using a small Illinois bus company as a front, it began buying up dozens of mass-transit companies. "Tracks were literally torn out of the ground, sometimes overnight," writes journalist Jonathan Kwitny. "Overhead power lines were dismantled, and valuable off-street rights of way were sold." In East St. Louis, for example, the transition from streetcars to buses took less than 24 hours. (*Harper's*)

• Soon the front company became too big for GM to finance. So GM transformed it into a holding company called National City Lines, Inc., and approached other companies that would also benefit from the destruction of electric transit. By 1937, Greyhound Bus Lines, the Firestone Tire and Rubber Company, Mack Manufacturing, Standard Oil of California, and Phillips Petroleum had also joined up, investing $10 million altogether.

• NCL finished dismantling transit systems after the end of World War II; by the time it was done, it had eliminated lines carrying hundreds of millions of passengers in more than 45 cities, including New York, Philadelphia, Baltimore, St. Louis, Oakland, Salt Lake City, and Los Angeles. By 1955, only 5,000 streetcars remained nationwide out of a fleet that had numbered 40,000 in 1936.

WAS IT A CONSPIRACY?

In 1949, GM and the other conspirators were indicted for violating antitrust laws. They defended themselves by claiming that their investments in the enterprise were small, that they had exerted no managerial control over National City Lines, and that a nationwide switch to buses had already begun.

SUSPICIOUS FACTS

• The conspirators claimed that they had put money into National City Lines because transit lines were a good investment. But internal documents showed they knew they were going to lose money. The real profits would come later, by selling products to the new *bus* lines. According to Kwitny, internal Mack memos admitted to "probable losses" on the bus stocks, but predicted that the losses would be made up by future sales to the newly created bus lines.

• The companies investing were very secretive about their involvement with National City Lines: Standard Oil of California invested its money through two other companies, because, a company official later admitted, "We didn't want to be criticized." Firestone channeled its investments through two of its employees who posed as independent investors.

• Though National City Lines was supposed to be independent, the agreements under which the conspirators provided money specified that all buses, tires, and petroleum products had to be purchased from the companies that owned stock in National City Lines. Moreover, NCL and its branches were run by employees of the stockholding companies.

• Kwitny also notes that the contracts forbade transit companies from buying streetcars or any other piece of equipment that ran on anything but gasoline. (The contracts were later changed to permit the purchase of *diesel* buses, which became popular in the 1940s).

END OF THE LINE

• Once the light rail systems were gone, big business got out of the transit business: GM, Standard Oil, Firestone, Phillips, Mack, and Greyhound all dumped their stocks. Even the holding company itself, National City Lines, got entirely out of mass transit.

• Meanwhile, a federal court decided that the companies had engaged in an illegal conspiracy. GM, National City Lines, Firestone Tire and Rubber, Phillips Petroleum, Mack Manufacturing, and Standard Oil of California were all convicted of violating the Sherman Antitrust Act.

• Their penalty? A slap on the wrist. Each company was fined $5,000. Company officials found guilty were each fined a dollar.

Why don't your eyes freeze in winter? There's lots of salt in your tears.

FAMILIAR PHRASES

More origins of everyday phrases.

RIDE PIGGYBACK
Meaning: Ride on the back of something.
Origin: "Piggyback" has nothing to do with pigs—it is a corruption of "pick-a-back"…which, in turn, came from "pick back" and "pick pack." All of these referred to packs that people threw on their back to carry things.

COAT OF ARMS
Meaning: Design showing a family crest.
Origin: In the Middle Ages, knights wore a special coat over their armor to keep it clean and protect it from the weather. The coat was usually decorated with the knight's family crest, showing that the knight was of noble birth and thus entitled to bear arms. As gunpowder made suits of armor obsolete, coats of arms became purely decorative.

HAVING A FIELD DAY
Meaning: Having a great time; easily overwhelming an opponent.
Origin: "Field days" began as special days set aside by the military for troop maneuvers and exercises. By the 19th century, the expression expanded to include civilian festivities as well. Eventually, it was used to mean any pleasurable experience.

GET COLD FEET
Meaning: Become wary; back out of a commitment.
Origin: In the early 17th century, having cold feet meant having no money (and thus no shoes). In the 18th century, the meaning changed, probably in reference to soldiers with cold or frozen feet, who are more likely to retreat than those with warm ones.

BEAT A HASTY RETREAT
Meaning: Leave quickly; back down.
Origin: In the 14th century, European armies used trumpets and other instruments to call troops back to camp. Centuries later, drums were used. Drummers literally "beat the signal to retreat."

Something to ponder: Elvis Presley got a "C" in his eighth grade music class.

BUTTONHOLE A PERSON

Meaning: Stop a passer-by; detain someone.

Origin: The expression was originally "buttonhold" a person. It referred to the practice of grabbing a person by their buttons and holding on while you tried to sell them something.

HEARD THROUGH THE GRAPEVINE

Meaning: Heard some gossip.

Origin: During the Civil War, soldiers said that rumors came in "on the grapevine telegraph"—a reference to the fact that there were no real telegraph lines in camp to supply accurate information...just grapevines.

INDIAN SUMMER

Meaning: The period of warm weather after summer has gone and before fall is over.

Origin: Dates back to the days of mistrust between settlers and Native Americans. The term "Indian" acquired a derogatory connotation and was used in expressions like "Indian giver" and "Indian summer"—weather that appeared to be summer but wasn't.

DRINK A TOAST

Meaning: Drink in honor of another person.

Origin: Literally comes from drinking toast. In the Middle Ages people added a piece of spiced toast to their tankards of ale to improve the taste. The practice was abandoned as brewing methods improved, but the term continued to apply to the practice of drinking to someone's health.

FLY IN THE OINTMENT

Meaning: One thing wrong with an otherwise-perfect situation.

Origin: Ointment used to mean a sweet-smelling cosmetic. The phrase comes from a verse in the Bible, Ecclesiastes 10:1: "Dead flies make the perfumer's ointment give off an evil odor."

DRESSED TO THE NINES

Meaning: Well-dressed.

Origin: Probably comes from the Old English expression *dressed to then eyne*, which means "dressed to the eyes."

Ho, ho, ho: More than 25 million kids visit Santa in malls nationwide each year.

CELEBRITY SWEEPSTAKES

Celebrity endorsements are a multi-billion-dollar business. If you get the right celebrity to pitch your product, it can be worth millions. But if you pick wrong...well, take a look at these examples.

GERALDINE FERRARO

Pepsi hired the 1984 Democratic vice-presidential candidate—the first woman ever nominated by a major political party—to do a Diet Pepsi commercial in 1985.

What they wanted: People "who represent America's new generation of leaders" to go with their "Choice of a New Generation" campaign. Roger Enrico, Pepsi's CEO, explained that "Ferraro is [no longer] a despised Democrat; she's a living symbol of women's possibilities." He added, "As the first woman vice-presidential candidate, she'll get us on every news show in America."

What they got: Angry customers. Liberals attacked Ferraro for selling out, conservatives attacked Pepsi for promoting a liberal agenda. But the worst criticism came from anti-abortion protesters, as Enrico recalled in his book, *The Other Guy Blinked:*

> As the commercial started to air, a whole other kind of protest began. It was about "The Choice of a New Generation." No, it was about the word *choice*....Did it ever enter our minds that, in politics, that word has a very different meaning? Nope. So we were very, very surprised when we start getting letters. Angry letters. Letters that said, "Your commercials are 'pro-choice.' You favor the right of women to have abortions on demand.'

What happened: Pepsi pulled the ads. "I felt sorry for Ferraro," Enrico writes, "but I learned to keep Pepsi's nose out of politics."

RUSH LIMBAUGH

In 1994, the Florida Citrus Department bought $1 million worth of ads on Limbaugh's show to get him to promote orange juice.

What they wanted: A big audience for their "health-oriented" ads. The 300-pound Limbaugh might not be a good spokesperson for health food, but he did have upwards of 15 million listeners. "True,

Mr. Limbaugh is no plain-vanilla guy," wrote *Advertising Age* in February. "He's popular because of his conservative opinions. And he dotes on baiting liberals. But that's a plus in today's market…where ad messages delivered by popular hosts carry extra weight with loyal listeners."

What they got: An instant public-relations disaster. Groups like the National Organization for Women (NOW) and the NAACP started a "Flush Rush–Drink Prune Juice" campaign. "Limbaugh's hate-mongering is being underwritten by state and federal tax dollars," NOW's president complained. And Democrats—particularly Florida's governor—were outraged. "We're looking for people who will present the best possible image for Florida citrus—not people who will engender hate, disregard for minorities or represent any political philosophy," said a Democratic state representative. Even the citrus commissioners' jobs wound up in jeopardy. The following month, Democrats held up the otherwise-routine appointment of three members of the Citrus Board in the Florida legislature as a protest.

What happened: Sales of orange juice dropped after the campaign went on the air, and the board dumped Limbaugh after his six-month contract expired. Limbaugh predictably blamed his firing on "liberals, both in government, in special interest groups like the militant National Organization for Women, and in the press."

❀   ❀   ❀

SELLING OUT?

Terri Garr on why she made a Yoplait commercial:
"They give you a lot of money, and I come from a…relatively poor background. So I go, '*That* much money for a day's work? Yessss!' But my management people said it's not enough. And I say, 'What do you mean it's not enough?' So they came back with even more money. It's crazy. But what am I going to do, be in the Motion Picture Country Home, 86 years old, saying to my pal, Farrah Fawcett: 'In 1986, I could have done a commercial for a million dollars but nooooo, I was too fine.' I don't want to be telling that story. I want to be on my own estate, in the south of France, telling my servants, 'I got this commercial….' "

THE TRUTH ABOUT "KILLER BEES"

Since 1964 we've read news reports of "killer bees" working their way up from South America to the United States. They finally arrived in 1990 ...and nothing much happened. Is the killer bee crisis for real, or is it an example of media exaggeration fueling public hysteria?

IN THE BEEGINNING

In 1956, the Brazilian government wanted to improve Brazil's honey industry. Although Brazil is the fifth-largest country in the world, it ranked only 47th in world honey production. So it hired Dr. Warwick E. Kerr, an American entomologist. Kerr's solution was to import African honeybees, which produce far more honey than the European bees that had been brought to Brazil by Western colonists in the 16th and 17th centuries.

Because African bees are more aggressive than Brazilian bees, Kerr decided not to release the bees directly into the environment. Instead, he planned to interbreed them with the gentler Brazilian bees, then release their hybrid offspring.

Kerr's plan didn't work as he had hoped. About a year after he began the project, 26 swarms of the purebred African bees escaped from his laboratory in São Paulo and quickly began overrunning the Brazilian honeybee population. His efforts to create a kinder, gentler honeybee had failed—and the aggressive bees were taking over.

NO BEEG DEAL

No one was too excited by this development. True, Africanized bees *are* more aggressive than European honeybees—for instance, they attack by the hundreds instead of by the dozens when their hives are disturbed. But they can still only sting once before they die. Brazil actually had a larger problem with its native wasps, which can sting someone many times without dying. About the only people who noticed the difference were Brazilian beekeepers, who found the new bees harder to manage.

POLITICAL ANIMAL

For the next eight years, the Africanized bees attracted little or no attention at all. Then, on April 1, 1964, the Brazilian army overthrew President Joao Goulart and set up a military dictatorship. When Kerr spoke out against human rights abuses, the new regime used the government-controlled press to portray him as a modern-day mad scientist. Professor Robert Morse describes what happened next in his book *Bees and Beekeeping*:

> In an effort to discredit Kerr as a scientist, the military played upon the fear that many people have of stinging insects. Since most people do not know the difference between bees and wasps, any stinging incident, many of which were caused by wasps, was blamed on Professor Kerr's [accidental release of Africanized bees].
>
> The Brazilian military called the bees, in Portuguese, the language of Brazil, *abelhas assassinas* (killer bees). So far as I can determine, the first mention of the words "killer bees" in the United States was in *Time* magazine in the September 24, 1965, issue that picked up one of these military press releases.

Some Brazilian newspapers even claimed that Dr. Kerr had *taught* the bees to be mean.

Other magazines and newspapers followed *Time*'s lead and printed the Brazilian junta's propaganda as if it were the truth. In the process, they created a wave of hysteria that swept across South America, then Central and North America as the Africanized bees moved inexorably northward.

HARD TO BEELIEVE

When will the killer bees arrive in the United States? Actually, they've been here since 1959, thanks to a U.S. Department of Agriculture program that distributed—no kidding—*Africanized bee semen* to domestic beekeepers. "It's common knowledge among larger commercial beekeepers," says Dee Lusby, an Arizona beekeeper. "The USDA bee lab in Baton Rouge, Louisiana, received Africanized bee semen from Brazil 30 years ago and made the offspring available to beekeepers in this country and around the world. It was part of an ongoing program to breed superior honey-producing bees, just like Dr. Kerr's experiments in South America."

Coincidence? William Shakespeare and Miguel De Cervantes died on the same day in 1616.

And that probably wasn't their first trip to the United States. According to *Bee World* magazine, other bee breeders may have brought them over from Africa as early as the mid-1800s. So the killer bees aren't coming, they're already here, and they've probably been here for over a century.

For that matter, most beekeepers say that the *German* bee, which has been in the United States for over two centuries, is even meaner than the Africanized bees. But even these extra-mean bees aren't much of a public nuisance, beekeepers note, and say many predict that the Africanized bees aren't either. "You're more likely to be killed by lightning than attacked by Africanized honeybees," says Dr. Anita Collins, a research geneticist with the Department of Agriculture.

SO WHAT'S THE DIFFERENCE?
• Anatomically speaking, Africanized bees are virtually indistinguishable from European bees, except that they're slightly smaller. Even the experts have a hard time telling them apart without studying them in a lab.

• Africanized bee venom is no stronger than that of European bees. In fact, Africanized bees carry slightly less venom than European bees do.

• The only real difference is behavior: Africanized honey bees are much more active, both as honey producers and defenders of the hive. They're more easily angered, and, once agitated, take longer to calm down—sometimes as long as 24 hours. They also defend the hive in greater numbers than European bees do. "They get eight to ten times as many bees out to defend the colony and sting," Dr. Collins says. "It's not any different sting for sting," adds Stormy Sparks, a Texas A&M entomologist, "but there's just a much bigger potential for multiple stings."

• A positive note: Africanized bees evolved in a hot climate, so they have very little tolerance for cold compared to European bees, and will probably never go above the southern third of the United States.

The average 10-gallon hat holds only 3 quarts of water.

DAVE BARRY'S FLAMING TOILET

Here's a Dave Barry column sent to us by a BRI member.
Barry seems to write about the bathroom fairly frequently
…which makes him our kind of humorist.

I f you were to ask me how I came to set my toilet on fire, I would answer you in two simple words: *Reader's Digest*. I am referring specifically to the February 1995 issue of *Reader's Digest*, which was sent to me by [an] alert reader who had spotted a startling article [about germs] originally written for *Health* magazine....

BATHROOM STUDIES

The…article concerns University of Arizona scientist Chuck Gerba, Ph.D., who is a serious student of bacteria found in bathrooms.

Consider the following absolutely true facts:

1. He routinely goes into public restrooms unarmed, and takes bacteria samples from the toilets.

2. His son's middle name is Escherichia, after *Escherichia coli*, also known as *E. coli*, which is a common type of fecal bacteria.

Needless to say I had to call this man. "You named your son after bacteria?" was my opening question.

"He finds it a good conversation starter," Gerba replied.

Gerba told me that there are definite hazards associated with his line of study. "When you spend a lot of time taking samples on your knees in the stalls of public restrooms," he said, "people tend to call the cops on you. I've had to do some fast talking."

TOILET FACTS

Gerba told me that in the course of his studies, he's learned some Amazing Toilet Facts:

Toilet Fact No. 1: Based on scientific measurements of the holes in public-toilet seats, "Americans have the biggest butts in the world."

Toilet Fact No. 2: In any group of public toilets, the first stall is likely to have the least bacteria, and the middle ones are likely to have the most, because more people use them.

Toilet Fact No. 3: The cleanest public toilets are found in national-chain restaurants; the worst are found in gas stations.

Toilet Fact No. 4: Every toilet user leaves a unique bacterial pattern; we know this thanks to a breakthrough technique Gerba developed called (I am not making any of this up) the Commode-A-Graph.

Toilet Fact No. 5: When you flush, a process called *aerosolization* takes place, in which the toilet shoots out an invisible cloud of germ-infested water droplets. In *Reader's Digest*, [the author] quotes Gerba as saying that if you keep your toothbrush within six feet of a commode, "you're basically brushing with toilet water."

THE FLAMING TOILET

So we see that a toilet is really nothing more than—to use scientific parlance—a Yuck Bomb. The question is, what can you do about it? Is there any way to get a toilet *really* clean? This brings us to the truly fascinating part of Roach's article, wherein Gerba and his family, demonstrating the only way to kill all the bacteria, put laboratory alcohol on their commode bowl and—this is right on page 64 of *Reader's Digest*, if you don't believe me—set it on fire.

Let me stress right here that Gerba is a recognized toilet expert, and he had a fire extinguisher ready, and the toilet-torching is very dangerous. You, the layperson, would be an irresponsible idiot to try it.

Fortunately, I am not a layperson; I am a trained humor columnist, and if there's one thing I enjoy, it's a clean toilet. So I tried Gerba's technique, and I have to say that, in a darkened room, a flaming toilet has a strange kind of beauty that can only be described as "a strange kind of beauty."

I'm tempted to speculate here on whether it might be possible to use this same technique to kill bacteria on other surfaces, such as the bodies of Tobacco Institute scientists, but I think I'm already in enough trouble as it is. So let me leave you with these important Toilet Health Reminders: (1) Avoid those middle stalls; (2) Move that toothbrush; and above all (3) Don't sit down until the bowl has completely cooled.

No wonder they grunt: Most of a hog's sweat glands are in its snout.

TEST YOUR GRAMMY IQ

Every year, the news media make a big deal about who won the Grammy Awards. Have you been paying attention? Here's a little quiz to see how much you really know about the "coveted" music awards.
(Answers on page 320.)

1. Which of these groups has never won a Grammy?
a) Alvin and the Chipmunks   **b)** The Beach Boys   **c)** Aerosmith

2. An assassination ended the meteoric career of the 1962 winner of Album of the Year. Who was it?
a) Vaughn Meader   **b)** Sam Cooke   **c)** Clark Taylor

3. In 1965, the bestselling record of the year was "Satisfaction"; the Beatles recorded *Help!*; Motown was tearing up the charts. The Grammy winner that year for Best Vocal Group was:
a) The Beatles   **b)** The Supremes   **c)** The Anita Kerr Quartet
d) Steve Brummet & His Polka Pals   **e)** The Mamas & the Papas

4. When did Elvis win his first Grammy?
a) 1960, for "Are You Lonesome Tonight?" (Best Male Singer)
b) 1965, for *Blue Hawaii* (Best Movie Sountrack)
c) 1967, for *How Great Thou Art* (Best Inspirational Performance)
d) 1974, for "In the Ghetto" (Song of the Year)

5. The first artist ever to refuse a Grammy was
a) Nina Simone   **b)** Bob Dylan   **c)** Sinead O'Connor

6. In the decade following the Beatles break-up in 1970, each member of the group won a Grammy for a non-Beatle effort… except one. Which one?
a) John   **b)** George   **c)** Ringo   **d)** Paul

7. Although this rock group—considered one of the world's best by most critics—had never won a Grammy, they received a Lifetime

There were two streetcars in Tennessee Williams' *A Streetcar Named*

Achievement Award in 1985. "Thank you," said the group's leader, "the joke's on you." What band was it?

a) The Doors   b) The Rolling Stones   c) The Who

8. What performer won a Best Vocalist Grammy for a song she'd written about *not* receiving the award a few years earlier?

a) Roseanne Cash   b) Dolly Parton   c) Carole King

9. Which Grammy winner told a reporter: "My nomination must have been an accident. Either that, or a lot of people have a perverse sense of humor."

a) Bobby McFerrin   b) Bob Newhart   c) Frank Zappa

10. What was notable about the Grammys won by Jimi Hendrix and Janis Joplin?

a) What Grammys?

b) They were withheld because of the artists' overt drug use.

c) They were given for a little-known duet they did of the Beatles' old hit, "She Loves You."

11. Who was the first African-American ever to win the *Best New Artist* award?

a) Chubby Checker, 1960   b) Little Stevie Wonder, 1962

c) O. C. Smith, 1968   d) Natalie Cole, 1975

12. What was surprising about 1966's Best Folk Artist winner, Cortelia Clark?

a) It turned out he'd undergone a sex-change operation.

b) He couldn't afford to rent a tux to go to the awards ceremony.

c) There *was* no Cortelia Clark—it was really B. B. King, recording under a different name.

13. In 1996 John Popper, harmonica player for Blues Traveler, pulled off a Grammy first when he jumped out of his seat to get an award, and...

a) Tore a ligament in his leg   b) His pants fell down

c) He tripped and fell

Desire. The other one was named Cemetery.

O'ROURKE-ISMS

P. J. O'Rourke, the "Republican party animal," on a few random topics.

"Never wear anything that panics the cat."

"Wearing a hat implies that you are bald if you are a man and that your hair is dirty if you are a woman."

"There is no way to make vomiting courteous. You have to do the next best thing, which is to vomit in such a way that the story you tell about it later will be amusing."

"People who don't smoke have a terrible time finding something polite to do with their lips."

"Drugs have taught an entire generation of American kids the metric system."

"How much fame, money, and power does a woman have to achieve on her own before you can punch her in the face?"

"Don't send funny greeting cards on birthdays or at Christmas. Save them for funerals, when their cheery effect is needed."

"Feminism seems to be a case of women having won a leg-wrestling match with their own other leg. There is only one thing for men to do in response to this confusing situation, which is the same thing men have always done, which is anything women want."

"Dates used to be made days or even weeks in advance. Now dates tend to be made the day after. That is, you get a phone call from someone who says, 'If anyone asks, I was out to dinner with you last night, okay?'"

"There is one thing women can never take away from men. We die sooner."

"After equality, wage parity, [and] liberation...Women still can't do the following: Start barbeque fires; hook up a stereo; shine shoes; anything on a roof; decide where to hang a picture; investigate mysterious house noises at night; kill and dispose of large insects; walk past a mirror without stopping to look."

If your stomach didn't produce a new layer of mucous every two weeks, it would digest itself.

THE CHEW-CHEW MAN

Where did the low-calorie diet come from? It started with a guy known as the "Chew-Chew Man" to critics and the "Great Masticator" to fans.

THE BIRTH OF "FLETCHERISM"

In 1895, 44-year-old Horace Fletcher was turned down for life insurance because he weighed 217 pounds (at 5'6" tall), and he drank excessively. "I was an old man at forty, and on the way to a rapid decline," he recalled years later.

In 1898, Fletcher performed an experiment on himself. He began chewing each bite of food 30 to 70 times—even milk and soup, which he swished in his mouth—and never ate when he was upset or wasn't hungry. After five months of "Fletcherizing" each morsel of food, he lost 60 pounds and regained his health. He also found that he could live happily on 1,600 calories a day, far less than the 3,500 to 4,500 calories recommended at the turn of the century.

THE GREAT MASTICATOR

The experience helped Fletcher find a new calling—pitching his chewing habits to the masses. His slogan: "Nature will castigate those who don't masticate." Fletcher's lecture tours and bestselling books attracted tens of thousands of followers, including John D. Rockefeller and Thomas Edison. Adherents formed "Fletcher clubs," where they met to eat slowly and chant ditties like:

> I choose to chew, Because I wish to do, The sort of thing that
> Nature had in view, Before bad cooks invented sav'ry stew;
> When the only way to eat was to chew! chew! chew!

Fletcher died from bronchitis in 1919 at the age of 69, and his chewing theories soon followed him to the grave. But one thing that did survive him was his low-calorie diet: In 1903, a Yale University professor named Russell Chittenden examined Fletcher, found him to be in excellent health, and decided to try the diet himself. Soon after, his rheumatic knee stopped bothering him and his chronic headaches went away, prompting Chittenden to launch a series of studies into diet and health. These and other pivotal studies led to a ratcheting down of the recommended calorie intake from 3,500 a day to the 2,000 recommended today.

The Sanskrit word for "war" also translates as "desire for more cows."

MISS AMERICA, PART III:
Creating An Institution

Here's where Miss America starts to look like the pageant we know today. It's interesting that one person is so responsible for its success—which makes her either an unsung hero, if you like the pageant…or the culprit, if you don't. It's also interesting to see that the key to turning a "moneymaking scheme" into an "institution" is finding a way to make it seem patriotic.

WONDER WOMAN

The 1935 pageant would probably have been another dud. But Eddie Corcoran, the person in charge of organizing the event, had a stroke of luck: he read an article praising Lenora Slaughter, assistant to Florida Baseball Commissioner Al Lang. The article lauded Slaughter's work on the "Festival of the States" parade and pageant in Saint Petersburg, Florida. Corcoran had never organized a pageant, and knew he needed help. He wrote a letter to Lang asking to "borrow" Slaughter for the six weeks leading up to the contest. He offered to pay her $1,000 for the work.

Slaughter hesitated…but Lang urged her to "go up there and show those damn Yankees how to do a *real* job with a pageant." Finally, she consented to go to Atlantic City. But only for the agreed-upon six weeks.

She ended up staying for more than 30 years.

CULTURAL REVOLUTION

Slaughter had spent her career working with civic-minded, upper-crust society women, and she put this background to work on the Miss America Pageant's #1 problem: its reputation for sleaze. For the rest of the 1930s and into the 1940s, she tore the pageant down to its barest essentials and rebuilt it into the kind of event that even high-class society matrons could love. Or as Bess Myerson, Miss America 1945, put it, "She picked the pageant up by its bathing suit straps and put it in an evening gown."

One of the ways Slaughter cleaned up the contest's image was by drawing attention away from the swimsuit competition. She did

---

Longest word typed entirely by one hand: "stewardesses."

this by adding a talent category to the competition, and by bringing back family-oriented events. She also excluded children from the competition for the first time, requiring that all entrants be 18 years old by the first day of competition.

MRS. ATLANTIC CITY

Despite all these changes, the pageant's surivival remained in doubt. Conservatives and women's organizations kept up their criticism, and groups like the Federated Women's Clubs of New Jersey denounced the contest as "the work of the devil."

Her back to the wall, Slaughter made a brilliant move to stave off an attack by the Atlantic City government—then run by conservative Quakers. She asked the wife of Mayor C. D. White to head the pageant's hostess committee, which organized the chaperones and escorts for contestants during Pageant Week. Mrs. White, whom Slaughter described as "the Quakerest of Quakers," was perfect for the job. She recruited people from the "best" families in town to volunteer in the pageant. The 1935 and 1936 pageants were considered successes.

CLOSE CALL

Putting Mrs. White in charge of the hostess committee helped the pageant survive its next big scandal. In 1937, a 17-year-old girl named Bette Cooper won the Miss America crown before anyone realized she was too young to compete. Then, the morning she was supposed to be crowned, she ran off with her pageant-appointed escort—an Atlantic City man named Lou Off. Cooper never returned, and the title remained vacant for the rest of the year.

It turned out later that Cooper ran away simply because she didn't want to drop out of Junior College to fulfill her "queenly duties," and didn't know how else to get out of them. Even so, newspapers all over the East Coast covered the drama in lurid—and inaccurate—detail. Ordinarily, the pageant would have been doomed, but not this time. "The pageant escaped a lot of heat," Deford writes, "because nobody wanted to take on Mrs. White."

FOR WOMEN ONLY

After the scandal blew over, Slaughter and White took steps to make sure it would never happen again. They instituted a ban,

forbidding contestants from having *any* contact with any men—
even their fathers—during Pageant Week. The young women were
also barred from nightclubs, bars, and taverns, and had to avoid any
public events where alcohol was served. They had to observe an
ironclad 1:00 a.m. curfew, and even taxicabs were declared off-
limits except in emergencies, to avoid even the hint of scandal.
Nearly all of the rules set down in the 1930s are still in effect today.

GOING FURTHER

Once Slaughter got the Miss America Pageant and its contestants
firmly under control, she set her sights on the pageant's other major problem: the cheesy state and local "franchise" pageants that
fed their winners into the Miss America contest.

Over the next several years, Slaughter phased out contests run
by newspapers and amusement parks and began regulating operators of the state and local pageants that were left. For-profit
pageants were out. One by one, Slaughter took control of them
and turned them over to local chapters of the nonprofit Jaycees
(Junior Chamber of Commerce) to run as a public service.

Today more than 300,000 volunteers around the country run the
2,000 local contests that feed into the Miss America Pageant.

ALL THIS AND WORLD WAR II

Slaughter was still implementing her reforms when the Japanese
bombed Pearl Harbor and the United States entered World War II.
Once again, the future of the pageant seemed in doubt (although
this time, at least, it wasn't the pageant's fault). Who could justify
all of the effort and expense that went into the pageant when
America's sons were shipping off to war?

The federal government, that's who.

The War Finance Department, which had the power to cancel
frivolous and wasteful public events during wartime, decided that
the pageant could—and should—continue during the war. Why?
"They knew we could do a good job selling war bonds," Slaughter
explained, "and agreed to pay $2,500 if I would chaperone Miss
America on a trip around America selling war bonds in 1943."

For the next three months, Slaughter and that year's Miss

America, a 19-year-old UCLA coed named Jean Bartel, toured the United States selling bonds. They made 469 appearances in 24 different states and autographed 50,000 pictures.

When it was done, they'd sold $2.5 million worth of bonds—more than any other individual Americans during the war.

WRAPPED IN THE FLAG

This was an amazing accomplishment. But it was even more amazing to see who *bought* the bonds. More than 80% of Bartel and Slaughter's customers were women—a total surprise, since traditionally, women did not like swimsuit contests or beauty pageants.

This illustrated how effective the bond sales had been as an image-building tool. Before the drive, the pageant was generally seen as an overhyped swimsuit contest. Afterward, it was regarded as a wholesome search for the ideal American woman—a beauty pageant the entire family could enjoy.

More than all of Lenora Slaughter's reforms combined, wrapping the pageant in the flag had transformed Miss America into an "all-American" institution.

☞   ☞   ☞   ☞

MISS AMERICA FACT

During a bond-selling visit to the University of Minnesota, the student council there approached Bartel and Slaughter with a suggestion. "I don't know any of the names," recalled Slaughter, "but I remember that an ugly little girl with spectacles—never a potential beauty—was at the head of it."

The ugly duckling noted that while plenty of scholarships were available for male students, there were almost none for females, and the pageant could help change that. Slaughter—always on the lookout for ways to improve the contest's image—was immediately enthusiastic.

Today, the Miss America Pageant is the largest source of scholarship money for U.S. women, handling over $25 million a year.

For Part IV of the story, turn to page 202

U.S. physicians treat an estimated 4 million broken bones a year.

OOPS!

More examples of Murphy's law—anyting that can goe wroong, will.

BORDER CROSSING
"If you closely examine a map of South Dakota, you'll see that the man-made western border of the state has a slight bump in it as it runs north-south. When the territory was being surveyed, the boundary was set to fall on the 27th meridian west from Washington, D.C. As the surveyors working down from the north met those coming up from the south, they missed each other by a few miles. This error remains on every map to this day."

—from *Oops*, by Paul Smith

HAPPY BIRTHDAY!
"A Dutch couple tried to have a baby for more than five years. Finally, they turned to the University Hospital at Utrecht, one of the Netherlands' most prestigious fertility clinics. An in-vitro fertilization took place in March, 1993; in December, the woman had twins—Teun and Koen.

"Apparently, however, the clinic made a mistake. 'Little Teun,' said news reports, 'is as white and blonde as his father and mother. Little Koen is black.' After first denying responsibility, the clinic had to admit they'd 'accidentally inseminated the mother's eggs with sperm from another man along with that of her husband.' "

—from the *San Francisco Chronicle*, 6/29/95

HEAR, HEAR
"In the 1950s Harold Senby of Leeds, England began experiencing difficulty hearing. He was fitted for a hearing aid, but his hearing did not improve.

In fact, he seemed to be hearing worse than before. During the next 20 years, he was refitted several times, but each time his hearing stayed the same. Finally, during a visit to his doctor in March 1978, the hearing aid was removed entirely.

Miraculously, Senby's hearing began to improve. After a closer medical examination, the doctor discovered that "in the 1950s,

---

Heavenly riches: 49% of Americans say they pray to God for financial advice.

the hearing aid had been made for his left ear, not the right ear, which was the one giving him trouble."

—from *The Blunder Book,* by M. Hirsch Goldberg

FUNNY MONEY

In 1960, the Brazilian government discovered that the cost of printing a 1-cruziero note was 1.2 cruzieros. They immediately stopped issuing it.

—from *Oops,* by Paul Smith

GOOD BET

In 1995, Pizza Hut scheduled a commercial featuring Pete Rose. According to news reports, "a young boy asks Pete Rose about his accomplishments in baseball. At the end, Rose asks if the boy likes Pizza Hut pizza, and the boy replies, 'You bet!' " After reviewing the script, the company canceled its plans. "That's not the best choice of words," explained Rose.

—from the *San Francisco Chronicle,* 6/21/95

WHAT A GAS!

"When a cow has an attack of bloat (actually methane gas generated in the stomach), it must obtain relief promptly or die.

"A Dutch veterinarian was summoned recently to treat a cow suffering from this affliction, an agricultural news service reported. He tried a standard remedy, which is to insert a tube carefully up the beast's rear end.

"A satisfying rush of gas followed. With misplaced scientific zeal, the vet, perhaps seeking a source of cheap heat and light, then applied a match. The resulting torchlike jet set the barn ablaze. It burned to the ground. The flames spread to the nearby fields, which were consumed.

"The vet was convicted of negligence and fined. The cow remained serene."

—from *Remarkabilia,* by John Train

Congress has proposed 10,679 amendments to the U.S. Constitution since 1789; 27 made it.

WHAT A DOLL!

*Here are five of the more unusual
dolls sold in America in recent years.*

THUGGIES

Introduced in the summer of 1993, Thuggies came with
something that no dolls had ever had before—criminal
records. There were 17 different characters, with names like "Motorcycle Meany," "Dickie the Dealer," "Bonnie Ann Bribe," and
"Mikey Milk 'em." They were outlaw bikers, dope pushers, white-collar criminals, even "check-kiting congressmen."

But despite their "personal histories," the dolls were designed to
discourage crime, not encourage it. Each one came packaged in a
prison cell and had its own rehabilitation program. Children were
supposed to set them on the straight-and-narrow. (Bonnie Ann
Bribe, for example, doing time for trying to bribe her way through
school, had to read to senior citizens one hour a day.) The dolls
even came with a gold star to wear when they successfully completed rehab.

"It works, believe me," Carolyn Clark, co-founder of Thuggies,
Inc., told reporters. "It's not going to turn the kid into a criminal.
…It lets them know that they can correct this kind of behavior."

TONY THE TATTOOED MAN

Comes with tattoos and a "tattoo gun," that kids can use to apply
the tattoos to the doll or to themselves. Additional tattoos—
including "brains, boogers, bugged-out eyes and other anatomical
atrocities"—are sold separately.

BABY THINK IT OVER

Like Thuggies, Baby Think It Over was designed to teach kids a
lesson—in this case, "Don't get pregnant." The dolls are issued to
junior-high and high school students so they can experience what
it's really like to have a baby. Each doll weighs 10 pounds, and contains electronics that make it cry "at random, but realistic, intervals, simulating a baby's sleeping and waking patterns to its

---

In 39 of the 50 U.S. states, the travel industry is the largest single employer.

demand for food," says Rick Jurmain, who invented the doll with his wife, Mary.

Like a real baby, there's no way to stop the doll from crying once it starts except by "feeding" it, which is done by inserting a special key into the baby's back, turning it, and holding the baby in place with pressure for as long as 15 minutes. The key is attached to the "parent's" arm with a tamper-proof hospital bracelet, which prevents them from handing off the responsibility to someone else. And the teenagers have to respond quickly—once the baby starts crying, a timer inside the baby records how long it cries. It also records any shaking, drops, or harsh handling that takes place. If the crying baby is left unattended for longer than two minutes, the timer registers that as neglect.

There's also a "drug-addicted" version that's more irritable, has a "higher pitch, a warbling cry," and a body tremor. Priced at $200 apiece, Baby Think It Overs are sold as instructional aids, not toys.

RHOGIT-RHOGIT

Sexual abstinence is simply not an option for Rhogit-Rhogit. "Elegant, intellectual, and extremely sexy, Rhogit-Rhogit will seduce you with his male prowess, his animal sexuality, his vision, and his depth," says the sales catalog from BillyBoy Toys, the Paris company that manufactures it. "He feels equally comfortable in butch, tough-boy clothes as he does in the most avant-garde French and Italian designer clothes and the most utterly formal attire."

Rhogit-Rhogit also has a male sidekick, Zhdrick, who, according to the catalog "is, perhaps, the most sophisticated, sensual, and provocatively sexual doll ever made." The dolls retail for $1,000 apiece, which includes one designer outfit and one condom. If you want wigs, jeans, lassos, boots, underwear, top hats, or other accessories from the company's "Boy Stuff" collection, you have to pay extra. (A lot extra—outfits run $600 to $900 apiece.)

TALKING STIMPY DOLL

From the cartoon series, *Ren & Stimpy*. "Yank the hairball in Stimpy's throat and he talks. Squeeze his leg and he makes 'rude underleg noises.' " Recommended for "ages 4 and up."

The average U.S. teenage girl owns seven pairs of jeans.

UNUSUAL AWARDS

*You've heard of the Oscars and the Emmys,
but how about these awards?*

THE BOZOS

Awarded during the 1980s by Bozo the Clown (Larry Harmon) to the "biggest bozos in the news." Winners included Jim and Tammy Bakker, Oliver North, Vanna White, Geraldo Rivera (twice), and Cher. The prize: a Bozo telephone.

SITTING DUCK AWARD

Presented annually by the National Society of Newspaper Columnists to "the target most useful to a columnist on a slow news day." Winners include: Roseanne Arnold, O. J. Simpson's houseguest Kato Kaelin, and Millie, the dog belonging to former first lady Barbara Bush.

HARLON PAGE HUBBARD LEMON AWARD

Awarded annually by consumer, public health, and environmental groups to "the year's most unfair, misleading, and irresponsible advertising." Hubbard pioneered America's first nationwide advertising campaign for "Lydia Pinkham's Vegetable Compound," a cure-all health tonic with a 20% alcohol content. Winners include: Walt Disney's "movie news" ads, which look like real news reports, and GMC truck, for bragging about the safety of its Safari minivan when it actually ranked "near the bottom" in crash tests.

GOLDEN FLEECE AWARDS

Awarded from 1975 to 1988, by Senator William Proxmire, to government agencies that wasted the most money. Winners included the Department of Agriculture, which spent $46,000 to find out how long it takes to cook two eggs for breakfast, and the National Science Foundation, which awarded a $9,992 grant to an anthropologist to study the "political significance of bullfighting in Spain."

Count 'em yourself: Ears of corn *always* have an even number of rows of kernels.

GOLDEN RASPBERRIES (RAZZIES)

Awarded by "460 film professionals, journalists, and fans for the worst films and performances of the year." Winners get a golfball-sized raspberry glued to a film reel and spray-painted gold. "It costs us about $2 to make and is every bit as tacky as the movies and performances they are given to," says John Wilson, the ceremony's organizer. Winners include *Showgirls*, *Mommie Dearest*, *Howard the Duck*, and Sylvester Stallone (who's won eight times, including a special award for worst actor of the decade).

MILLARD FILLMORE MEDAL OF MEDIOCRITY

Presented by "The Society for the Preservation and Enhancement of the Recognition of Millard Fillmore, the Last of the Whigs" to "recognize mediocrity in high places." The award is named after America's 13th president, who was denied his own party's nomination for re-election in 1852. "We felt that underachievers needed somebody to look up to, or down on, and that's Fillmore," says the group's president. "He was the Gerald Ford of the 19th century."

Winners include ex-President Bush (for winning a 90% approval rating at the end of the Gulf War...and then losing the 1992 election to the governor of Arkansas); Roseanne Arnold (for botching the national anthem at a baseball game in 1990); the canceled baseball season of 1995; former Vice President Dan Quayle (do we need to explain?); Billy Carter; Ed McMahon; Prince Charles and Princess Diana; and James Watt, Reagan's Secretary of the Interior.

✦   ✦   ✦

BRI's nominee for the "Did-We-Really-Need-This Award?" Award: The Liberace Legend Award. Presented since 1994 by the Liberace Foundation, in "a gala benefit at the famed Liberace Mansion." Winners are selected "for major contributions to the community and the world of entertainment." They include Debbie Reynolds, Siegfried and Roy, and Liza Minelli. According to a press release: "The presentation is the highlight of a series of festivities surrounding the May 16 birthday celebration of Liberace."

Approximately 14% of U.S. homes have a TV in the kitchen.

THE MYSTERIOUS OUIJA BOARD

Why did Uncle John write this chapter? Maybe his porcelain Ouija board told him to.

GHOSTWRITER

In the 1890s, spiritualism was a big fad. In the midst of it, someone came up with a new tool for communicating with the dead: a small piece of wood called a "planchette." People would gather around a table or other flat surface, place their hands on the planchette, and watch how it moved. Some had pencils attached that wrote out messages; others pointed at letters, numbers, and words painted on the table and spelled out messages that way. No one could explain why the planchette moved. Skeptics charged that the people who held the planchette were moving it—perhaps unconsciously. But true believers insisted that spirits guided the little thing across the table.

SPELLING IT OUT

William and Isaac Fuld thought the whole thing was a bunch of nonsense, but wanted to cash in on it. They owned a toy company in Maryland, and figured the planchette would make a good game. So they took a board about the size of a cafeteria tray, painted the letters of the alphabet across the middle, and put the numbers 0 through 9 underneath. They also put the words "Yes" and "No" in the left and right corners, and the word "Goodbye" across the bottom. Then they painted the name of the game, "Ouija"—a combination of *oui* and *ja*, the French and German words for "yes" — across the top. Their "Ouija Talking Board" was patented in 1892.

DEAD SERIOUS

It wasn't until World War I that Ouija boards became a big commercial success.

Company legend has it that not long before the war broke out, William Fuld's favorite Ouija board told him to "prepare for big business." So he expanded production...and sure enough, during the war people began using the Ouija to "keep in touch" with loved ones who'd been sent into battle. Sales skyrocketed, and the money poured in.

Since then, Ouija sales have always boomed in times of national crisis, tailed off when conditions improved, then increased again when the next crisis hit. The Ouija board sold well during World War II, the Korean War, and the Vietnam War, and dipped in between. The Fuld Family manufactured Ouija Boards until 1967, when they sold the rights to Parker Brothers.

OUIJA FACTS

• At the time World War I started, the IRS collected a 10% tax on every game sold in the United States and the Fulds didn't want to pay. So they declared the Ouija board to be a "scientific instrument" that didn't qualify for the tax. They fought the case all the way to the Supreme Court...and lost.

• No one can explain how the Ouija planchette moves across the board. "There's nothing special about Ouijas to give it any supernatural powers," one Parker Brothers spokesperson insists. "It's simply a game."

• One reasonable theory: the game works through an "idiomotor action" in much the same way that a dowsing rod finds water. "Unconsciously picturing what you want to have happen can cause your muscles to make it happen," psychology professor Ray Hyman explains. "People think they're not doing anything and that some outside force is making it happen."

*　　*　　*　　*

TRUE STORY

At age 47, the Rolling Stones' bassist, Bill Wyman, began a relationship with 13-year-old Mandy Smith, with her mother's blessing. Six years later, they were married, but the marriage only lasted a year. Not long after, Bill's 30-year-old son Stephen married Mandy's mother, age 46. That made Stephen a stepfather to his former stepmother. If Bill and Mandy had remained married, Stephen would have been his father's father-in-law and his own grandpa.

The spiral shaped part of a corkscrew is called a "worm."

WEIRD TALES OF THE OUIJA BOARD

Here are some of the strangest stories from the annals of the Ouija board.

GHOST WRITING?

The most famous Ouija board user in history was Pearl Curran, a St. Louis, Missouri, housewife. She was playing the game with some friends in 1913 when, legend has it, the planchette began moving around the board with surprising strength. It spelled out this message: "Many moons ago I lived. Again I come, Patience Worth my name." The "spirit" identified itself as a woman who'd been born in 1625 in Dorsetshire, England, and had migrated to New England…where she was murdered by an Indian.

For the next six years (according to Curran), the spirit fed her poems, aphorisms, and other works through the Ouija board. Paul Sann writes in *Fads, Follies and Delusions of the American People*,

> Between 1913 and 1919 the pent-up Patience transmitted to Curran no less than 1,500,000 pearls of wisdom heavy with moral and religious dissertations, garnished with 2,000 items of blank verse and six novels. Mrs. Curran said that in one busy ten-day stretch alone her whirling planchette recorded 30,000 words. She said she could take 2,000 words an hour off the board when both she and the virginal puritan were on the right wavelength.

One thing that made Curran's story believable was the fact that while she'd had no formal training as a writer, the prose she produced was surprisingly good, often using very antiquated language. All of it was "far beyond the ken of Mrs. Curran, who," one critic wrote, "has never exhibited a shred of literary talent or enthusiasm." Curran's story was still intact when she died in 1937 at the age of 46—although many psychology experts explained away her writings as either a fraud or the product of an "alternating personality," the same phenomenon that causes people to speak in tongues.

The country of Brazil is named after the brazilnut.

COMMAND PERFORMANCES

A handful of people have actually committed murder when their Ouija boards "told" them to.

• In the early 1930s, for example, a 15-year-old girl named Mattie Turley murdered her father with a shotgun, apparently with the help of her mother, Dorothea Turley, who wanted to leave Mattie's father for another man. "The Ouija board told me to do it so that Mama can be free to marry a handsome cowboy, that's all that happened," the 15-year-old testified at her trial, "Mother told me the Ouija board couldn't be denied and that I would not even be arrested for doing it." Both mother and daughter were convicted of murder: Mrs. Turley's 10- to 25-year sentence was overturned three years later, and she was freed, but Mattie Turley didn't get out until she was 21.

• In 1932, a 77-year-old railroad worker named Herbert Hurd murdered his wife after their Ouija board falsely accused him of having an affair. As he later testified:

> The spirits told her through her Ouija board that I was too fond of another woman and had given her $15,000 of a hidden fortune. The Ouija board lied. I never was friendly with another woman and I never had $15,000, but Nellie beat me and burned me and tortured me into confessing all those lies, so I finally had to kill her.

• In 1956, a wealthy Connecticut woman named Helen Dow Peck left nearly her entire $178,000 estate to John Gale Forbes, a name her Ouija board had spelled out in 1919. The only problem: There was no John Gale Forbes—a court-ordered search failed to turn up a single person by that name in the entire United States.

OUIJA BOARDS IN THE NEWS

"Britain's Appeal Court was asked today to review a murder trial because three jurors allegedly used a Ouija board to contact one of the victims before finding a man guilty. Lawyers for Stephen Young told the court they had received information from another juror about a seance in the hotel where the jury stayed the night before they found Young guilty of shooting newlyweds Harry and Nicola Fuller. The three jurors 'contacted' Harry Fuller, who named Young, 35, as the killer, they said. The 12-person jury went on to convict Young unanimously." —*San Jose Mercury News*, 1994

Whale oil was used in automobile transmission fluids as late as 1973.

PRIMETIME PROVERBS

Pearls of television wisdom from Primetime Proverbs,
compiled by John Javna and Jack Mingo.

ON BEAUTY
"You could throw her in the river and skim ugly for two days."

—Granny,
The Beverly Hillbillies

ON WISDOM
"A truly wise man never plays leapfrog with a unicorn."

—Banacek,
Banacek

"What insight could you possibly hope to gain from a man whose I.Q. wouldn't make a respectable earthquake?"

—Diane Chambers,
Cheers

ON HISTORY
L.P.: "She's from one of California's first families."
Chico Rodriguez: "Oh, is she Mexican, too?"

—*Chico and the Man*

ON MATH
"If you've enjoyed this program just half as much as we've enjoyed doing it, then we've enjoyed it twice as much as you."

—Michael Palin,
Monty Python's Flying Circus

ON RELATIONSHIPS
"You're nothing but a tiny dot, a speck, a minute insignificant nothing. But I'm proud to call you my friend."

—Warren Ferguson,
The Andy Griffith Show

"I've never felt closer to a group of people. Not even in the portable johns of Woodstock."

—Jim Ignatowski,
Taxi

ON THINGS TO LOOK FORWARD TO
"If you make it to one hundred, that fat weather guy will say your name on TV."

—George Utley,
Newhart

ON THE LEGAL PROFESSION
"It's not enough that all the lawyers are crooks. Now the crooks are becomin' lawyers."

—Donegan,
Kaz

ON HOPE
"One good, solid hope is worth a carload of certainties."

—The Doctor,
Dr. Who

When a cat died in ancient Egypt, its owners shaved off their eyebrows as a sign of mourning.

FAMOUS TIGHTWADS

Who are the cheapest guys around? Often, the richest ones.
Here are more examples of extreme tightfistedness.

JOHN D. ROCKEFELLER, founder of Standard Oil. Gave a groundskeeper a $5 Christmas bonus...then docked it from the man's pay when he took Christmas Day off to spend with his family.

WALT DISNEY. Timed employees' trips to candy and soda machines.

CLARK GABLE, movie star. Often argued with his grocer about the price of jelly beans.

PAUL VOLCKER, chairman of the Federal Reserve Board. Rather than pay for a laundromat, he packed dirty laundry into a suitcase every week and drove it to his daughter's house.

TY COBB, baseball legend. As an early investor in Coca Cola stock, he was extremely wealthy—but still collected bars of soap from locker room showers and hotel rooms and sent them back to his Georgia farm.

J. PAUL GETTY, oil baron.
• When his son was kidnapped and held hostage, he refused to pay ransom money until the kidnappers sent the boy's ear to him in the mail.

• He calculated the wages of his gatekeeper by counting the number of times the main gate of his estate was opened and closed on a given day, then multiplied the number "by some minute sum" to arrive at a salary.

CALVIN COOLIDGE, U.S. president. Personally oversaw and approved all White House expenditures; reportedly bought food for state dinners at the local Piggly Wiggly.

ARTHUR FIEDLER, conductor of the Boston Pops. Rather than repair the holes in the walls of his home, he stuffed them with "moldering bits of carpet." He was also famous for skipping out on the tab when dining with his musicians.

The average caterpillar has 2,000 muscles in its body; the average human, 700.

THE PINBALL STORY

If you like pinball (and who doesn't?), here's the next best thing to actually having a machine in the bathroom. Hmm…interesting idea. Imagine what it would sound like to people waiting to use the toilet. "What are you doing in there? What's that noise? Hey, are you playing pinball?!!?"

ROLLING STONE

Have you ever heard of a game called Bagatelle? No one plays it anymore, but for centuries it was one of the most popular pastimes of the European upper classes. Originally, it was played outside. People threw stones up a hill and hoped that, as the stones rolled down, they'd fall into holes that had been dug in the hillside.

By the middle of the 17th century, the game was played indoors. Players pushed small balls up an inclined felt board with a stick, then let the balls go. Again, the object was to get the balls to drop into holes. But now each hole was surrounded by small pins (actually brass nails) to make it harder. The more points a hole was worth, the more pins were nailed around it. That, of course, is how *pinball* got its name.

THE NEXT STEP

Bagatelle remained popular in various forms for centuries. But modern pinball didn't evolve until 1931, when game manufacturer David Gottlieb created a version called Baffle Ball. He made two important changes to Bagatelle:

1. He incorporated a spring-loaded mechanism (virtually indistinguishable from modern-day pinball shooters), so balls were *launched* rather than pushed or dropped.

2. He made it a coin-operated machine, designed to sit on retailers' countertops.

There weren't any lights, bells, mechanical bumpers, or even flippers. Players shook and jostled the machine (technically, they weren't even supposed to do *that*) to get the ball into one of the high-scoring holes.

But it was an appealing diversion during the Great Depression, and was very popular.

Female canaries cannot sing.

As Russell Roberts wrote in the *Chicago Tribune*:

> To an American public haunted by economic disaster, facing day upon dreary day of hanging around street corners with nothing to do and no hope in sight, the new games were a welcome respite. For either a penny or a nickel (for which you got 7 or 10 balls, respectively), you could forget, for a few minutes anyway, the world and all its troubles. Soon every drugstore, bar and candy store had at least one.

Baffle Ball was also a source of employment. The games sold for only $16. Anyone who had the money could buy one, put it in a store, and split the profits with the store owner. "Pinball routemen," explains Candice Ford Tolbert in *Tilt: The Pinball Book*, "were anyone and everyone who could come up with a little cash and who had the time to service and collect from machines out on locations."

THE BIG THREE

Demand for Baffle Ball was so great that Gottlieb couldn't fill all his orders. So some of his distributors started to build their own games. In 1932, Gottlieb's biggest distributor, Ray Moloney, invented a game called Ballyhoo. It was so successful that he formed the Bally company and began designing games full-time.

Another distributor—an aspiring Disney cartoonist named Barry Williams—came up with so many innovations that Gottlieb offered him a royalty for his designs. (Later, Williams formed his own company.) Their first joint venture was a game called Advance. Roger Sharpe writes in *Popular Mechanics*:

> One of the breakthrough attractions of Advance was its delicately counterbalanced gates, which were vulnerable to jabs and nudges from players. One day, in 1932, Williams went to a drugstore and saw a player hit the bottom of Advance to score points without having to aim. This so enraged Williams that he took the game off location and hammered five nails through the bottom of the machine. In Williams' words, "Anybody who tried to affect the play of the game by slapping the flat of his hand against the game's undersurface, would now think twice before trying it again."

> However, Williams knew this was a cruel and temporary solution. So, he developed a simple, effective device that stopped play if the machine was handled roughly. The device consisted of a small ball

---

Good reason for ear plugs: The average newborn cries 113 minutes a day.

balanced on a pedestal. If the game was shaken or pounded, the ball fell from the pedestal and struck a metal ring that immediately stopped play.

Williams called the device a stool pigeon…but not for long. "I never quite liked the name 'stool pigeon,' " he recalled years later, "but I just couldn't come up with anything else." So he set one of the games up in a nearby drugstore and waited to watch the response. Sure enough, a player came along and handled the game too roughly, setting off the stool pigeon. "Damn, I tilted it!" he exclaimed. From then on, the mechanism was known as the *tilt*.

OTHER MILESTONES

There were four other important steps in creating the pinball machine as we know it:

1. Themes. In 1933, David Rockola (later a jukebox tycoon) came up with *Jigsaw*. Players could put a puzzle together by hitting certain targets and holes. Its popularity showed that the public wanted variety and novelty in their pinball games.

2. Electricity. Williams introduced *Contact*, the first pinball game to use electricity, also in 1933. It had an electrified "kick-out hole" that returned a ball to play after awarding points, and a bell that rang every time a player scored. Features like automatic scoring and "lighted back glass" quickly appeared on new machines.

3. Bumpers. Bally introduced *Bumper* in 1937. It used the first "electrically operated wire and spring bumpers."

4. Flippers. The first flippers appeared in a Bally game called *Humpty Dumpty*, in 1947. Before this breakthrough—created by accident when a technician touched two loose wires together—pinball machines were almost entirely games of chance. In *Humpty Dumpty*, the balls jumped around at the player's command. This feature quickly became indispensable on the machines…and turned pinball into a worldwide phenomenon. "In most of Europe, in fact, they're called flipper games and flipper machines," Roger Sharpe writes in *Pinball!* "Today, we have ramps, drop holes, underground networks, multiball games, drop targets and spinners, but they all don't necessarily have to be on every game. A flipper does."

PINBALL AND THE LAW

In 1933, pinball manufacturers made a mistake that would haunt them for decades. They decided to compete directly against slot machines, electronic bingo, and other gambling machines by building "payout" pinball machines, which rewarded successful players either with cash or tokens that could be redeemed for cash.

To many people, the move made pinball machines synonymous with gambling. And when communities outlawed other types of gambling machines—before and after World War II—they often got rid of all types of pinball machines as well.

Fighting Back. Pinball manufacturers countered by introducing "free play," machines that rewarded players with extended games instead of cash. But even these were controversial. Free games are objects of value, and therefore a kind of gambling payoff. Tamer "add-a-ball" features were condemned, too. In fact, it wasn't until America was exposed to the excesses of the 1960s that pinball finally regained acceptance as the lesser of many evils.

Believe it or not, however, many cities and states still have anti-pinball laws on the books, although they're seldom enforced anymore. Ironically, Chicago—home of Gottlieb, Bally, and Williams, the big three manufacturers of pinball machines—is one of the cities that had a long-term ban on the game. It wasn't until 1976 that pinball was finally legalized in its own hometown.

PINBALL FACTS

• David Gottlieb may have invented pinball, but he didn't have much faith in it. His second game was called *Five Star Final*, supposedly named after his favorite newspaper, the *Chicago Tribune*'s end-of-the-day edition. Actually, though, Gottleib figured the pinball "fad" was over and this was his "final" game. A few decades later, in the "golden age" of pinball, new machines were being designed and shipped every *three weeks*.

• It takes a team of six designers about nine months to invent and perfect a pinball game.

• Pinball designers work toward these ideals: the game should be easy enough to keep novices from getting discouraged, yet challenging enough to keep "wizards" interested; the average game should last from 2 1/2 to 3 minutes, or roughly 47 seconds a ball; and the player should get one free game for every four played.

MAKING HIS MARK

Mark Twain is one of America's greatest humorists...and maybe one of our great philosophers, too. Here are examples of what we mean.

"A banker is a fellow who lends you his umbrella when the sun is shining and wants it back the minute it begins to rain."

"Clothes make the man. Naked people have little or no influence on society."

"Every time you stop a school, you have to build a jail. What you gain at one end you lose at the other. It's like feeding a dog on his own tail. It won't fatten the dog."

"If you pick up a starving dog and make him prosperous, he will not bite you. This is the principal difference between a dog and a man."

"The human race has one really effective weapon, and that is laughter."

"The man who sets out to carry a cat by its tail learns something that will always be useful and which never will grow dim or doubtful."

"The surest protection against temptation is cowardice."

"There is no distinctly native American criminal class ...except Congress."

"Keep away from people who try to belittle your ambitions. Small people always do that, but the really great make you feel that you, too, can become great."

"The rule is perfect: in all matters of opinion our adversaries are insane."

"It usually takes more than three weeks to prepare a good impromptu speech."

"The best way to cheer yourself up is to try to cheer somebody else up."

"Nothing so needs reforming as other people's habits."

"Put all your eggs in the one basket and WATCH THAT BASKET!"

It's against the law to stare at the mayor of Paris.

CRANK CALLS

Ever make a "phony phone call"? What if you tried it and reached the
president or vice president...and they took you seriously?
Here are a few times when it really happened.

THE PRESIDENT IS DEAD!

Call for: Vice President Thomas Marshall

What happened: Marshall was in the middle of a speech at Atlanta's Civic Auditorium on November 23, 1919, when he was interrupted by a member of his staff. They'd just received a call from the White House telling them that President Woodrow Wilson, who'd recently had a stroke, had died. "I cannot continue my speech," the stunned vice president told his shocked audience, "I must leave at once to take up my duties as chief executive of this great nation."

Aftermath: Marshall was stunned again when he found out the call was a fake. He denounced it as a "cruel hoax."

WE WANT TO NEGOTIATE

Call for: President George Bush

What happened: In March 1990, an Iranian official called the White House to say he'd been instructed to set up a phone conference between Bush and Iranian president Ali Akbar Hashemi Rafsanjani concerning U.S. hostages held in Lebanon. Bush took the call "on the off chance that it might be real." Two days later, when the White House tried to return the call, they realized it had been a put-on.

Aftermath: Even the Iranians thought the Bush administration's response to the crank call was a little weird. "Can it be that such a global power, with all its intelligence capabilities, talks to a person it cannot identify?" the real President Rafsanjani asked in Teheran. "This is a strange occurrence."

THE PRESIDENT IS DEAD!

Call for: CNN (Cable News Network)

What happened: In 1992, three hours after President Bush had collapsed during a banquet in Tokyo and vomited in the Japanese

---

The most popular Campbell's soup in Hong Kong is watercress and duck gizzard.

prime minister's lap, the CNN newsroom got a call from the president's personal physician, who was with Bush in Japan. He had terrible news: the president had just died. CNN staffers thought the story was real and typed it into their news computer. Fortunately for them, the caller had left his phone number…and they traced it to Idaho, not Tokyo.

The story was quickly wiped off the computer and never made it onto CNN's main news channel. But downstairs at Headline News, staffers saw it moments before it was erased. They rushed the tragic information to anchor Don Harrison. "This just in to CNN Headline News!" he told viewers urgently. Then, as he opened his mouth to read the bulletin, he heard someone off-camera yell, "No! Stop!" "We are now getting a correction…," he ad-libbed.

Aftermath: The call was traced to the Garden City, Idaho, home of James Edward Smith, 71, who was arrested and placed in a mental hospital.

WHAT DO YOU THINK OF QUEBEC?

Call for: Queen Elizabeth

What happened: In October 1995, Pierre Brassard, a disc jockey at Montreal's Radio CKOI, called Buckingham Palace and said he was Canadian Prime Minister Jean Chretien; he asked to speak to the queen. Palace officials checked with Chretien's office to verify that the call was genuine, but Chretien wasn't in. Still, an official said that Chretien "probably wanted to speak with her."

So Queen Elizabeth got on the line…and chatted for 17 minutes. She didn't realize it was a prank, even when Brassard "started talking about Halloween and suggesting she put on a nice hat."

Aftermath: The English public was not amused. "We think it's annoying," a Palace spokesperson said. In retaliation, one British newspaper published Radio CKOI's phone number and urged readers to call when Brassard was on the air. Another paper had a reporter call Brassard, posing as a Scotland Yard detective, and threaten legal action. But the London tabloid *News of the World* got the best revenge: it offered Brassard an $80,000 trip to London for an exclusive story…then reneged on the deal when he accepted, telling him it was a prank.

Spinach consumption in the U.S. rose 33% after the Popeye comic strip became a hit in 1931.

ALL ABOUT CHESS

For chess lovers, books about how to play the game are essential bathroom reading. For the rest of us, three pages about chess—one of the oldest and most popular board games in history—are plenty.

FIRST MOVES

• Chess began in northern India sometime before 500 A.D. and was probably based on an Indian military game called *chaturanga* —*chatur* meaning "four," and *anga* meaning "parts of an army." Like real Indian armies of the day, the game had four types of pieces: elephants, chariots, cavalry, and infantry. It was largely a game of chance; how well you did depended on how well you rolled the dice.

• Chaturanga was later combined with *petteia*, a Greek game of reason. The result was a game close to modern chess. The dice were eliminated, and the emphasis of the game shifted from chance to strategy. There were 16 pieces per player, just like in modern chess: one king, one vizier, or adviser, two elephants, two horses, two chariots, and eight foot soldiers.

• The new game became a worldwide phenomenon. By 800 A.D., it had spread east to China, Korea, and Japan…and west to the Arab world. In Persia, the game was known as *shāh māt*—"the king is dead." This is the direct linguistic predecessor to the English word "checkmate."

• When the Moors conquered Spain in the ninth century, they brought chess with them. From there it spread all over Europe, and continued to evolve into the game we know today.

THE PIECES

How did the game go from the original pieces to what we have now?

• **The elephant.** According to *The Greatest Games of All Time*, Arabs didn't approve of the elephant piece because "physical representations are forbidden in the Islamic religion." They replaced it with "a minaret-shaped piece with a nick cut into it." Later, when Europeans saw it, the pointed top with a nick reminded them of a bishop's hat…so they called it a bishop.

- **The chariot.** Hadn't been used for centuries in European war-fare. It was changed to something more familiar: a castle (or rook).

- **The vizier.** Never a part of European culture, it was replaced by the queen—a king's most important *un*official advisor.

- **The cavalry pieces and foot soldiers.** Stayed the same—the names were simply changed to knights and pawns.

SLOW MOTION

About the only thing that separated medieval chess from today's version was the way the pieces moved. Most were considerably weaker. The queen, for example—the most powerful piece today—could only move one space at a time. But in the 15th century, the rules abruptly changed.

- The queen was suddenly able to go any distance in any direction, as long as she wasn't blocked by other pieces.

- The bishop became able to move any distance diagonally, as long as no one was in the way.

- Even the pawns were strengthened a little: they became able to move two spaces on the first move.

Chess historians believe these changes were connected to the introduction of artillery into modern warfare. Artillery enabled armies to shoot weapons over previously unthinkable distances, so the short distances traveled in chess no longer made military sense. When the game was brought up to date, pieces naturally became more powerful.

THE RIGHT MOVES

Today, the way some pieces move seems pretty arbitrary. For example, the pawns can only move straight ahead, except when they are attacking; then they can only move diagonally. And the knight (horse) can jump over other pieces. But these moves actually made a lot of sense when they were introduced:

- The pawn is based on a soldier known as a *pikeman*. As pikemen marched forward into battle, they held their shields directly in front of them and stuck their pikes (spears) out on either side. The shield was so bulky that it was literally impossible for the pikeman to attack anything directly in front of him. That's why a pawn can

Q: Why is pound cake called pound cake?   A: The original recipe called for a pound of butter.

only attack pieces that are diagonally to the left or right.

• Knights were the only people in the battlefield on horseback—and thus are the only ones who can leap over their opponents.

CHESS AND REVOLUTION

Because many court officials—kings, queens, etc.—are represented in chess, the pieces have traditionally been seen as symbols of the establishment. This has made them unpopular with revolutionaries. Often, when a king was overthrown, the people who toppled him would try to replace the country's chess pieces as well.

• After the Revolutionary War, for example, many American chessmakers replaced kings with acorn-shaped pieces. One editor who hoped to make chess "better adapted to our feelings as citizens of a free republic," suggested calling the kings, queens, and pawns *governors*, *generals*, and *pioneers*. The idea never caught on.

• At the beginning of the French Revolution, the Convention decreed that kings, queens, knights, rooks, bishops, and pawns would henceforth be known as *flags*, *adjutants*, *dragoons*, *cannons*, *volunteers*, and *troops of the line*. These changes were rejected by chess players...although many French sets still contain crownless queens.

CHANGING SIDES

The most bizarre example of "revolutionary chess" came in the late 1920s, when the Marx and Engels Institute in Moscow invented a communist chess board for the USSR. The board was divided into red and white teams, with Joseph Stalin serving as the red king and other prominent Communists filling out the ranks of the red queen, bishops, knights, and rooks. Prominent opponents of the Communists filled out the white ranks.

But as Stalin began wiping out his political enemies in the purges of the 1930s, many Communists represented by the red pieces fell out of favor—which meant they could no longer be represented on the red side. These "enemy of the people" pieces had to be bleached white and moved to the other side of the board; owners who didn't comply risked being sent to Siberia. As the purges progressed, it became so difficult to keep track of who belonged on which side of the board that the chess sets had to be abandoned.

How many languages in the world? About 5,000.

IS *THIS* BATHROOM READING?

Here's a surprise entry—the Bill of Rights. Actually, Uncle John's been thinking about including this for some time. After all, what better chance to read the document than in the bathroom? You know, you can read one of the Amendments, then flip to the history of bubblegum or something. If they'd taught it that way in school, we'd all know it by heart now. We at the BRI like to think that the Founding Fathers would be proud of us.

BILL OF RIGHTS

Here's the complete text of the first 10 Amendments to the U.S. Constitution.

1. Congress shall make no law respecting an establishment of religion, or prohibiting the free exercise thereof; or abridging the freedom of speech, or of the press; or the right of the people peaceably to assemble, and to petition the Government for a redress of grievances.

2. A well regulated militia, being necessary to the security of a free State, the right of the people to keep and bear Arms, shall not be infringed.

3. No Soldier shall, in time of peace be quartered in any house, without the consent of the Owner, nor in time of war, but in a manner to be prescribed by law.

4. The right of the people to be secure in their persons, houses, papers, and effects, against unreasonable searches and seizures, shall not be violated, and no Warrants shall issue, but upon probable cause, supported by Oath or affirmation, and particularly describing the place to be searched, and the persons or things to be seized.

5. No person shall be held to answer for a capital, or otherwise infamous crime, unless on a presentment or indictment of a Grand Jury, except in cases arising in the land or naval forces, or in the

---

There are more fatal traffic accidents in July than any other month.

Militia, when in actual service in time of War or public danger; nor shall any person be subject for the same offence to be twice put in jeopardy of life or limb; nor shall be compelled in any criminal case to be a witness against himself, nor be deprived of life, liberty, or property, without due process of law; nor shall private property be taken for public use, without just compensation.

6. In all criminal prosecutions, the accused shall enjoy the right to a speedy and public trial, by an impartial jury of the State and district wherein the crime shall have been committed, which district shall have been previously ascertained by law, and to be informed of the nature and cause of the accusation; to be confronted with the witnesses against him; to have compulsory process for obtaining witnesses in his favor, and to have the Assistance of Counsel for his defence.

7. In Suits at common law, where the value in controversy shall exceed twenty dollars, the right of trial by jury shall be preserved, and no fact tried by a jury, shall be otherwise re-examined in any Court of the United States, than according to the rules of the common law.

8. Excessive bail shall not be required, nor excessive fines imposed, nor cruel and unusual punishments inflicted.

9. The enumeration in the Constitution, of certain rights, shall not be construed to deny or disparage others retained by the people.

10. The powers not delegated to the United States by the Constitution, nor prohibited by it to the States, are reserved to the States respectively, or to the people.

*   *   *   *

FOOD FOR THOUGHT

In a recent survey, a randomly selected group of American citizens were shown a list of freedoms. Then they were asked by pollsters if they would vote for those rights. Not only did many respondents fail to recognize that the freedoms on the list were already guaranteed by the Bill of Rights—they said they'd vote *against* the rights if they were on the ballot.

The average 1995 luxury car had more than one mile of wiring.

BRAND NAMES

You already know these names. Now you know where they come from.

KOOL-AID. Originally named Kool-Ade, until bureaucrats in the Food and Drug Administration banned the use of "ade" because it means "a drink made from…" So inventor E. E. Perkins simply changed the spelling to "aid," meaning "help."

SONY. Originally called Tokyo Tsushin Kogyo. Founder Akio Morita wanted a name he could market internationally. He looked through a Latin dictionary, picked out the word *sonus* (sound), and combined it with "sunny."

CHEERIOS. Originally Cheery Oats. In 1946, Quaker Oats threatened to sue, claiming it had exclusive rights to the name "Oats." Rather than fight, General Mills switched to Cheerios.

BISSELL CARPET SWEEPER. Melville Bissell owned a crockery shop in Grand Rapids, Michigan. He was so allergic to the straw his crockery was packed in that he started sneezing whenever he had to sweep it up. So he invented—and ultimately manufactured—the first carpet sweeper.

HAMILTON-BEACH. L. H. Hamilton and Chester A. Beach perfected a "high-speed, lightweight universal electric motor" and used it in the first commercial drink mixer in 1912. They went on to build small appliances for home use.

GREY POUPON DIJON MUSTARD. Sound classy? Actually, it's named for the Briton who invented it—a Mr. Grey—and his French business partner—Monsieur Poupon—who put up money to open a mustard factory in (where else?) Dijon, France.

CARNATION. In 1901, while walking down a street in Seattle, the head of the Pacific Coast Condensed Milk Company noticed a box of Carnation Brand cigars in a store window. He decided it was a good name for his milk, too. With a picture of a flower on the label, it would be recognizable even to children.

Sound like someone you know? An ostrich's eyes are bigger than its brains.

PHRASE ORIGINS

More origins of everyday phrases.

TURN OVER A NEW LEAF

Meaning: Start over.

Origin: Trees have nothing to do with it—the leaf in the expression is actually the page of a book. Just as the plot of a novel changes from page to page, so too can people change their lives.

IN THE DOLDRUMS

Meaning: Unhappy or depressed; sluggish.

Origin: *Doldrum* is believed to be a corruption of the word *dullard* —meaning "dull or sluggish person." Early cartographers applied it to the dullest areas of the ocean, near the equator, where the waters are calm and winds are very light. With little or no wind in their sails, ships might literally spend weeks "in the doldrums."

WORKING FREELANCE

Meaning: Working independently, for more than one employer.

Origin: The novelist Sir Walter Scott first used this term to describe soldiers-for-hire in the Middle Ages. Because they owed loyalty to no one, he reasoned, they were *free* to hire out their skill with *lances* to anyone who could afford them.

PUT SOMEONE ON THE SPOT

Meaning: Put someone in a difficult position.

Origin: Gangster slang from the 1920s. A person *on the spot* was marked for execution. Probably originated in reference to witnesses, who were "on the spot" where a crime was committed.

ON THE NOSE

Meaning: Perfect; right on time.

Origin: In the early days of radio broadcasting, directors used hand signals to communicate with announcers in soundproof studios. A finger across the throat meant "cut," and a finger *on the nose* meant that the show was right on schedule.

The man who created the Thighmaster was once a Bhuddist monk.

PLEASE LEAVE A MESSAGE...

Telephone answering machines are a bathroom reader's friend. We owe the inventor a debt of gratitude, because they let us read in peace. After all, who wants to jump off the toilet and race madly for the phone every time it rings?

THE FIRST EFFORT

You may not know this, but when Thomas Edison played "Mary Had a Little Lamb" on his first crude recording device in 1877, he was really trying to create a telephone answering machine. The problem with the telephone, he reasoned, was that—unlike the telegraph—it didn't take messages. Unfortunately, the Wizard of Menlo Park couldn't come up with a viable answering device; he had to "settle" for the phonograph instead.

THE FIRST MACHINE

A Danish technician named Valdemar Poulsen invented the answering machine in the summer of 1898. Poulsen's device, called the "telegraphone," was meant to be used exclusively as an answering machine, but was actually the world's first magnetic recorder—the direct precursor to the tape recorder. In 1903, his company, the American Telegraphone Company, tried to crack the U.S. market. It failed miserably, for three reasons:

1. Poor sound quality.

2. It was too expensive for most homes or businesses.

3. The Bell companies refused to allow "outside" machines to be hooked up to their phone lines—which virtually eliminated the entire U.S. market.

American Telegraphone then tried to market their machine as a dictaphone instead, but that failed, too. They went bankrupt in 1919.

THE PHONEMATE

Then, in the late 1960s, Neal Buglewicz, a California inventor, decided to buck the phone company. He developed an answering machine that used two tape recorders and called it the Phonemate 700. His second version, the "streamlined" Phonemate 400, became the first answering machine made widely available to consumers. By today's standards, it was laughably primitive: It weighed 10 pounds, used reel-to-reel tapes, could only record voice messages 30 seconds long, and required earphones to retrieve messages. But it opened the door for other designs. Soon other companies were offering similar machines.

AT&T did what it could to prevent the answering machine from succeeding. In 1972, they announced that phone customers had to buy special equipment to connect answering machines to the telephone company network. But Phonemate and its competitors went to court to have the regulations thrown out, and in 1976 they won.

☞   ☞   ☞   ☞

FARTS IN THE NEWS

• Frank Lathrop is the proud inventor of the TooT TrappeR, a special seat cushion that instantly absorbs the odor of unwanted gas. Lathrop got the idea after too many complaints from his wife. "You just sit on it, and it goes to work," Lathrop explains. "We call this the perfect thing for the person who has everything, including gas." The TrappeR's air filter "uses the same technique that was used in gas masks during the Desert Storm War."

• Biologist Dr. Colin Leakey has devoted his entire career to figuring out what makes people pass wind. "We believe that by looking at chemicals in the flatus, we can look at what is being broken down and where these particular chemicals come from," he says. To accomplish this, Leakey (*Leakey?!!?*) has invented the *flatometer*, a device that measures flatulence.

• Johnson & Johnson, which produces drugs for gas and indigestion, once conducted a survey and found that almost one-third of Americans believe they have a flatulence problem. However, according to Terry Bolin and Rosemary Stanton, authors of *Wind Breaks: Coming to Terms with Flatulence*, most flatulence is healthy. What is unhealthy, the authors argue, is that we spend too much time dwelling on it.

THE ODD TITLE AWARD

*Q: What do the Pulitzer Prize and the Odd Title Award have in common?
A: None of Uncle John's Bathroom Readers have won either of
them. Here are some real-life books that have won* Bookseller
magazine's annual award for the most unusual book title.

THE NAME GAME

Every year, tens of thousands of new books are published.
Some are pretty strange…and in 1978, the staff at *Bookseller*
magazine decided to honor a few with the Odd Title of the Year
Award. Every year, they give a bottle of champagne to the person
who finds the most unusual book title of the year. The only rules:
the book itself has to be serious, and "gratuitously eye-catching academic works" are automatically disqualified. The title has to be
weird without trying to be. (That's why *New Guinea Tapeworms &
Jewish Grandmothers; Tales of Parasites and People*, lost out in 1994.)
Here are all the winners. Remember: These are *real* book titles!

1978: *Proceedings of the Second In-
ternational Workshop on Nude Mice*
(Also won the Oddest of the Odd
Book Title Award, given in 1994
to the oddest title in the contest's
15-year history)
Runners-up:
• *Cooking with God*
• *Iceberg Utilization*
• *Fight Acne and Win*

1979: *The Madam as Entrepreneur:
Career Management in House
Prostitution*
Runners-up:
• *Macrame Gnomes*
• *100 Years of British Rail Catering*

1980: *The Joy of Chickens*
Runner-up:
• *Children Are Like Wet Cement*

1981: *Last Chances at Love:
Terminal Romances*
Runner-up:
• *Waterproofing Your Child*

1982: Two winners: *Braces Own-
ers' Manual: A Guide to the Care
and Wearing of Braces*, and *Popula-
tion and Other Problems*
Runners-up:
• *Tourist Guide to Lebanon*
• *Scurvy Past and Present*
• *Keeping Warm with an Axe*

1983: *The Theory of Lengthwise Rolling*
Runners-up:
- *Practical Infectious Diseases*
- *Nasal Maintenance: Nursing Your Nose Through Troubled Times*
- *Atlas of Tongue Coating*

1984: *The Book of Marmalade: Its Antecedents, Its History and Its Role in the World Today*
Runners-up:
- *Big and Very Big Hole Drilling*
- *Picture Your Dog in Needlework*
- *Napoleon's Glands and Other Ventures in Biohistory*

1985: *Natural Bust Enlargement with Total Power: How to Increase the Other 90% of Your Mind to Increase the Size of Your Breasts*
Runner-up:
- *Anorexia Nervosa in Bulgarian Bees*

1986: *Oral Sadism and the Vegetarian Personality*

1987: No prize awarded

1988: *Versailles: The View from Sweden*
Runner-up:
- *Detecting Fake Nazi Regalia*

1989: *How to Shit in the Woods: An Environmentally Sound Approach to a Lost Art*

1990: *Lesbian Sado-masochism Safety Manual*

1991: No prize awarded

1992: *How to Avoid Huge Ships*
Runner-up:
- *Watermark Diseases of the Cricket Bat*

1993: *American Bottom Archaeology*
Runners-up:
- *Liturgy of the Opening of the Mouth for Breathing*
- *The Complete Suicide Manual*

1994: *Highlights in the History of Concrete*
Runners-up:
- *Septic Tanks and Cesspools: A Do-It-Yourself Guide*
- *Butchering Livestock at Home*
- *Best Bike Rides in the Mid-Atlantic*
- *Gymnastics for Horses*
- *Psychiatric Disorders in Dental Practice*

1995: *Reusing Old Graves* ("a study of cemetery etiquette")
Runners-up:
- *Amputee Management: A Handbook*
- *Mucus and Related Topics*
- *Simply Bursting: A Guide to Bladder Control*
- *Fun Games and Big Bangs: The Recreational Use of High Explosives*
- *Rats for Those Who Care*
- *Teach Your Cat to Read*
- *Virtual Reality: Exploring the Bra*

The U.S. Post Office sold a record 123 million Elvis Presley commemorative stamps in 1993.

INCOME TAX TRIVIA

You may not like to pay them, but reading about them isn't so bad. And when you're done with the page, you can always tear it out and...

AUDIT INFO

Do you worry about being audited? Actually, the odds you'll be audited are pretty low: In 1994 the IRS audited about 93,000 individual income tax returns out of 114 million submitted, or about .08% of all returns filed. That's way down from 1914, when every single one of the 357,598 tax returns submitted was audited. The IRS didn't take any chances with the signatures that year, either: each taxpayer had to sign their return under oath in the presence of IRS officials.

KISS & TELL

Believe it or not, the IRS actually pays people to tattle on tax cheats. In fiscal year 1993, for example, it payed out $5.3 million to tipsters. The money was rewarded to more than 14,000 different informants, whose tips led to the collection of $172 million in previously unpaid taxes. The most "useful" tattlers earned an average of $1,772 apiece. But they had to file Form 211, the official IRS informer form, to claim their "reward."

TAX RANKINGS

Sweden has the highest taxes of any modern economy on earth—its taxes make up 56.9% of the country's total income. The United States comes in ninth behind Sweden, France, Italy, Germany, Canada, Britain, Switzerland, and Japan. Taxes make up about 29.9% of its total income.

LEGAL DEADBEATS

According to a 1990 IRS study, 1,219 taxpayers with incomes over $200,000 legally paid *no* federal income tax at all that year—and 1,114 of these people paid no income taxes anywhere else in the world, either.

Sonny & Cher originally called themselves Cleo and Caesar.

DEDUCTIONS

According to the 1995 tax code, Nobel Prize money is exempt from taxation, and the cost of a police officer's uniform can be deducted. But the meals a firefighter eats in the firehouse are taxable, because the IRS considers the fire station to be a "home."

THE FIRST "LOOPHOLE"

In 1915 a U.S. Congressman, complaining about the increasing complexity of the tax code, lamented, "I write a law. You drill a hole in it. I plug the hole. You drill a hole in my plug." His words were reported in newspapers all over the country, and a new word—*loophole*—was born.

IT'S OUR TIME, TOO

How much time do you spend each working day to pay your federal income taxes? Over the years the National Tax Foundation, an income tax lobbying group, has kept track of how much of the average American's working day is used to earn enough to make payments to Uncle Sam. Their findings:

1929: 19 minutes per day	1969: 1 hour, 48 minutes
1939: 40 minutes	1979: 1 hour, 48 minutes
1949: 1 hour, 16 minutes	1989: 1 hour, 47 minutes
1959: 1 hour, 36 minutes	

CHANGING VIEWS

In a 1972 poll by the Advisory Commission on Intergovernmental Relations, Americans ranked the federal income tax as "the fairest of all taxes." In a similar study in 1989, American taxpayers ranked the tax as "the *least* fair of all taxes."

THE DREADED DATE

In 1954, the IRS moved the deadline for filing tax returns back a month, from March 15 to April 15. Reason: The tax code had become so complicated that Americans needed more time to fill out the forms.

The oldest pig in the world lived to the age of 68.

AS SMART AS BAIT

A lot of stuff on the internet makes great bathroom reading. For example:
Here's a list of "35 Politically Correct Ways to Say Someone's Stupid,"
taken off the Internet and sent to us by BRI member John Dollison.

1. A few clowns short of a circus.
2. A few fries short of a Happy Meal.
3. An experiment in Artificial Stupidity.
4. A few beers short of a 6-pack.
5. Dumber than a box of hair.
6. A few peas short of a casserole.
7. Doesn't have all his corn flakes in one box.
8. The wheel's spinning, but the hamster's dead.
9. One Fruit Loop shy of a full bowl.
10. One taco short of a combination plate.
11. A few feathers short of a whole duck.
12. All foam, no beer.
13. The cheese slid off his cracker.
14. Body by Fisher, brains by Mattel.
15. Has an IQ of 2, but it takes 3 to grunt.
16. Warning: Objects in mirror are dumber than they appear.
17. Couldn't pour water out of a boot with instructions on the heel.
18. Too much yardage between the goal posts.
19. An intellect rivaled only by garden tools.
20. As smart as bait.
21. Chimney's clogged.
22. Doesn't have all his dogs on one leash.
23. Doesn't know much but leads the league in nostril hair.
24. Elevator doesn't go all the way to the top floor.
25. Forgot to pay his brain bill.
26. Her sewing machine's out of thread.
27. Her antenna doesn't pick up all the channels.
28. His belt doesn't go through all the loops.
29. If he had another brain, it would be lonely.
30. Missing a few buttons on her remote control.
31. No grain in the silo.
32. Proof that evolution *can* go in reverse.
33. Receiver is off the hook.
34. Several nuts short of a full pouch.
35. He fell out of the Stupid tree and hit every branch on the way down.

"The Alphabet Song," "Twinkle, Twinkle Little Star," and "Baa, Baa Black Sheep" are

THE ROOSEVELTS

The Roosevelt family has been a big part of the American 20th century. They're quotable, too.

"The best executive is one who has sense enough to pick good people to do what he wants done, and self-restraint enough to keep from meddling."
—*Theodore Roosevelt*

"A conservative is a man with two perfectly good legs who has never learned to walk forward."
—*Franklin D. Roosevelt*

"No man is justified in doing evil on the ground of expediency."
—*Theodore Roosevelt*

"No one can make you feel inferior without your consent."
—*Eleanor Roosevelt*

"To destroy our natural resources, to skin and exhaust the land instead of using it so as to increase its usefulness, will result in undermining, in the days of our children, the very prosperity which we ought by right to hand down."
—*Theodore Roosevelt*

"Every time an artist dies, part of the vision of mankind passes with him."
—*Franklin D. Roosevelt*

"I think we consider too much the good luck of the early bird, and not enough the bad luck of the early worm."
—*Franklin D. Roosevelt*

"If you can't say something good about someone, come and sit by me."
—*Alice Roosevelt Longworth* **(Theodore's daughter)**

"My father gave me these hints on speechmaking: Be sincere… be brief…be seated."
—*James Roosevelt* **(FDR's son)**

"Never underestimate a man who overestimates himself."
—*Franklin D. Roosevelt*

"Calvin Coolidge looks like he was weaned on a pickle."
—*Alice Roosevelt Longworth*

"When they call the roll in the Senate, the Senators do not know whether to answer 'Present' or 'Not guilty.'"
—*Theodore Roosevelt*

"The gains of education are never really lost. Books may be burned and cities sacked, but truth…lives in the hearts of humble men."
—*Franklin D. Roosevelt*

---

all sung to the same music: a 1765 French song titled "*Ah! Vous Diraije Maman.*"

THE ICEMAN COMETH

*Not all mummies are wrapped in bandages. Here's one
who was buried in ice, fully clothed, for 5,000 years.*

SURPRISE ENCOUNTER

On September 19, 1991, some people hiking in the Alps along the Austrian/Italian border spotted a body sticking out of a glacier. The corpse was brown and dried out and looked like it had been there for a long time. But neither the hikers nor the Austrian officials who recovered it four days later had any idea *how* long.

When scientists carbon-dated the remains, the "Iceman" (as he was dubbed in the press) turned out to be more than 5,300 years old. It was the world's oldest fully preserved human body, and the first prehistoric human ever found with "everyday clothing and equipment"—including an axe, dagger, and bow and arrows. Other bodies that have been found were either buried following funerals or sacrificed in religious ceremonies…which means they had ceremonial objects and clothing that didn't shed much light on what everyday life was like.

CLOSE CALL

Because no one realized how old or valuable the Iceman was until five days after he was discovered, no one took any precautions to ensure he wasn't damaged during removal and shipment to the morgue. In fact, it seems they did just about everything they could to *damage* him. An Austrian police officer tried to free the Iceman from the ice by using a jackhammer—shredding his garments and gashing his left hip to the bone. He probably would have done more damage, except that he ran out of compressed air for the jackhammer and had to quit.

Next, as word of the unusual discovery spread, locals and gawkers traveled to the site to view the remains. Many pocketed the Iceman's tools and shreds of garment as souvenirs. And when forensics experts finally removed the body from the ice, they did so using clumsy pickaxes, destroying the archaeological value of the site in the process.

By now the Iceman, clothed from the waist down when initially discovered, was buck naked save for pieces of a boot on his right foot and shards of clothing strewn around the body. Even worse, his private parts were missing, perhaps stolen by one of the visitors to the site. They were never recovered.

MODERN PROBLEMS

When scientists did get around to studying him, they found a dark-skinned male between the ages of 25 and 40 who stood 5'2" tall. The Iceman surprised archaeologists with his shaved face, recently cut hair, and tattoos; experts thought that people did not "invent" shaves, haircuts, and tattoos until thousands of years later.

He also suffered from some surprisingly modern ailments. A body-scan revealed smoke-blackened lungs—probably from sitting around open fires, but definitely not from smoking—as well as hardening of the arteries and blood vessels. He also had arthritis in the neck, lower back, and hip. But he didn't die from any of them.

CAUSE OF DEATH

The fact that the Iceman's body survived so long may provide a clue about how he died. Most bodies recovered from glaciers have literally been torn to pieces by slow-moving ice. But the Iceman's wasn't. He was found in a small protective basin, 10 to 15 feet deep, that sheltered him as glaciers passed overhead. This leads archaeologists to speculate that he sought shelter in the basin when a surprise winter storm hit. "He was in a state of exhaustion perhaps as a consequence of adverse weather conditions," a team of experts theorized in *Science* magazine in 1992. "He therefore may have lain down, fallen asleep, and frozen to death." Snow covered the body, the glacier eventually flowed over it…and the body remained completely preserved and undisturbed for the next 53 centuries.

FINAL RESTING PLACE

The Iceman now resides in a freezer in Austria's Innsbruck University, kept at 98% humidity and 21°F, "the glacial temperature he had grown accustomed to over more than 5,000 years." Scientists only examine the body for 20 minutes every two weeks—anything more than that would cause the mummy to deteriorate.

About 75% of U.S. families put up a Christmas tree; 54% of the trees are artificial.

FOOD FLOPS

How can anyone in the food industry predict what people will buy, when Frankenberry Cereal and Cheez Whiz are wild successes? It's anyone's guess what America will eat…which is how they come up with clunkers like these.

LA CHOY "FRESH AND LITE" EGG ROLLS. A quick snack? Not exactly. The big, fat egg rolls took half an hour to thaw and eat, so by the time the center was hot, the shell was damp and gooey. Even the name "Fresh and Lite" was half-baked. "It sounded like a feminine hygiene product," one of the company's ad executives admitted. "And it was hard to say it was fresh anyway, because it was frozen."

MCDONALD'S MCLEAN DELUXE. In 1991, McFood scientists were ordered to come up with a burger that even health nuts could love. Their solution: to replace most of the fat with carrageenan (seaweed extract) and water to create the "91% fat free" McLean Deluxe. It was a product with no market: health-conscious eaters still avoided the Golden Arches; fast-food aficionados were revolted by the concept of a seaweed burger. After years of slow sales, McDonald's finally threw in the towel in 1996.

WINE & DINE. According to *Business Week* magazine, Wine & Dine was "the upscale answer to Hamburger Helper—noodles and a sauce mix bundled with a tiny bottle of Chianti. Sad to say, the labeling didn't make it clear that the Chianti in that bottle was salty cooking wine. Consumers thought they had bought a little vino for dinner. When they discovered their error, they took their wining and dining elsewhere."

I HATE PEAS. If kids won't eat peas in their natural shape, why not mash them into a paste and make them look like French fries? Answer: Because, as one kid put it, "they still taste disgusting." Consumer researcher Robert McMath summed it up: "Kids said, 'A pea is a pea is a pea….I don't like peas. In fact, I hate peas, even if they're in the shape of French fries." I Hate Beans also flopped.

None of the Beatles knew how to read music. (Paul McCartney eventually taught himself.)

MILLER CLEAR BEER. In the wake of huge publicity generated by Crystal Pepsi, Tab Clear, and other colorless soft drinks (most of which flopped), Miller came up with this clearly stupid idea. Unlike soft drinks, which are artificially colored, a beer's color is *natural*. So it's just about impossible to remove the color without destroying the flavor and body at the same time. One newspaper critic described Clear Beer as "a lager the color of 7-Up, with little head and a taste like sweetened seltzer…with the faintest touch of oily, medicinal hoppiness in the finish." Born: 1994; died: 1996.

NESTEA'S TEA WHIZ. Would you give a "yellowish, carbonated, lemon-flavored drink" a name like *Whiz*?

VIN DE CALIFORNIE. "For the first time in history, American wines will cross the sea to France!" boasted three California winemakers in 1966. The ship might as well have sunk on the way over. Novelty shops were the only stores willing to stock "Vin de Californie" (the brand name they marketed it under)—and even there, sales were poor. "French customers approached the displays gingerly," *Newsweek* magazine reported, "almost as if they were afraid the wines might explode."

Critics considered the wine a joke. And the Californians unwittingly seemed to agree. "Vin de Californie," it turned out, is French slang for Coca-Cola.

JUMPIN' JEMS. The soft drink equivalent of the lava lamp. Introduced in 1995 by Mistic Brands, it was supposed to have "jelly balls" floating in the liquid. A major flaw: The "jelly balls" settled to the bottom of the bottle. Consumers figured the product had gone bad and wouldn't touch it. "Even *I* didn't drink it," admitted Mistic's president.

• Okay, then. A year later, the Clearly Canadian Beverage Company tried again with Orbitz. This time, the "flavored gel spheres" stayed suspended in the drink and were small enough to fit through a straw, but large enough so they "didn't look like a mistake." Reaction: "I think it's gross," one consultant told reporters. "It's like, when you drink a glass of milk, do you want to find lumps?"

REVENGE!

"Don't get mad, get even" was John F. Kennedy's motto. All of us want to get back at someone, sometime. Here are six reports we've found about people (and a rabbit) who actually did.

T RIGGER HAPPY
"Two gangsters, James Gallo and Joe Conigliaro, set about to murder a stoolpigeon, Vinny Ensuelo, alias Vinny Ba Ba. On November 1, 1973, they jumped him on Columbia Street, Brooklyn, and took him for a ride. Gallo pointed a gun at his head from the right; Conigliaro covered him from the left. The car swerved violently. The two gangsters shot each other."

As the New York *Daily News* described it:

Conigliaro, hit in the spine, was paralyzed. Every year after that Vinny Ensuelo sent wheelchair batteries to Conigliaro. A small card with the batteries always said, "Keep rolling, from your best pal, Vinny Ba Ba."

—*Remarkable Events*, **by John Train**

COMMON CENTS
"A shabbily dressed man went up to a teller yesterday at the U.S. Bank of Washington in Spokane, and asked her to validate his 60¢ parking ticket. She refused. The man asked to talk to a bank manager about the matter. The manager also refused. So 59-year-old John Barrier withdrew all the money he had on deposit—$1 million—and took it down the street to the Seafirst Bank. 'If you have $1 in a bank, or $1 million, I think they owe you the courtesy of stamping your parking ticket,' he said."

—**UPI, Feb. 21, 1989**

MASHED
In 1974, after three seasons as Col. Henry Blake on "M*A*S*H" (CBS), McLean Stevenson suddenly announced he was leaving to star in a sitcom for NBC.

The show's producers paid him back in kind. "One story around Hollywood," wrote Tom Shales in the *Washington Post*, "was that

---

That's fast: Peregrine falcons can dive at speeds up to 240 miles an hour.

Stevenson was so disliked on the set that Blake's death was written in to make sure there was no way he could ever come back." John Carman updated the story 20 years later in the *S.F. Chronicle*:

> To be *McLeaned* is to be blotted out fully and finally and with extreme TV prejudice.
>
> Reserved for actors who've been naughty and unappreciative, the process is named for McLean Stevenson, who wanted off M*A*S*H and saw his wish come all too true. His irate producers packed Stevenson's character, Henry Blake, into a helicopter and had it plunge from the sky. Message to McLean: You're crop dust now. You can't come home again.

LETTERS FROM HELL

"When attorney Theresa McConville sold her vacant lot in Ventura Country in 1985, a losing bidder was Reynaldo Fong, a local anesthesiologist. Fong, embittered by the loss, devised a novel form of revenge. Over ten years he took out nearly 100,000 magazine subscriptions in her name, asking in each case that the magazine bill McConville. He also sent McConville a refrigerator—C.O.D. McConville spent $50,000 to straighten out the mess."

—*Forbes* **magazine, June 5, 1995**

FROM THE X-(RATED) FILES

"An employee of the St. Louis Blues apparently couldn't resist a parting shot at the team after he was fired.

"On the page listing playoff records in the hockey team's media guide, between the date of the Blues' last overtime game on the road and their last overtime loss at home, the anonymous employee slipped in a crudely worded 'record' for sexual favors.

"The red-faced Blues have recalled the guide and will have to amend it, at a reported cost of $70,000."

—*L. A. Times*, **Oct. 16, 1995**

I'M GAME

"Near Louisville, Kentucky, a rabbit reached out of a hunter's game bag, pulled the trigger of his gun, and shot him in the foot."

—*New Yorker*, **May 1947**

Lake Nicaragua in Nicaragua is the only freshwater lake in the world that has sharks.

TREK WARS

As "Star Trek" creator Gene Roddenberry conceived it, the Starship Enterprise was a metaphor for an ideal world—a multiracial, multinational crew working together to achieve humanity's highest goals. In real life, however, the crew of the Enterprise was bogged down in typical 20th-century politics. Here are four examples.

CAPT. KIRK VS. EVERYBODY

William Shatner (Capt. Kirk) was originally intended to be the only star of "Star Trek." That meant he made a lot more money than everyone else—$5,000 per episode, compared to Leonard Nimoy's $1,250, and $600 to $850 for the other actors. And it meant he got what he wanted, even at other cast members' expense. In virtually every script, for example, he had more lines than any other actor. But that didn't stop him from taking other people's lines if he felt like it. As George Takei (Mr. Sulu) writes in his book *To the Stars*:

> [The script consultant] would occasionally give us an advance peek at an early draft of a script, which might contain a wonderful scene for our respective characters or even a fun line or two of dialogue.... But when the final shooting script was delivered, the eagerly awaited scene or line would now be in someone else's mouth, and invariably, it was Bill's... Even if an idea had originated with one of us, if Bill wanted it, he got it.

CAPT. KIRK VS. MR. SPOCK

Spock was conceived as a minor character, but Leonard Nimoy was so good in the role that the part kept growing. This apparently drove Shatner nuts, as J. Van Hise writes in *The History of Trek*:

> Shatner was so concerned over the situation that he counted his lines in each new script to be certain that he had more than Nimoy. If he didn't, either more were added for him at his insistence, or Nimoy's lines were cut....[One scriptwriter] witnessed the director trying to come up with an alternative way for Nimoy to react to Shatner in a scene, because for Nimoy to utter a line would have given him one line too many as far as Shatner was concerned.

The rivalry started interfering with production schedules. During the first season, for example, *Life* magazine decided to shoot a photo essay on Spock's makeup. They sent a photographer to the set, and everything went smoothly until Shatner arrived. When he saw what was going on, he turned and walked away. Shortly afterward, a production assistant insisted that the photographer leave. Takei writes:

> Leonard, understandably, was livid. He got up and refused to have his makeup completed until the photographer was allowed back. Until then, he announced, he would wait in his dressing room with his makeup only half done. And with that, he exited.

For the next few hours, studio executives shuttled back and forth between Nimoy's and Shatner's dressing rooms trying to resolve the dispute. The photographer was finally allowed to finish the job, and the article appeared in *Life* as planned. By then, however, half a day's shooting had been lost.

LT. UHURA VS. NBC
Nichelle Nichols (Lt. Uhura) was the only main character who wasn't signed to a contract when she was hired. In her autobiography, *Beyond Uhura*, Nichols writes that contract talks broke down when NBC executives found out she was a black woman:

> ["Star Trek" creator Gene Roddenberry] told the network that he wanted to add a little "color" to the bridge. They assumed he was merely redecorating the set....The network men had a fit when they saw that not only was there a woman in the command crew and on the bridge, but a Black one! When they realized that Uhura's involvement would be substantial and her lines went beyond "Yes, Captain!" they furiously issued Gene an ultimatum: Get rid of her!

Roddenberry refused to fire Nichols, but couldn't get the network to hire her as a permanent cast member. So he hired her as an uncontracted "day player" for each episode. Ironically, thanks to the union wage scale, Nichols made more money than she would have under contract. "Not only did Gene get what he wanted," Nichols writes, "he made sure NBC paid—literally and dearly—for it."

An Unlikely Fan
By the end of the first season, Uhura was nearly as popular as Capt. Kirk and Mr. Spock—and got nearly as much fan mail. But

Nichols didn't know it. Studio officials had ordered that she not receive her fan mail. Near the end of the first season, a mailroom employee finally told her of the embargo. "To say I was stunned does not even begin to convey how I felt," she writes in *Beyond Uhura*.

In fact, she was so upset that she decided to quit. The following evening, however, she met Dr. Martin Luther King at an NAACP fundraiser. He turned out to be a fan of the show and urged her to stay on, arguing that "Uhura was the first non-stereotypical black character in television history"…and that *white* Americans, as well as black Americans, needed to see that character. Nichols agreed to stay and fight it out.

MR. SPOCK VS. GENE RODDENBERRY

What about the Great Idealist himself? It turns out that the creator of "Star Trek" could be just as much of a pain to work with, especially when money was involved. "My business dealings with him were always miserable," Nimoy recalled in 1994. "Gene always had an agenda—his own." One example: Early in the show's history, a Connecticut amusement park offered Nimoy $2,000 to make a personal appearance on a Saturday morning. But the only flight available was on Friday evening—which meant Nimoy had to get permission from Roddenberry to leave work a few hours early.

Rather than give Nimoy a direct answer, Roddenberry mentioned he was forming "Lincoln Enterprises," his own talent agency, and he wanted to represent Nimoy when he made public appearances. Nimoy wasn't interested; he already had an agent and didn't want someone else getting a percentage of his salary. But Roddenberry pressed the issue, as Joe Engel writes in *Gene Roddenberry: The Myth and the Man Behind Star Trek*:

> "The difference between your agent and Lincoln Enterprises," Roddenberry said, "is that Lincoln can get you off the lot at five p.m. every Friday."
>
> "Gene," Nimoy said, "I already have the job. I'm asking if you can help me out of here so I can pick up two thousand dollars this weekend."
>
> "The problem with you," Roddenberry said, "is that you have to learn to bow down and say 'Master.' "

When boxer dogs get excited, they stand on their hind legs and jab the air with their front paws.

MILLENNIUM MADNESS

*There are some pretty strange goings-on associated with the millennium.
This page, excerpted from* The Bathroom Reader's Guide
to the Year 2000, *gives you an idea of what we mean.*

WORTH WAITING FOR
The *Warsaw Voice* reports that a group called "Atrovis,"
in the Polish village of Niebo, expects a select group of
people to be evacuated by extraterrestrials in 1999. They believe
144,000 white people and 600,000 from other races will enter eternity. The men will get new 25-year-old bodies, the women will
look like 20-year-olds.

SERMON ON THE MOUNTAIN
In Cuzco, Peru, 50,000 pilgrims a year are climbing Mount Auzangate to worship an image of Christ that is painted on a rock. The
image, according to the *Daily Telegraph*, was discovered in 1780—
the same year the Spanish killed the last great Inca leader, Tupac
Amaru II. Reportedly, the pilgrimage has become popular among
Peruvians because of the widespread belief that Tupac's body will
re-emerge at the site in the year 2000 to liberate his people.

JUST WAIT!
In South Korea, a "doomsday" preacher named Lee Jang-rim was
sent to jail for convincing his followers—including some in the
United States—that the apocalypse would occur at midnight October 28, 1992. Members sold their homes and possessions; a few
even committed suicide. Many followers are still convinced. One
told the *Chicago Tribune* that doomsday has only been postponed.
"1999 is the end of the earth," he says. "That's for sure."

MARY, MARY
The New York Times reports that there are now so many sightings
of the Virgin Mary that a newsletter called "Mary's People" is being
published. People studying the visions speculate that the recent increase is connected to the approach of the year 2000.

THE HONEY BUCKET

You think you got troubles? At least you're not sitting on a honey bucket. This article, by John Foley, was published in Alaska *magazine in April 1994.*

On camping trips when nature beckons, I usually seek out a tree. It goes without saying that in urban areas I find a toilet. But now I live in a place with neither trees nor toilets, and I have, to my everlasting regret, discovered the honey bucket.

Many fortunate folks from Outside are not familiar with honey buckets. When I told my mother in Iowa we had a honey bucket, she said, "Isn't that charming. Are the bees much of a nuisance?" Honey buckets, at least in these parts, do not hold honey. A honey bucket is a foot-high pail lined with a plastic bag. A child-size seat and lid are attached to the rim.

A small percentage of homes in Gambell [Alaska], have running water and thus flush toilets. The rest of the village—located on the northwestern tip of St. Lawrence Island—makes do (so to speak) with honey buckets. I took a teaching job in Gambell in mid-August. Within moments of my arrival I had to give the honey bucket a test run. Situating my 6-foot-3 frame on the low bucket was a challenge at first, but I soon mastered the technique—save for those groggy 3 a.m. visits, when my form suffers and I have a tendency to fall overboard.

My initial impulse was to put the honey bucket in the bathroom, where it belonged, by God, even if I had to brush my teeth while holding my nose. Our neighbors explained that it's best to put the bucket in the Arctic entry, as the cold cuts down the smell.

The cold has also entered my personal habits. For the first time in my adult life I don't bring reading material along when I am anticipating a sit-down visit. Nor do I linger. Some habits die hard, however, and I still find myself reaching over my shoulder to flush the honey bucket. There should be a psychological term for this tendency. Air flush, perhaps.

We adjusted to the bucket

life as well as can be expected, but some newcomers did not. Kris Lucas, another first-year teacher, had a terrible time with her honey bucket at first, primarily because it didn't have a handle.

The locals were greatly amused to see her hauling her bucket to the dump like a load of laundry; she clutched it to her chest and, for obvious reasons, threw her head back.

While Kris was suffering this indignity, her husband, Luke, was back home in Wisconsin tidying up details for his own move to Gambell. Kris decided …it would be wise marital strategy not to mention the honey bucket until he set foot on the island. Needless to say, Luke was surprised by the local plumbing. But he adjusted quickly. He had to, as he was put in charge of the honey bucket detail.

Hauling heavy buckets over soft gravel is a workout…. So we were appreciative when the principal decided to loan us the school four-wheeler once a week for honey bucket runs.

The honey bucket dump is a foul sight—not to mention smell—however you get there. Still, it's more tolerable on a weekly basis. We've designated Thursday as Honey Bucket Day and fallen into a resigned pattern.

This pattern no longer includes our wives. Amy and Kris are independent and capable women but their feminist attitudes are conspicuously absent on Honey Bucket Day, when they assume traditional roles faster than you can say "Barbara Bush." In short, they cook dinner while we haul buckets.

Luke and I have become fast friends—partly because we share this distasteful chore. It's impossible to put on airs or be standoffish when you tiptoe through a honey bucket dump with someone. As far as male-bonding activities, it ranks right up there with watching pro football.

Occasionally we get into heavy discussions during our dump run. Once we debated the etymology of "honey bucket." Luke surmised that the phrase entered the language as an ironic term, like Peacekeeper Missile or rap music. My guess is that it was a shortened form of a longer expression. This first came to mind in the pre-four-wheeler stage, when Amy would say, all too often, "Honey, go dump the bucket!" Hence, honey bucket.

Stretched end-to-end, the blood vessels in your body would go around the equator 2-1/2 times.

PRIMETIME PROVERBS

More TV wisdom from Primetime Proverbs.

ON PRIDE
"I hate to blow my own horn, but 'Beep beep!'"
—**Alex P. Keaton,**
Family Ties

ON GUNS
"The intellect is a much more powerful weapon than the gun, particularly when the gun doesn't work."
—**Dorian,**
Blake's 7

ON LAWYERS
"Lawyers and tarts are the oldest professions in the world. And we always aim to please."
–**Horace Rumpole,**
Rumpole of the Bailey

ON THE BATTLE BETWEEN THE SEXES
"Did you know the male bee is nothing but the slave of the queen? And once the male has, how should I say, serviced the queen, the male dies. All in all, not a bad system."
–**Phyllis Lindstrom,**
The Mary Tyler Moore Show

Jules: "Roseanne, listen to this. 'Utah Housewife Stabs Husband 37 Times.'"
Roseanne: "I admire her restraint."
—*Roseanne*

ON THE MEDIA
"There's a standard formula for success in the entertainment medium—beat it to death if it succeeds."
—**Ernie Kovacs,**
The Ernie Kovacs Show

ON DRINKING
"Never cry over spilt milk. It could've been whiskey."
—**Pappy Maverick,**
Maverick

ON HOME
"A man's home is his coffin."
—**Al Bundy,**
Married...with Children

ON BRAVERY
"Wanna do something that's really courageous? Come on over to my mother-in-law's house and say, 'You're wrong, fatso!'"
–**Buddy Sorrell,**
The Dick Van Dyke Show

ON FAMILY
Maddie Hayes: "I didn't know you had a brother."
David Addison: "I never thought of him as a brother. I thought of him as Mom and Dad's science project."
—*Moonlighting*

Science fact: Goldfish remember better in cold water than in warm water.

MISS AMERICA, PART IV:
There She Is...

When you think about it, the Miss America contest is more a TV show than a pageant. Sure, we get a national figure (or figurine) out of it—but the thing that keeps it going is ratings. So just like any sitcom or talk show, it has to have a theme song. Here's how Miss America got hers.

O**N THE AIR**
After the war, the Miss America Pageant was flying high. It was oh-so-respectable, financially sound, and as popular with women as with men. Its survival was no longer in doubt.

In fact, thanks to strong media coverage, it was regarded as a national institution. Millions of Americans followed the contest in the newspapers, on the radio, and in movie newsreels. But if they wanted to watch the pageant in its entirety, they had to go to Atlantic City and view it in person. There was no other way.

Then in 1953, the fledgling American Broadcasting Company (ABC) offered $5,000 to broadcast the event over its small network of TV stations. Miss America officials seriously considered the offer, but turned it down when ABC refused to black out the broadcast in nearby Philadelphia. (The pageant had just doubled its ticket prices and was afraid too many people would stay home and watch it on TV.)

The next year, ABC upped the ante. It doubled the offer to $10,000, and lined up the Philco Television Company as a sponsor. Philco even offered to introduce a new line of "Miss America" television sets. This time pageant officials accepted. The Miss America Pageant was broadcast live on September 11, 1954; a record breaking 27 million people—39% of the viewing audience—tuned in to watch. All through the '50s, TV ratings were astronomical.

MUSIC MAN
One of the people who got caught up in the excitement was Bernie Wayne, a songwriter. He learned about the first TV broadcast in a newspaper article, and it inspired him to write a song. "Although I

Oldest ex-president: John Adams, America's second president, was 90 years old when he died.

had never seen a pageant before," he explained years later, "somehow the words and melody for the song suddenly came into mind….I just sat down in my little office, and started writing. I wrote the whole song in the space of an hour…I just tried to put myself in the place of the lucky girl—walking down the runway— an ideal, walking on air." He called his song "There She Is."

Wayne performed the song for the pageant's producer and musical director. "They loved it," he says, and told him they would use it in the pageant. Wayne phoned his mother and told her to watch for the song during the broadcast.

Then the producer called him over during final rehearsals and said they'd changed their minds—they weren't going to use the song. The reason: Bob Russell, host of the broadcast, wanted some songs *he'd* written, "This Is Miss America" and "The Spirit of Miss America," included—and he got his way. "I was brokenhearted," Wayne recalled years later….The next night I was too disappointed to go see the show. I watched it on TV from some broken-down bar."

LUCKY BREAK

"There She Is" might never have made it into the pageant, if Wayne hadn't been invited to a Park Avenue party a few months later. While performing a piano medley of his songs, he sang "There She Is." "As I sang, the place quieted down like magic. When I finished, there was such a hush I thought I'd laid an egg." Someone in the audience asked him, "Why haven't I heard this song before!"

He was Pierson Mapes, the advertising executive in charge of both the Philco account and the upcoming 1955 pageant. Mapes pressured Miss America officials to make the song a centerpiece of the broadcast—a task made all the easier by the fact that host Bob Russell did not return in 1955. Crooner Bert Parks took his place, and both Parks and "There She Is" became hits.

Still interested? We continue the story on page 257.

FAMILIAR PHRASES

More origins of everyday phrases.

IN ONE FELL SWOOP
Meaning: All at once.

Origin: Falling has nothing to do with it. *Fell* comes from the Middle English word *fel*, meaning "cruel, deadly, or ruthless" and is related to the word *felon*. The expression "one fell swoop" first appeared in *Macbeth* (Act 4, Scene iii), when Shakespeare compares the sudden death of a character to an eagle *swooping* down on some chickens and carrying them off.

HAVE YOUR WORK CUT OUT FOR YOU
Meaning: Have a difficult task ahead.

Origin: According to Christine Ammer in *Have a Nice Day—No Problem!*, the term refers to "a pattern cut from a cloth that must be then made into a garment." When the easier task of cutting out the cloth is finished, the more difficult job of sewing the garment is still left.

CALLED ON THE CARPET
Meaning: Admonished or reprimanded by a superior.

Origin: In the 19th century, carpets were prohibitively expensive, so usually, only the boss's office was carpeted. When employees were "called on the carpet," it meant the boss wanted to see them —which frequently meant they were in trouble.

SIGHT FOR SORE EYES
Meaning: Welcome sight.

Origin: According to ancient superstition, unpleasant sights could make eyes sore...and pleasant sights made sore eyes feel better.

TEN-GALLON HAT
Meaning: Big cowboy hat.

Origin: Measurements have nothing to do with it. The name comes from *sombrero galon*, which means "braided hat" in Spanish.

MORE OLYMPIC CHEATERS

Here are four Olympians who might have cheated...and then again, maybe they didn't. We'll never know.

HAMMOU BOUTAYEB AND KHALID SKAH, members of the Moroccan track team
Year: 1992

Place: Barcelona, Spain

What happened: Boutayeb fell so far behind in the 10,000-meter event that the two front-runners, Khalid Skah and Kenya's Richard Chelimo, were about to lap him. Rather than let them pass, Boutayeb blocked Chelimo for an entire lap before officials finally dragged him from the track and disqualified him. But by then it was too late—he'd allowed his teammate, Khalid Skah, to sprint past Chelimo into first place and win the race.

Reaction: Skah's excitement was short-lived. Spectators booed loudly and pelted him with garbage as he made his victory lap; 30 minutes later, Olympic officials disqualified him and took away his gold medal, figuring that he and Boutayeb had been in cahoots. Skah appealed the decision...and won: the next day the appeals committee took the gold medal back from Chelimo and returned it to Skah.

STELLA WALSH, Polish 100-meter runner
Years: 1932 and 1936

Places: Los Angeles and Berlin

What happened: Walsh won the gold medal in the 100-meter race in Los Angeles and a silver medal in Berlin. But she aroused suspicions. "She ran like a man," says Roxanne Andersen, a women's track coach in the 1930s, who also noted that at the 1936 Olympics, Walsh appeared to have a "five o'clock shadow."

Walsh's victories went unchallenged until 1980, when she was gunned down by a man robbing a Cleveland, Ohio, discount store. An autopsy revealed that she had a genetic condition known as *mosaicism*, which gave her "traces of male *and* female genitalia," as well as male and female chromosomes. Walsh had kept her condition secret her entire life and would probably have taken it to the grave had she not been murdered. If people had known about her condition in the 1930s, she would almost certainly have been barred from competing as a woman. "Maybe that's why she refused to room with anybody else," Andersen remarked to reporters.

Reaction: In 1991, the U.S. Women's Track and Field Committee decided not to strip Walsh of her titles, concluding that her gender identity was more complex than it seemed, and that "allegations Walsh either masqueraded as a woman or was definately a man were unfair." (Gender testing of female athletes has been standard since 1966.)

BORIS ONISCHENKO, member of the USSR pentathlon team
Year: 1976
Place: Montreal
What happened: The defending silver medalist was in the middle of the fencing competition, when the British team noticed that he scored points even when his sword didn't touch his opponent's body. Olympic officials examined his sword...and discovered it had been rigged with a "hidden push-button circuit-breaker" that enabled him to score a hit every time he pushed the button.

Reaction: Soviet officials initially protested, but later "admitted" Onischenko's guilt and apologized. "He lost many of his privileges and his career was left in ruins," says Carl Schwende, fencing director for the Montreal Games. "I heard he was working as the manager of an aquatic center in Kiev...Then I learned he was found dead at the pool. Drowning, suicide, accident? My Soviet colleagues won't talk about it."

Onischenko denied any knowledge of the rigging for the rest of his life, and no one knows if he really *was* responsible. The sword may not even have been his: "The Russians had about 20 identical-looking weapons lined up for their use," Schwende says. "A fencer is handed his mask and weapons by a coach only when his name is called....It's possible someone else rigged the weapon, but we had no proof. If we had, we would have disqualified the entire Soviet team." One theory: Onischenko was sacrificed by the Soviets to save the rest of the team. But no one will ever know.

MORE LUCKY FINDS

Here are more examples of valuable things that people have stumbled on—including one that Uncle John found...and lost.

BURIED IN THE LIBRARY

The Find: *The Inheritance*, Louisa May Alcott's first novel

Where It Was Found: On a shelf in a Harvard University library.

The Story: The manuscript, hand-written by Alcott, represents one of the grossest oversights in Western literature: it was listed in the Harvard card catalog under "*The Inheritance,* a manuscript; Boston, 1849; 166 pages, unpublished, her first novel."

Even so, probably fewer than a dozen people even knew it existed, and it didn't occur to any of them to publish it. At least five people had checked it out since the library acquired it, and a microfilm copy was made for a scholar. But that was it—the manuscript sat virtually ignored for nearly 150 years, until Joel Myerson and Daniel Shealy, two professors researching a book on Alcott, came across it in the late 1980s. They made a Xerox copy of it, took it home, and transcribed it. In 1996, they submitted it to an agent... who began shopping it to publishers and movie studios. Estimated worth: $1 million.

MESSAGE IN A BOTTLE

The Find: The will of Daisy Singer Alexander, of the Singer sewing machine family

Where It Was Found: In a bottle on a beach near San Francisco.

The Story: In 1937, the eccentric Alexander, who lived in England, made out her will, stuffed it into a bottle, and tossed it into the Thames River in London. The will read:

> To avoid any confusion, I leave my entire estate to the lucky person who finds this bottle, and to my attorney, Barry Cohen, share and share alike—Daisy Alexander, June 20, 1937.

Almost *12 years* later, in March 1949, a unemployed man named Jack Wrum (or Wurm, depending on which version you read) was wandering along a San Francisco beach when he found the bottle. To his credit, he not only opened it and read its contents, he also took it seriously enough to find out if it was real. It was—Wrum inherited $6 million up front, and $80,000 a year in income from Alexander's Singer stock.

UNCLE JOHN'S CONFESSION

The Find: A first edition of Dr. Seuss's first book, *To Think That I Saw It on Mulberry Street*…inscribed to the mother of the boy who inspired Seuss to write it

Where It Was Found: In a farmhouse in Worcester, Vermont.

The Story: In the 1970s, Uncle John rented a woodworking shop from a woman named Phyllis Keyser. It was located next to her house, and occasionally John would wander in to chat. One day, he picked up a copy of *To Think That I Saw It on Mulberry Street* from her coffee table and noticed an inscription that read something like: "*To _____, the real Marco's mother. Thanks for the inspiration. From your neighbor, Ted Geisel.*" Uncle John knew that Dr. Seuss's real name was Theodore Geisel and that the boy in the story was named Marco. He asked Phyllis for an explanation.

"Oh," she replied, "that's my sister. She lived next to Ted Geisel in Boston. Her son, Marco, used to make up these wild stories every day when he came home from school, and that gave Geisel the idea for the first book he ever published."

Apparently, she didn't have any idea of the book's value. Uncle John offered to check it out, but the used bookstores he talked to wouldn't touch it. "You've got to bring it to a rare book dealer," they said. Unfortunately, Uncle John dropped the ball. Keyser died a few years later, and her possessions were disposed of.

First editions of Dr. Seuss's books (as well as Dr. Seuss memorabilia) have become extremely collectible since then. And until now, most experts weren't aware that this "first of the first" edition ever existed.

So, if someone out there in Bathroom Readerland has picked it up at a garage sale, you may have something worth tens of thousands of dollars!

A "beer can fancier" is called a *canologist*.

THE EVOLUTION OF THANKSGIVING

In "Thanksgiving Myths" (see page 10), you read about how the pilgrims ate deer, not turkey, at the first Thanksgiving celebration. So how did turkey become the food of choice? Here's more info on how Thanksgiving, as we know it, came to be.

GOING NATIONAL

As late as the 1860s, Thanksgiving was exclusively a Yankee holiday. Every Northern state celebrated it (not all on the same day), but no Southern states did. There had been several efforts to make it a national holiday—the Continental Congress tried in 1777, and George Washington proclaimed a National Day of Thanksgiving in 1789. But it never caught on, thanks to people like Thomas Jefferson, who denounced the idea as a "monarchical practice" unfit for the new republic.

Early presidents occasionally proclaimed their own days of thanksgiving to mark victories on the battlefield or other good fortune. But such occasions were one-time affairs, not annual events.

ABE STEPS IN

Then, in 1863, President Abraham Lincoln proclaimed *two* national days of Thanksgiving: one on August 6, to honor Union victories at Gettysburg and Vicksburg, and one on November 26, the last Thursday of the month, to celebrate a year "filled with the blessings of fruitful fields and healthful skies."

Lincoln didn't intend to make Thanksgiving an annual event, but when General Sherman captured Atlanta in September 1864, the president declared the last Thursday in November a day of thanksgiving for the second year in a row. And after Lincoln was assassinated, succeeding presidents turned it into a tradition in his honor. As the wounds of the Civil War healed, the popularity of the holiday grew. By the 1890s, the last Thursday in November was celebrated as Thanksgiving by nearly every state in the Union.

What counterculture? About 60 million Baby Boomers commute to work every day.

THE BUSINESS OF THANKSGIVING

The Pilgrims aren't responsible for making turkey the center of the Thanksgiving feast (see page 11), so who is? Business historian Thomas DiBacco believes that poultry companies deserve the credit. "There is no rhyme or reason for us to have turkey on Thanksgiving, except that business promoted it," he says, adding that poultry producers in New Jersey, Pennsylvania, and Maryland began promoting turkey as Thanksgiving food after the Civil War. Why? Because at 10¢ a pound, it was more profitable than any other bird.

Illustrators followed their lead and painted Pilgrim dinners with roast turkey on the table. Soon a brand-new "tradition" was born.

The next group of businesses to cash in on Thanksgiving were turn-of-the-century retailers, who used the holiday to jump-start Christmas sales. Newspaper ads began counting down the number of shopping days until Christmas, and in 1921, Gimbel's department store in Philadelphia came up with a retailer's tour-de-force: they held the first Thanksgiving Day parade, designed to kick off the shopping season. By 1930, department stores all over the country sponsored parades to get shoppers into their stores.

FRANKSGIVING

By the late 1930s, Thanksgiving was as much the start of the Christmas shopping season as it was a holiday in its own right. That's why retailers—still trying to dig their way out of the Great Depression—were worried in 1939. Thanksgiving was traditionally the last Thursday of the month, and since there were *five* Thursdays in that November instead of the usual four, Thanksgiving fell on the very last day of the month. That meant only 20 shopping days until Christmas. In the spring of 1939, the National Retail Dry Goods Association lobbied President Franklin Roosevelt to move Thanksgiving back one Thursday to November 23, arguing that it would boost retail sales by as much as 10%. Roosevelt agreed, and announced the change during the summer.

The decision made headlines around the country. It became a political issue as traditionalists (unaware of the day's true roots) and Republicans both condemned it. "What in the name of common sense has Christmas buying to do with it?" the Rev. Norman Vincent Peale bellowed from his pulpit. "It is questionable thinking and contrary to the meaning of Thanksgiving for the president of this great nation to tinker with a sacred religious day on the specious excuse that it will help Christmas sales. The next thing we may expect Christmas to be shifted to May 1 to help the New York World's Fair of 1940."

Like the proclamations that had proceeded it, Roosevelt's Thanksgiving proclamation was only binding with federal employees and in the District of Columbia—the governors of individual states had to ratify the decision for it to apply to their own states. Usually this was only a technicality...but Republican governors seized on the issue as a means of discrediting Roosevelt. As Diana Carter Applebaum writes in *Thanksgiving: An American Holiday, an American History*:

> Politician watchers...began to call November 23 the Democratic Thanksgiving and November 30 the Republican Thanksgiving Day....Colorado law required that the state observe both holidays, but Republican Governor Ralph Carr vowed to eat no turkey on the 23rd. Republican Senator Styles Bridges of New Hampshire said that he wished that while he was at it, "Mr. Roosevelt would abolish winter;" and Republican Governor Nels Hanson Smith of Wyoming commended Roosevelt for finally instituting a change "which is not imposing any additional tax on the taxpayers."

FINAL SETTLEMENT

In the end, 23 states celebrated Thanksgiving on November 23 and another 23 celebrated it on November 30, with Texas and Colorado celebrating it on both days and the city of Minneapolis celebrating it from 12:01 a.m. November 23 to 11:59 p.m. November 30. The controversy might have continued to this day if retail sales had gone up as predicted. But they didn't—some retailers even suspected that the confusion caused sales to *drop*. So in May 1941, President Roosevelt announced that, beginning in 1942, Thanksgiving would again be held on the last Thursday in November.

Several congressmen, who feared that future presidents might pull similar stunts, introduced legislation to make the change permanent. On November 26, 1941, Roosevelt signed a compromise bill: Thanksgiving would always fall on the fourth Thursday in November, whether it was the last Thursday of the month or not. (Five years out of seven, it *is* the last Thursday of the month). Thanksgiving has been celebrated on that day ever since.

The Eiffel Tower (984 ft.) is more than three times taller than the Statue of Liberty (305 ft.)

DOLL DISASTERS

*Some dolls, like Barbie and Cabbage Patch Kids, are enormous successes.
Others seemed like good (even brilliant) ideas at the time, but they fell
on their little plastic butts. Here are some "sure things" that bombed.*

T HE "MOST WONDERFUL STORY" DOLL

Background: In 1957, Ben Michtom, president of the Ideal
Toy Company, had a brainstorm: why not sell a Jesus doll?
The majority of kids in America were Christian, so he figured parents would jump at the opportunity to make playtime a religious
experience. Other Ideal executives were horrified, but Michtom
was convinced it was a great idea. To prove it, he took his case to a
higher authority; while on vacation in Italy, he got an audience
with the Pope and pitched the idea to him. The Pope gave his
blessing, as did every other Christian leader Michtom consulted.

What Happened: Unfortunately for Ideal, Michtom didn't consult
any parents, who probably would have told him the idea was a loser...which it turned out to be. As Sydney Stern describes the doll
in *Toyland: The High-Stakes Game of the Toy Industry:*

> No one bought them because parents were horrified at the idea of
> undressing the Jesus doll, dragging it around, sticking it in the bath-
> tub. Nothing sold. Ordinarily, there is a no-return policy on prod-
> ucts already shipped. But in this case it was such a horrible mistake
> that Ideal took them back....It appears that what Ideal did with
> them was give each of its employees a doll and then ground up the
> rest and put them in landfills.

Jesus dolls—packaged in a box that looked like the Bible—were
probably the biggest doll flop in American toy history.

THE JOEY STIVIC DOLL

Background: In 1976, Ideal came out with another product that
it thought was a sure thing: the "drink-and-wet" baby Joey Stivic
doll, based on Archie Bunker's grandson in TV's "All in the Family." The show was the most popular sitcom of the decade, and Ideal
officials figured the hype surrounding Joey's birth (on an episode of

the show) would be as huge as when Lucille Ball had her TV baby on "I Love Lucy" in the 1950s.

What Happened: "All in the Family" was daringly realistic—the first of its kind on TV, and Ideal execs decided to be just as realistic with the Joey doll. They gave him something that few little boy dolls had in the 70s: a penis. Big mistake. America was not ready for reality-based "anatomically correct" male dolls.

CHAIRMAN MAO DOLL

Background: In 1968, a U.S. company tried to import Chairman Mao dolls into the country. The dolls—manufactured in Ireland, not China—were really a joke: they showed Mao holding a copy of his little red book in front...and a bomb behind his back. Furthermore, *Newsweek* magazine reported, "each doll comes with twelve voodoo pins, just in case anyone misses the point."

What Happened: They never got off the boat. Figuring the dolls were part of a subversive plot, the Longshoreman's Union refused to unload the shipping crates. "That's definitely Communistic!" a union member exclaimed when a U.S. Customs official opened the crate, "We'd rather lose work than handle this cargo."

"I don't believe these dolls come from Ireland," one union official told reporters. "This stuff is being pushed through by some subversives—but we're on the lookout."

THE "HAPPY TO BE ME" DOLL

Background: If Barbie were life-sized, her measurements would be 38-18-28—an outrageously impossible role model for girls. That's what prompted Cathy Meredig, a 38-year-old software designer, to develop her own doll, "Happy to Be Me," in 1989. It has measurements of 36-27-38, with "rounded tummies and hips, normal sized waists, legs, chest, neck and feet." Traditional toy manufacturers balked at selling the doll, so Meredig founded High Self-Esteem Toys and began marketing it herself.

What Happened: Happy to Be Me was the toy equivalent of boiled carrots. Grown-ups loved them, but kids overwhelmingly preferred Barbie...no matter how much their parents tried to get them to switch. Meredig's company was still in business as late as 1994, but by then the dolls were only available by mail.

ZAPPED!

Irreverent comments from the late, great Frank Zappa.

"It would be easier to pay off our national debt overnight than to neutralize the long range effects of our national stupidity."

"Remember, there's a big difference between kneeling down and bending over."

"Life is like high school with money."

"It is always advisable to become a loser if you can't become a winner."

"There will never be a nuclear war—there is too much real estate involved."

"The whole universe is a large joke. Everything in the universe are just subdivisions of this joke. So why take anything too seriously?"

"Anything played wrong twice in a row is the beginning of an arrangement."

"Seeing a psychotherapist is not a crazy idea–it's just wanting a second opinion of one's life."

"Bad facts make bad laws."

"Politics is the entertainment branch of industry."

"Thanks to our schools and political leadership, the U.S. has an international reputation as the home of 250 million people dumb enough to buy 'The Wacky Wall Walker.' "

"Stupidity has a certain charm. Ignorance does not."

"Without music to decorate it, time is just a bunch of boring production deadlines or dates by which bills must be paid."

"The only thing that seems to band all nations together is that their governments are universally bad."

[*When asked by Tipper Gore whether he feels music incites people toward deviant behavior.*] "I wrote a song about dental floss, but did anyone's teeth get cleaner?"

"People who think of music videos as an art form are probably the same people who think Cabbage Patch Dolls are a revolutionary form of soft sculpture."

THE 10 WORST SNAKES TO BE BITTEN BY

In his book, Dangerous to Man, *Roger Caras included a list of the 10 snakes he'd least like to be "trapped in a phone booth with." Here's the list, with some extra info gathered by our own herpetologists.*

1. KING COBRA

The largest poisonous snake in the world. According to many experts, it's also the most dangerous. Its venom is so powerful, it can kill an elephant…and in some known instances, it actually has. Adults measure 14 feet (longest on record is 18 feet). When angered, its hoodspring expands and it "stands" with its head 5-6 feet in the air. It's found in Southeast Asia, southern China, and India.

2. TAIPAN

A 10-footer from Australia. There's enough venom in one Taipan bite to kill 100,000 mice. Also known as the "Fierce Snake," it is normally shy and prefers to escape rather than attack. Fortunately, it lives in sparsely populated areas. A person bitten by a Taipan will die in a matter of minutes.

3. MAMBA

A black or green snake from Africa. The 10- to 14-foot black mamba, which lives among rocks and in tall grass, is the largest and most feared snake in Africa. It is the world's fastest snake (burst of speed up to 15 mph) and may be the only poisonous snake known to stalk humans. Two drops of black mamba venom can kill a person in 10 minutes. The green mamba is about half as long and spends most of its life in trees. But it's just about as deadly.

4. BUSHMASTER

The world's largest viper. Found mostly in Central America, where it occupies the abandoned burrows of other animals. Particularly dangerous because, when confronted, it attacks people rather than fleeing from them, as most snakes do. Has one-inch fangs and carries enough poison to kill several people.

5. WESTERN DIAMONDBACK RATTLER

The name comes from the diamond- or hex-shaped blotches on its skin. Measures anywhere from 3 to 8 feet. Because it's aggressive and abundant, it's the cause of more serious bites and deaths than any other snake in North America. Its poison can kill a mouse in a few seconds, and a person within an hour.

6. FER-DE-LANCE

Also known as the Terciopelo (Spanish for "velvet"), it is relatively small (about 4 feet), but especially dangerous to humans because it's nervous and quick to bite. Its venom spreads through the body and causes internal bleeding. Found in tropical areas in the Americas, such as Martinique.

7. TROPICAL RATTLESNAKE

Has a venom 10 times more potent than its cousin, the Western Rattler. This variety is found predominantly in Central and South America.

8. TIGER SNAKE

Named for the yellow stripes covering its body. Usually feeds on mice, frogs, and rats. Occasionally, this 6-footer also dines on Australians. A single dose of venom induces pain, vomiting, and circulatory collapse. Mortality rate from a bite is 40%. Considered the most dangerous reptile Down Under.

9. COMMON COBRA

Also known as the Indian Cobra. It's the kind of snake tamed by Indian snake charmers and is normally a shy hunter that eats frogs and rats. However, because it lives in populated areas, it is actually more dangerous than the King Cobra. Just one bite has enough venom to kill 30 people. It grows to 4 to 5 feet long.

10. JARRACUSSU

An aquatic snake from South America with a deadly bite. Usually, a bite from one of these water-dwellers isn't necessarily fatal. But it *will* cause blindness and tissue damage.

Australia is the only continent where poisonous snakes outnumber nonpoisonous kinds.

THE HISTORY OF THE INCOME TAX

"In this world," Benjamin Franklin wrote in 1789, "nothing can be said to be certain, except death and taxes." We at the BRI have written about death once in a while, but never about taxes. We figure it's time to make amends.

A braham Lincoln isn't remembered as the "Father of the Income Tax"...but he could be. In 1862, in order to raise money to pay for the Civil War, he signed the country's first income tax into law.

However, under this law, only people with an income over $800 a year had to pay any tax. And only 1% of the American people made more than $800 a year in 1862...so the government wound up having to look elsewhere for a source of money to finance the war (they borrowed it).

TAX CONTROVERSY

From the start, the income tax was very controversial. No one was even sure if it was legal. The Constitution had authorized the federal government to collect taxes "to pay the debts and provide for the common welfare of the United States"—but it didn't explicitly state that the government had the right to levy taxes on *income*. And as this was hotly debated, public opposition grew. The first income tax was repealed in 1872.

But it wasn't dead. By the 1890s, an overwhelming majority of Americans supported re-establishing an income tax—as long as it applied only to the super-rich. Farm, labor, and small-business interests promoted it as a means of taking money away from millionaires and robber barons and redistributing it for the common good.

In 1894, they succeeded in passing a 2% tax on all personal and corporate net income over $4,000. Few Americans were in that income bracket...but those who were had the incentive and resources to oppose the tax. They battled it all the way to the Supreme Court, and in 1895 the Court declared that an income tax was unconstitutional.

Weird coincidence: Ex-presidents Thomas Jefferson and John Adams both died on July 4, 1826.

THEODORE ROOSEVELT

Opinion was divided along party lines—Democrats and Populists supported the income tax; Republicans opposed it. But in 1908, outgoing Republican president Theodore Roosevelt broke with his party and called for both an income tax *and* an inheritance tax. He wasn't able to enact either before his term ran out, but the momentum had shifted.

In the election of 1908, America sent a pro-tax Congress and an anti-tax president—Republican William Howard Taft—to Washington. Taft tried to derail the issue by proposing a Constitutional amendment permitting the personal income tax. He figured the hurdles for such an amendment were so great that the amendment would fail and the income tax issue would go away.

But he was wrong. By February 1913, less than four years after it was introduced, 36 states had ratified the 16th Amendment to the Constitution. For the first time in U.S. history, income taxes were indisputably constitutional. On October 3, 1913, President Woodrow Wilson signed the first modern income tax into law.

POPULAR TAX?

The 1913 tax was simple—the entire tax code was only 16 pages long (compared to 9,100 pages today). The rate was 1% on income over $3,000 for a single person and $4,000 for a married person, with "super taxes" as high as 6% applied to income over $500,000. In general, the tax was popular with just about everyone…because it applied to almost no one.

The few Americans who were required to pay income taxes in 1913 paid an average of $97.88 apiece.

WEAPON OF WAR

But America's entry into World War I in 1917 changed everything. The federal budget shot up from $1 billion in 1916 to $19 billion in 1919. Faced with enormous, unprecedented expenses, the Wilson administration was forced to raise the tax rate…and to broaden the tax base to include millions of Americans who had never before paid income taxes.

To insure that the new taxes were paid promptly and in full, Wilson expanded the IRS. The agency's total number of employees

A year on the planet Jupiter is 12 times longer than a year on Earth.

mushroomed from 4,000 workers in 1913 to 21,300 in 1920.

Compared to earlier income taxes, Wilson's were pretty severe. The top tax rate, applied to income over $1 million, was 77%. These taxes revolutionized the finances of the federal government; its total tax revenue went from $344 million to *$5.4 billion*...and the percentage of government revenues collected from income taxes went from 10% to 73%.

In the 1920s, income taxes were cut five different times, but they would never again be as low as they were before the war.

WORLD WAR II

The 1930s, too, were a period of relatively low taxes. The Great Depression had wiped out the earnings of most Americans. In 1939, for example, the average blue-collar employee paid no taxes, the average doctor or lawyer paid about $25 a year, and a successful business person earning $16,000 paid about $1,000. But taxes changed once more when America began gearing up for World War II.

Like the previous "Great War," World War II was a budget buster. Government expenses rose from $9.6 billion in 1940 to $95 billion in 1945—prompting the government to raise the tax rate again (the highest bracket rose to 94%).

The tax base broadened, too. In 1939, before the war, there were 6.5 million Americans on the tax rolls; they paid about $1 billion a year. By the end of the war in 1945, 48 million Americans paid $19 billion annually. To handle this, the IRS nearly doubled in size, going from 27,000 employees in 1941 to 50,000 in 1945.

For the first time, even people with ordinary incomes had to pay taxes. As the *Chicago Times* put it, World War II transformed America's income tax "from a *class* tax to a *mass* tax."

WITHHOLDING BEGINS

Another development that came about as a result of World War II was income tax withholding, which enabled the government to collect estimated taxes every pay period, not just once a year. The federal government's cash needs were so great during the war that it couldn't wait until the end of the year, and it began withholding estimated taxes from every paycheck. Similar "pay-as-you-go" plans had been used during the Civil War and World War I, but they were abandoned. This time the change was permanent.

There was a second reason for withholding: Taxes were collected from so many new taxpayers that the IRS could no longer handle the flood of tax payments that came in on tax day. It had no choice but to spread the payments out over the entire year.

INCOME TAXES TODAY

By the end of World War II the pattern for taxation had been set: wars and other crises pushed taxes up, peace and prosperity sent them back down, although rarely to where they had been before. Today's taxes seem higher than ever, but believe it or not, when you correct for inflation they're about the same as they were in the 1960s.

On the other hand; the IRS's job *is* bigger than ever—it is now the world's largest law-enforcement agency, with more than 115,000 employees. In fiscal year 1993 it processed more than 207 million tax returns, collecting more than $586 billion in personal income taxes and $1.2 trillion in other taxes. It also paid out more than $84 billion in personal refunds, and cost taxpayers more than $7.1 billion to operate. That comes to about 60¢ for every $100 collected.

☛   ☛   ☛   ☛

TAX QUOTES

"A hand from Washington will be stretched out and placed upon every man's business; the eye of the federal inspector will be in every man's counting house. . . . The law will of necessity have inquisitorial features, it will provide penalties, it will create complicated machinery. Under it men will be haled into courts distant from their homes. Heavy fines imposed by distant and unfamiliar tribunals will constantly menace the tax payer. An army of federal inspectors, spies, and detectives will descend upon the state."

—**Virginian House Speaker Richard E. Byrd,
predicting in 1910 what would happen if
a federal income tax became law**

The average human has 50 trillion cells in their body; the average elephant, 6.5 quadrillion.

"Those citizens required to do so can well afford to devote a brief time during some one day in each year to the making out of a personal return...willingly and cheerfully."

> —The House Ways and Means Committee,
> recommending passage of the landmark
> 1913 income-tax law

"The hardest thing in the world to understand is income taxes."
> —Albert Einstein, 1952

☆   ☆   ☆   ☆

BY THE YEAR 2000...

For decades, "experts" have been making predictions about what the year 2000 will be like. Here are a few, from The Bathroom Reader's Guide to the Year 2000.

"A trip down an air street to see a neighbor may be on top of an individual flying platform; a trip to Europe by rocket may take only half an hour."
> —*The New York Times,* 1967

"Housewives [will] wash dirty dishes—right down the drain! Cheap plastic would melt in hot water." And homes will be waterproof, so "the housewife of 2000 can do her cleaning with a hose."
> —*Popular Mechanics,* 1950

"We will press a button to formulate our clothing. We will have alternatives: what color, should it give off steam, do we want it to light up, do we want it to sparkle or do we prefer a matte finish, do we want it to glow in the dark, do we want an invisible shield?"
> —Betsy Johnson, *fashion designer*

"Men of the year 2000 could enjoy exotic extras like orgasmic earlobes, replaceable sex organs, electronic aphrodisiacs, ultrasensory intercourse, and a range of ecstasy options that would make current notions of kinkiness look sedate by comparison."
> —Howard Rheingold, *Excursions to the Far Side of the Mind: A Book of Memes* (1988)

TAKE A DRINK

The background info on three of America's favorite drinks.

MOUNTAIN DEW. Invented in the 1940s by Ally Hartman of Knoxville, it was intended as a chaser for Tennessee whiskey. The original version looked and tasted like 7-Up, but after Hartman sold the formula in 1954, a succession of new owners tinkered with it. According to one account, credit for the final version goes to William H. Jones, who bought the formula in 1961 and sold it to Pepsi three years later. "He fixed it so it had just a little more tang to it, mainly by adding citrus flavoring and caffeine," a business associate recalls. "He'd take little cups marked A, B, C and D around to high schools and factories and ask people which mixture tasted best. That's how he developed his formula."

V-8 JUICE. In 1933, W. G. Peacock founded the New England Products Company and began manufacturing spinach juice, lettuce juice, and other vegetable juices. Even though the country was in the midst of a health craze, few people wanted to drink Peacock's concoctions. So he began mixing the drinks together, hoping to find something more marketable. It took about a year, but he finally came up with a drink he called Vege-min—a combination of tomato, celery, carrot, spinach, lettuce, watercress, beet, and parsley juices. The label had a huge V for Vege-min and a large 8 listing the different juices. One day, as he gave a free sample to a grocer in Evanston, Illinois, a clerk suggested he just call the product V-8.

A&W ROOT BEER. Roy Allen made a living buying and selling hotels...until he met an old soda fountain operator who gave him a formula for root beer. "You can make a fortune with a five-cent root beer," the guy told him. It was during Prohibition when beer was illegal, so Allen decided there was a market for a root beer stand that looked like a Wild West "saloon"—including a bar and sawdust on the floor. The first stand, opened in Lodi, California, in 1919, did so well that Allen opened a second one in nearby Stockton and made one of his employees, Frank Wright, a partner. In 1922, they named the company A&W, after their own initials.

MOVIE RATINGS

This page is rated PG for reading by general audiences. Parental Guidence is advised.

NEW KID IN TOWN

In 1966, Jack Valenti quit his job as a senior White House aide to become president of the Motion Picture Association of America. Three weeks into his new job, he attended a meeting with studio head Jack Warner concerning some foul language in Warner Bros. upcoming film, *Who's Afraid of Virginia Woolf.*

At issue were the expressions "screw you" and "hump the hostess," which had never been heard in films before. Valenti—whose job was to protect Hollywood's image—wanted the words taken out of *Virginia Woolf*; Warner—whose job was to make money—wanted to leave them in. After three hours of arguing, Warner agreed to substitute "goddam you" for "screw you," but insisted on keeping "hump the hostess." He also agreed to include the words "Suggested for Mature Audiences" in ads promoting the film.

"As I listened to Jack Warner and his associates debate whether they should cut a 'screw' and leave in a 'hump the hostess' or vice versa," Valenti recalled years later, "it dawned on me that ...the old Production Code wasn't adequate to deal with these changes anymore."

SPEAKING IN CODE

Valenti was referring to the Motion Picture Production Code, established by Hollywood executives in 1930 to keep the government from getting involved in movie censorship. The Hollywood Code served as the official list of filmmaking dos and don'ts—complete with taboo subjects like extramarital sex—for nearly 40 years. At first, if you followed The Code, your film made it into theaters. If you didn't, your film was shut out and nobody saw it. It was that simple.

But while the Production Code remained static over the next 35 years, while world changed dramatically. In fact, it became such a ridiculous standard by which to judge films that even the censors began to ignore it. By the early 1960s, movies like the double-

---

Actor Sean Connery was once selected Scotland's "Mr. Universe."

entendre-laden James Bond films sailed through the censorship process virtually untouched, when in earlier years they would have been banned.

As the film industry's censorship powers waned, increasingly controversial films made it into the theaters. The result was the movie industry's worst nightmare—local censorship groups began to spring up all over the country. The industry challenged these groups...and lost. In April 1968, the U.S. Supreme Court handed down two rulings guaranteeing the legality of state and local censorship efforts.

LETTERS OF APPROVAL

As Valenti saw it, Hollywood had to act. If local groups began setting different standards all over the country, it would be impossible to make and market films to national audiences. Movies that were acceptable in one community would be illegal to show in others. The film industry stood to lose millions.

"It didn't take long," he recalled in 1978, "to figure out that the movies would be inundated by classification systems....We could see 200 to 300 regulating bodies across the country, each with its own ideas of what was obscene and what wasn't....So we started discussing a self-regulatory system in May 1968, and had it put together by the fall."

THE ORIGINAL CODE

After more than 100 hastily called meetings, the MPAA announced its ratings system on November 1, 1968. It included four categories:

G: *General* audiences, all ages admitted

M: *Mature* audiences, parental guidance suggested, but all ages admitted

R: Restricted, children under 16 not admitted without an accompanying parent or adult (the age was later lifted to 17)

X: No one under 17 admitted

PARENTAL GUIDANCE

Now that there was a ratings system, who would rate the films? Valenti and other Hollywood executives figured that since the ratings

---

The Statue of Liberty's index finger is eight feet long.

were designed primarily with parents in mind, parents should be the ones to rate the films. The MPAA set up a board of 13 parents to watch and issue ratings on an estimated 1,200 hours' worth of films per year. This board is still in effect today: People who serve on it are paid for their time, and for some of them, it has become a full-time career. After the board rates a film, the producer can withdraw it from release for 90 days and then re-submit it for rating, with or without re-editing.

CHANGES

• Not all the original ratings survived. When the MPAA discovered that parents mistakenly thought M was stricter than R, they changed it to GP (*General audiences, Parental guidance suggested*) …then to PG (*Parental Guidance*). When parents expressed concerns that PG had become too broad a category, they split it into PG and the stricter PG-13 (*Not recommended for children under 13*).

• The X rating posed another problem. The MPAA intended that it be used for "serious" films with adult themes, such as *Midnight Cowboy, A Clockwork Orange,* and *Medium Cool.* But when they trademarked all of the other motion picture codes in 1968, the Association either declined or forgot to trademark the X rating. This left filmmakers free to use it however they wanted. It quickly became synonymous with pornography, which made it virtually useless to the MPAA and the kiss of death to serious filmmakers. Even so, the MPAA didn't change it until 1990, when it replaced X with NC-17, "No Children Under 17"—which it trademarked.

MOVIE MISCELLANY

• How successful has the ratings system been? When it was introduced in 1968, there were more than 40 local censorship boards around the country. By 1996, there were none—the last one, in Dallas, Texas, closed up shop in 1993. The City Council of Dallas abolished it, saying that the movie industry does a better job.

• Unlike the original Motion Picture Code, the MPAA's rating system is entirely voluntary, with the exception that members agree not to release films that haven't been rated. Exhibitors are responsible for enforcement; an estimated 80% to 85% follow the guidelines and keep children out of R and NC-17 films.

In 1870, it took eight days to cross the United States by train.

IRONIC DEATHS

Here's a look at more ironic deaths.

MAJOR GENERAL JOHN SEDGWICK, *commander of the Sixth Army Corps during the Civil War*
On May 9, 1864, he was sitting under a tree making battle plans with an aide when he observed that some of his soldiers were not properly positioned for the upcoming battle.

As Sedgwick got up and started walking toward the men, a lone Confederate sniper opened fire. Rather than return fire, most of the soldiers ducked or ran for cover, which made Sedgwick laugh. "What, what men!" he told them, "Dodging for single bullets? I tell you they could not hit an elephant at this distance."

Final Irony: One of Sedgwick's aides later recounted,

> before the smile which accompanied these words had departed from his lips...there was a sharp whistle of a bullet, terminating in a dull, soft sound; and he fell slowly and heavily to the earth.

Sedgwick was killed instantly.

ALAN SIMPSON, *a U.S. airman during World War II*
In 1942, he was shot down off the coast of Sicily. He was captured and spent three years in a German prisoner-of-war camp, where he was "starved, tortured, and tossed in isolation for months at a time." According to his daughter Catherine, "He always hated the Germans for what they did to him."

Final Irony: In 1989, the 67-year-old Simpson went to London, England, for a reunion with his POW buddies. As he was crossing the street on his way to the meeting place, he was run down by a bus...filled with West German tourists.

"It took forty years, but they finally got him," his daughter was quoted as saying. "He took all the punishment they could dish out during World War II, but now they've nailed him with a bus."

Hawaii is the only U.S. state that was once a kingdom.

JEAN BAPTISTE LULLY, *orchestra conductor*
Lully liked to stamp out the beat of the music on the floor with a long, pointed staff as he conducted.

Final Irony: According to one account, "One time he missed the floor, hit his own foot, got blood poisoning from the accident, and died."

RICHARD VERSALLE, *opera tenor*
In January 1996, the 63-year-old Versalle joined the cast of New York's Metropolitan Opera House to perform in a Czech opera called *The Makropulous Case.* He played an elderly law clerk who sings about a legal case that's nearly a century old.

Final Irony: In the opening scene, Versalle climbed a 10-foot ladder to reach a file cabinet in the "law office." As he reached the top, he sang the words "You can only live so long." At that moment, he fell backward from the ladder to the stage. According to the Associated Press:

> Many of the 3,000 spectators at first thought the seemingly graceful drop from the ladder was deliberate. But admiration quickly gave way to gasps and murmurs of alarm as he lay motionless on his back with his arms outstretched.

In fact, Versalle had died from a heart attack.

JIM FIXX, *author*
Fixx, who almost single-handedly started the jogging craze of the 1970s with his 1977 bestseller *The Complete Book of Running*, ran an average of 10 miles a day. He championed its health benefits: "Research has repeatedly shown that with endurance training such as running, the heart becomes a distinctly more efficient instrument."

Final Irony: In July 1984, he had just started off on a run when he suffered a massive heart attack. An autopsy revealed that two of his arteries "were sufficiently blocked to warrant a bypass operation." He was 52.

Pierre Michelin, inventor of super-safe Michelin tires, died in a car accident.

YOU'RE MY INSPIRATION

Often, fictional characters are around long after the people who inspired them have been forgotten. Ever heard of these three people, for example?

FRANCES "FRANKIE" BAKER

Inspired: The song "Frankie and Johnny"

The Story: In 1899, when she was 22 years old, Frankie shot and killed her boyfriend, Allen (not Johnny). She pled self-defense and was acquitted. But that was just the beginning of her problems. When "Frankie and Johnny" became a popular tune, she was the talk of St. Louis. She tried to get away by moving to Omaha, then to Portland. But when *Frankie and Johnny* was released as a film in 1936, she sued the film studio for defamation of character. Ironically, she lost because she convinced jurors she was *not* a "woman of easy virtue," like the character in the film. She was committed to a mental hospital in 1950 and died two years later.

GEORGE TRAIN

Inspired: *Around the World in 80 Days*

The Story: In 1870, wealthy American businessman/eccentric George Frances Train made a highly publicized trip around the world in only 80 days—an incredible speed for that time. Two years later, Jules Verne published his acclaimed novel, but called his hero Phileas Fogg. Train, the self-described "advocate of speed," was incensed. "Verne stole my thunder," he complained. He made the round-the-world trip three more times, finally breaking his own record by completing the journey in a mere 60 days.

DENNIS PATRICK CASEY

Inspired: The poem "Casey at the Bat"

The Story: Baseball fans have long wondered about the hero in Ernest L. Thayer's 1888 poem. Who was he? Convincing evidence points to Dennis P. Casey, a popular star with the Baltimore Orioles at the time. Casey's pitching and hitting elevated the team into "First Division" in the American Association, a feat no Baltimore team had accomplished.

The word "television" means to "see at a distance."

THE MUNSTERS

Here are some things you didn't know about
TV's weirdest sitcom family.

HOW IT STARTED

In 1963, Joe Connelly and Bob Mosher were considering ideas for a new sitcom. Their 1950s hit *Leave It to Beaver*, was about to go off the air. Their 1961 sitcom *Ichabod & Me* had flopped.

Universal Pictures had recently dusted off its classic horror films —*Frankenstein, Dracula, The Mummy*, etc.—and sold them to TV. Monsters had quickly become a fad, with baby boom kids buying monster models, wallets, cards, toys, and dozens more products.

Connelly and Mosher saw a chance to bring back the Cleavers: turn them into monsters. A family of middle-class monsters in a typical suburb would make the same old sitcom plots seem new.

They were excited about the prospect, but weren't sure how the networks would react. So they assembled a crew of experienced actors—including Fred Gwynne and "Grandpa" Al Lewis (both fresh from *Car 54, Where Are You?*), and shot a 15-minute pilot episode. "It was pretty bizarre" Gwynne recalled. "They hadn't figured out the costumes or the laughs. God only knows how they ever sold it on those fifteen minutes, because it was just awful."

But they did sell it—right away. According to Norman Abbot, who directed the pilot: "We had everybody from the studio at the soundstage watching the filming. Somebody called the people from the head office and told them to come down and see it. It was wild. Jim Aubrey, [president of] CBS, bought it instantly."

INSIDE FACTS

Start and Stop

The Munsters premiered on April 30, 1964 —the same week that ABC first aired its own monster sitcom, *The Addams Family*. And it was cancelled in 1966—ironically, the same week *The Addams Family* was dumped. Which show was more popular? *The Munsters*. It ranked #18 on the list of the most popular shows of 1964-5. The

---

The first Chamber of Commerce in the U.S. was organized in 1912.

Addamses ranked 23rd. By the second season, however, the novelty of both shows had worn off, and ratings were only mediocre.

Making the Monster
• It took two hours to transform the bony 6' 5", 180-pound Fred Gwynne into Herman Munster. His face was covered with grease, balloon rubber, and yellow-green makeup (even though the show was filmed in black-and-white).

• He wore pants stuffed with foam and a shrunken jacket stuffed with foam in the shoulders and arms. The costume was so heavy and hot that he lost 10 lbs. during the first weeks of shooting.

• Gwynne's boots had 5" heels and weighed 10 lbs. They were intentionally hard to walk in, so he'd have a clumsy, "lurching" walk.

Yvonne to Be Alone
• Yvonne De Carlo's (Lily's) makeup wasn't as difficult as Gwynne's, but she hated it as much—and had five different hairdressers fired during the show's two-year run. She complained that her makeup made her look older, and even tried to paint out the grey streak that ran through her wig (the producers made her put it back in).

• She also refused to paint her own nails black, which meant she had to have fake nails glued on every day. They wouldn't stay attached; often shooting had to be suspended while De Carlo and the crew looked around the set for the nails that had fallen off.

• De Carlo didn't even want the part. "I did the show in the beginning for one reason only—I needed money at the time." Her husband, a stuntman, had been critically injured during the filming of *How the West Was Won*, and De Carlo had exhausted her savings nursing him back to health.

THE COFFIN CAPER
• Grandpa's car, the *Dragula*, was a dragster with a real coffin as a body. It wasn't easy to build. When George Barris, the car's designer, tried to buy a coffin for it, he couldn't find a funeral home that would cooperate. "They wouldn't sell one unless you were dead." Finally, Barris had someone leave an envelope full of money at a funeral home while "my guys picked up a casket and walked out with it. We literally spooked off with the casket."

The average human sheds 40 lbs. of dead skin in their lifetime.

THE 10 MOST-WANTED LOST FILMS

Only about 20% of the silent movies made between 1895 and the late 1920s (when talkies began) still survive. Many were discarded as worthless. Others, made on fragile film, have crumbled into dust. Today people are searching for—and sometimes finding—masterpieces of the silent era. In 1980, the American Film Institute (AFI) compiled this list of the 10 most historically and artistically significant "lost films." It is supplied by Gregory Lukow at AFI.

THE LIST, IN ALPHABETICAL ORDER

1. CAMILLE (1927). Norma Talmadge played the title role in one of her last triumphs. A legend of the silent screen, Talmadge watched her career all but vanish with the arrival of the "talkies." Apparently her voice did not match her image, and when audiences stopped buying tickets, the studios—which she'd helped to build—unceremoniously dropped her. Not a frame of this film (which was remade in 1937 with Greta Garbo) is known to exist.

2. CLEOPATRA (1917). This lavish half-million dollar epic featured Theda Bara, the original vamp of the silent era, as the sexy queen of the Nile. Sadly, only two of Bara's 38 films have survived. Her body of work is considered one of the lost treasures of the silent era, with *Cleopatra* the crown jewel.

3. THE DIVINE WOMAN (1928). Greta Garbo starred in 10 silent films before shifting to sound in 1930. *The Divine Woman* was her first starring role, and the only one of her films that hasn't survived. One reel was recently located in the former Soviet Union; the rest is still missing.

4. FRANKENSTEIN (1910). The first horror film (see p. 80). This version, made by Thomas Edison, has turned up in a private collection. But because the American Film Institute has no access to the film, they keep it on their list.

Sarah Josepha Hale's 1830 poem "Mary Had a Little Lamb" was inspired by a little

5. GREED (1925). Scholars and film critics consider this the Holy Grail of lost films. The original version—40 reels and 10 hours—was the masterpiece of one of film's most talented directors, Erich von Stroheim. It was released in a butchered version over von Stroheim's vociferous protests. The rest of the film was discarded. No one knows what happened to it.

6. THE KAISER, BEAST OF BERLIN (1918). Part of a series of short anti-German propaganda films made during the World War I period. Directed by and starring Rupert Julian as the Kaiser. U.S. historians are especially interested in this one.

7. LITTLE RED RIDING HOOD (1922). This was Walt Disney's first cartoon, produced six years before the introduction of Mickey Mouse in *Steamboat Willie*. Posters and a few sketches are all that remain.

8. LONDON AFTER MIDNIGHT (1927). Produced at the height of horror star Lon Chaney's short career, and hailed as a masterwork when it was released. Chaney stars as a detective who turns into a vampire at night. The false teeth he wore caused him so much pain that he was unable to keep them on for more than a few minutes at a time. Directed by Tod Browning.

9. THE ROGUE SONG (1930). Would be considered just another forgettable operetta, if it didn't contain a few non-musical scenes of Laurel and Hardy in their only known color film. It's also Laurel and Hardy's last short film. (In the '30s, they worked exclusively in features.) A three-minute segment, the original trailer, and the soundtrack (which was released as an album in 1980) are all that remain.

10. THAT ROYALE GIRL (1925). The story of an innocent girl saved from her accusers by a loving district attorney was the second film that legendary director D. W. Griffith made with W. C. Fields. Griffith was reportedly uncomfortable with the contemporary setting (he liked historical epics). However, given his status as one of the great directors of all time, and Fields's as a great comedian, film scholars would love to get another chance to see this.

FAMILIAR ORIGINS

More origins of everyday phrases.

THAT'S A LOAD OF BULL

Meaning: It's a lie or exaggeration.

Origin: It's logical to assume that this phrase started with cow-chips…but it turns out that *boule* is an Old French verb meaning "to lie."

CLAP-TRAP

Meaning: Meaningless talk; empty speech.

Origin: "Claptrap" comes from the theater. It describes any line that the playwright inserts—often knowing it's terrible—just to get applause. It's literally "a trap to catch a clap."

RED-LETTER DAY

Meaning: Special occasion or day.

Origin: As far back as the Middle Ages, Christian church calendars and almanacs had feast days, saint days, and other holy days printed in red ink; everything else was printed in black ink.

IF YOU CAN DO IT, I'LL EAT MY HAT

Meaning: I don't believe you can do it.

Origin: Why would anyone offer to eat a hat under *any* circumstances? Answer: The original hat in this expression was "hatte," an English dish that contained eggs, veal, dates, saffron, and salt. Over time, the meaning of the phrase evolved into the ridiculous proposition it *sounded* like.

MY BETTER HALF

Meaning: My spouse.

Origin: The Puritan view of people was that we're made up of two halves: a body and a soul. The soul—our spiritual side—was considered our better half. In the 16th century, the English writer Sir Philip Sidney became the first person to apply the term to the union between a married couple. By the 18th century, his use of the expression had become the most common.

Of the top 10 moneymaking Hollywood films, only *Forrest Gump* won the Best Picture Oscar.

CELEBRITY SWEEPSTAKES

Three big stars—three big products. What could go wrong with these endorsements? Try divorce, sex, and alcoholism. Here are more surefire celebrity promotions that didn't quite turn out as expected.

MADONNA

In January 1989, Pepsi agreed to pay Madonna $5 million for a two-minute commercial featuring her brand-new single, "Like a Prayer."

What they wanted: Publicity. Pepsi planned to show its "Like a Prayer" ad the night *before* the world premier of Madonna's video on MTV. So it was the first chance for Madonna fans to see her sing it. Madonna was so popular—and the deal so unusual—that Pepsi's "coup" became front-page news. They showed the ad simultaneously on all three TV networks, and in 40 countries.

What they got: A scandal. Incredibly, nobody at Pepsi previewed Madonna's video before they built their campaign around it. Their ad featured Madonna going back to her eighth birthday. But the *video* was full of sexually suggestive scenes and provocative religious symbolism—including "a scantily clad Madonna singing in front of burning crosses, suffering wounds on her hands like Jesus and kissing a saintly statue that turns into a man."

What happened: Pepsi had purposely linked its ad campaign to the video, and they were stuck with it. Fundamentalist Christians turned their wrath on the "blasphemous" soft drink company. Sensing a consumer boycott in the making, Pepsi cancelled the whole deal within 24 hours. Madonna cried all the way to the bank. "It's just what I'd expect from her," a friend said, "She doesn't have any obligations to Pepsi…and still gets to keep their money."

BURT REYNOLDS

In 1992, the Florida Department of Citrus hired Reynolds to promote Florida orange juice in a $16 million ad campaign.

What they wanted: A believable spokesperson. Reynolds was a native Floridian with a pleasant, good ol' boy image. Plus, he and his wife, actress Loni Anderson, had actually *left* Hollywood to live in the Sunshine State. "I'm kind of Mr. Florida," he told reporters modestly. "I know a lot of the growers, and I'm proud to speak for them."

What they got: "The world's ugliest and most public divorce." Anderson filed for divorce in June 1993, and nearly every detail of the split was played out in the tabloids. Most accounts blamed Reynolds for the breakup. And he didn't do much to help the situation when he admitted to the *National Enquirer* that he'd had a two-year affair with a Florida cocktail waitress.

What happened: The Citrus commission pulled the ads. "What was happening in his personal life, at the level it was being played out, overshadowed the message we were trying to communicate," a spokesman told reporters. Reynolds no longer drinks Florida orange juice, and blames the Florida Citrus commission for cashing in on his failed marriage. "They took the opportunity . . . to cash in on the P.R. from my divorce, saying I wasn't the right image for them. Yeah, like Anita Bryant is. Or Rush Limbaugh."

BRUCE WILLIS

In the mid-1980s, Willis was hired to plug Seagram's Wine Coolers for an estimated $2 to $3 million a year.

What they wanted: A macho, good-time spokesman to make their wine coolers acceptable to young male drinkers.

What they got: A huge success—albeit with some bad publicity. Seagrams' brand-new product quickly became the bestselling cooler in the country. Then, in May 1987, Willis was arrested for "scuffling" with police officers who were called to his home to break up a loud, drunken party. The charges were dropped after Willis apologized to his neighbors and promised to move away.

What happened: Seagrams stuck by its man, apparently thinking that his drunk and disorderly behavior was *good* for their product—or at least didn't hurt it.

But Willis was finally dumped in 1988 after:

1. The *National Enquirer* ran a story saying he had an alcohol problem, and

2. His wife, Demi Moore, began a public campaign against alcohol abuse.

Sure, and they can quit any time: 21% of U.S. smokers say they don't believe nicotine's addictive.

SEINFELD ON...

Comments by Jerry Seinfeld, sent to us by BRI member Ben Brand.

PAPERWEIGHTS

"Nothing compares with the paperweight as a bad gift. To me, there's no better way...to [say] to someone, 'I refused to put any thought into this at all.'...And where are these people working that papers are just blowing right off of their desks, anyway? Is their office screwed to the back of a flatbed truck going down the highway? Are they typing up in the crow's nest of a clipper ship? What do you need a paperweight for? Where's the wind coming from?"

DOCTORS

"People love to recommend their doctor to you. I don't know what they get out of it, but they really push them on you. 'He's the best. This guy's the best.' There can't be this many 'bests.' Someone's graduating at the bottom of the classes. Where are these doctors? Is someone somewhere saying to their friend, 'You should see my doctor, he's the worst. He's the absolute worst there is. Whatever you've got, it'll be worse after you see him. The man's an absolute butcher.' "

BOXING

"The simplest, stupidest sport of all. It's almost as if these two guys are just desperate to compete with each other, but they couldn't think of a sport. So they said, 'Why don't we just pound each other for forty-five minutes? Maybe someone will come watch that.' "

PLANE CRASHES

"I don't know why people always have the same reaction when they hear about a plane crash. 'Plane crash? What airline? Where was it going?' As if it makes a difference, like you're going to go, 'Oh that flight. Oh, OK, that I can understand.' Like there's some planes that are expected to crash.

"You go up to the ticket agent. 'Excuse me, this flight generally goes down quite a bit, doesn't it?'

" 'Actually it does, yes. We do have another flight, but it explodes on take-off. It is, however, a snack flight.' "

New York's Central Park is almost twice as big as the entire country of Monaco.

TOY FACTS

*The BRI takes a look at random info on some
childhood (and adulthood) classics.*

NERF BALLS

After successfully inventing the game Twister (see p. 87),
Reynolds Guyer decided to become a full-time toy designer.
He quit his family's business and formed his own toy design firm.
One of his company's first efforts was a game based on a caveman
theme. It involved hiding money under foam rubber rocks and de-
fending the loot by throwing some of the rocks at an opponent.

"Pretty soon," Guyer recalls, "we found we really enjoyed throwing the rocks. Then someone decided that the rocks were not as
round as they would like, so they began shaping them, cutting
them with scissors," until they were balls. Guyer soon abandoned
the caveman theme entirely and focused on the balls. He made up
the name "Nerfs" to communicate what he thought of as their
"soft, friendly nature." Within a decade Nerf became one of the
largest lines of sports/action toys on earth.

MAGIC SLATE

In the early 1920s, R. A. Watkins, owner of a small printing plant
in Illinois, was approached by a man who wanted to sell him the
rights to a homemade device made of waxed cardboard and tissue.
You could write on it, but the messages could be easily erased by
lifting up the tissue. Watkins couldn't make up his mind; he told
the man to come back the next day.

In the middle of the night, Watkins's phone rang; it was the man
calling from jail. He said that if Watkins would bail him out, he'd
give Watkins the rights to the invention. The printer agreed. He
wound up getting a patent for the device—which he called Magic
Slate. Since then, tens of millions have been sold.

PICTIONARY

Robert Angel, a Seattle waiter, used to entertain his friends at parties by selecting a word from the dictionary, drawing it, and having

them guess what it was. He didn't think about developing it into a game until Trivial Pursuit became popular. Then he spent eight months looking up 6,000 words in the dictionary (2,500 made it into the game) while a friend designed "word cards" and the board. He borrowed $35,000 to manufacture the game and started selling it to stores in Seattle out of the trunk of his car.

He got his big break when Nordstrom ordered 167 games. They didn't even have a game department. "They let us set up a table in the accessories department," Angel recalls. "If anybody glanced in our direction, we would yell at them to come and watch us play the game." Tom McGuire, a salesman at Selchow & Righter (manufacturer of Trivial Pursuit), played Pictionary at Nordstrom with his family. He was so impressed that he quit his job and began marketing it full time. By the end of 1987, over $90 million worth of Pictionary games had been sold in the United States alone.

MISCELLANY

• Tonka Toys was originally called the Mound Metalcraft Company. It was renamed *Tonka* after Lake Minnetonka, which dominated the scenery around their factory.

• Mattel got its name from its two founders—Harold *Mat*son and *El*liot Handler. Handler was in the picture frame business in L.A. In 1946 he had a bunch of extra frame slats, so he and Matson built doll furniture out of them.

• Mattel was the first toy company to advertise on national TV. In 1955 they sold toy burp guns on "The Mickey Mouse Club."

• Mr. Potato Head used to come with a pipe—which bugged anti-smoking activists. "It's not only dangerous to his health," complained Surgeon General C. Everett Koop, "it also passes on the message to kids that smoking is okay." In 1987, Hasbro gave in; after 35 years of smoking, Mr. Potato Head surrendered his pipe to the Surgeon General. Koop was so pleased that he named Mr. Potato Head "Official Spokespud" for the Great Smokeout.

• World record: A game of Twister was played by 4,160 participants on May 2, 1987 at the University of Massachusetts.

There are more bagpipe bands in the U.S. than there are in Scotland.

MORE STRANGE LAWSUITS

Here are more real-life examples of unusual legal battles.

THE PLAINTIFF: Mary Verdev, a 73-year-old Milwaukee resident

THE DEFENDANT: St. Florian Catholic Church

THE LAWSUIT: In 1990, the church's 300-pound electronic bingo board fell on Verdev. She sued, claiming it had caused $90,000 worth of injuries. She also said that as a result of the accident, she now found herself sexually attracted to women and had begun to experience spontaneous orgasms, "sometimes in clusters."

THE VERDICT: Verdev wouldn't undergo a psychological exam ordered by the judge. He dismissed the case.

THE PLAINTIFF: Three-year-old Stacy Pevnev

THE DEFENDANT: Three-year-old Jonathan Inge

THE LAWSUIT: In February 1996, the two children were playing in the sandbox at a local park in Boston. Jonathan apparently kicked Stacy, and the parents argued heatedly. Then Stacy's mom went to court and asked that Jonathan be restrained from using the playground when Stacy was there. "Maybe it's a little emotional, maybe it's overprotective, but you do what you can," she said.

THE VERDICT: Amazingly, Superior Court Judge Charles Spurlock actually granted a temporary restraining order. Then he called the families to court and ordered them to stay separated at the playground.

THE PLAINTIFF: Richard Loritz

THE DEFENDANT: San Diego County

THE LAWSUIT: Loritz was imprisoned for three months in 1995. During that time, he says, he asked for dental floss and was refused. As a result, he developed four cavities. He sued for $2,000 in dental expenses.

THE VERDICT: The case was thrown out of court.

President Lyndon Johnson used to give electric toothbrushes with presidential seals as gifts.

THE PLAINTIFF: Sharon Silver

THE DEFENDANT: Gerald Pfeffer, her ex-husband

THE LAWSUIT: After the couple divorced in 1985, Silver moved out of state. Pfeffer stayed in their St. Paul, Minnesota, home. In 1988, the reunion committee of Silver's high school class sent an "update" questionnaire to her old address. Pfeffer filled it out and returned it. A sample of his answers:

Current occupation: "Retired on third husband's divorce settlement."

Current interests / hobbies: "Night clubbing and partying. Looking for new and wealthier husbands."

Recent outrageous / unusual / interesting experience: "Going to W. Virginia on the job and having an affair with two different guys while my third husband was in Minnesota working two jobs."

The committee printed these (and other) answers in its newsletter. Silver sued for libel; her ex-husband argued that it was all true.

THE VERDICT: After three years of litigation, the case was settled out of court for $75,000—$50,000 from Gerald, $25,000 from the Harding High School Class of 1958. "Well, I thought they were pretty good answers at the time," Pfeffer commented afterward.

THE PLAINTIFF: Kenneth Parker

THE DEFENDANT: Nevada State Prison

THE LAWSUIT: Parker was an inmate, serving 15 years for robbery. He wanted to buy two jars of chunky peanut butter from the prison canteen. (Cost: $5.) But the canteen had only one jar of chunky peanut butter. When they had to substitute a jar of creamy for the second one, Parker sued for "mental and emotional pain," asking for $5,500 and the imprisonment of a prison official.

THE VERDICT: The case went on for two years. It was finally dismissed.

THE PLAINTIFF: Jeannine Pelletier and her husband

THE DEFENDANT: Fort Kent Golf Club in Portland, Maine

THE LAWSUIT: Pelletier hit a golf ball in the spring of 1995 that bounced back and bonked her on the nose. She and her husband sued—she for physical damages, he for "loss of consortium."

THE VERDICT: The Maine Supreme Court awarded her $40,000. Her husband got zilch.

In his entire lifetime, King Louis XIV bathed three times.

CELEBRITY GOSSIP

*A few random bits of gossip you've probably never heard. They're
supplied by Jack Mingo, whose book* The Juicy Parts
is full of great tidbits like these.

MICK JAGGER

"About the time Mick started dating girls, his mother
started selling Avon. When his parents were out, he
would invite a girl to the house where they would sit at his mother's dressing table trying on her makeup. One of his dates remembers, 'He just seemed happy letting me put lipstick and mascara on him. Then he'd do the same for me. It did strike me as very strange at the time, but it was all in fun. Dating Mick was more like being with one of the girls.' "

HENRY FORD

"The automobile tycoon believed in reincarnation. Since he was born a few weeks after the battle of Gettysburg, he decided he had been a soldier killed in that battle. And later in life, he decided his niece was really the reincarnation of his mother."

W. C. FIELDS

"He didn't like to carry a lot of cash while on the road, so wherever he was, he opened a bank account. He claimed to have 700 of them in banks all over the world—including London, Paris, Sydney, and Cape Town. Usually these accounts were open under his real name, but sometimes he used odd aliases like Figley E. Whitesides, Sneed Hearn, Dr. Otis Guelpe, and (in Madrid, Spain), 'Señor Guillermo McKinley.' After his death, only about three dozen accounts were located."

MICHAEL JACKSON

• "What started him on plastic surgery? According to one report, it was because he hated the fact that he was growing up to look like his father."

• "He once met Andy Warhol and Alfred Hitchcock and thought, for some reason, that they were brothers."

• "He's been reported as saying he believes human beings can fly."

HARPO MARX

"In Harpo's professional debut with the Marx Brothers, he looked out at the audience…and immediately wet his pants."

WALT DISNEY

• "The animator shared an apartment with his brother Roy until Roy got married. Then Walt, feeling abandoned, decided that he (as he put it) 'needed a new roommate' and three months later, took a bride himself. His honeymoon night was spent on a train from Idaho to California; his behavior was strictly Mickey Mouse: he developed a 'toothache' and spent the entire night shining shoes in the porter's car 'to keep his mind off the pain.' "

• "Walt's famous 'trademark' signature was designed by a studio artist. He often had to insist he really *was* Walt Disney to autograph seekers who thought he was putting them on."

RICHARD NIXON

• "In first grade, his mother made a point of telling his teacher, 'Never call him Dick—I named him Richard.' Every day he wore a freshly starched white shirt with a black bow tie and knee pants, and his teacher was quoted as saying later that she could not remember him ever getting dirty."

• "He took great pains in brushing his teeth, was careful to gargle, and before he left for school asked his mother to smell his breath to make sure he would not offend anyone on the bus. He didn't like to ride the school bus, because the other children didn't smell good."

THE BEATLES & MUHAMMAD ALI

"In 1963, during their first American tour, the world-famous Beatles tried to meet heavyweight boxing champion Sonny Liston, who was going to fight Cassius Clay (later known as Muhammad Ali) for the championship in a few days. He refused to have anything to do with 'a bunch of faggots.' Instead, they met Clay. He bossed them around for the photographers, commanding them to the canvas with 'Get down, you little worms!'

"Lennon, however, got the last laugh. While Clay was talking with them, he used one of his favorite lines: 'You guys ain't as dumb as you look.' John Lennon looked him in the eye and said, 'No, but you are.' "

MUCH ADO ABOUT SNORING

*They say that if your spouse snores loudly enough to keep you awake,
one of the best things to do is lay down on the living room couch
and read until you fall asleep. Uncle John suggests saving
this chapter for just such an occasion.*

A SNORE BY ANY OTHER NAME

There's an old saying: "Laugh, and the world laughs with you. Snore, and you sleep alone." But you won't *snore* alone. It's estimated that every night, as much as half the population of the world is snoring, too.

What, exactly, *is* snoring?

• When you go to sleep, the muscles that control the soft tissue in your mouth—your tongue, soft palate, uvula (the piece of flesh hanging down in the back of your mouth), tonsils, and adenoids—begins to relax.

• The deeper you sleep, the more these soft tissues relax. In some people, they actually begin to obstruct the airway. When this happens, the air that flows in and out of your mouth makes the tissues vibrate, causing the snoring sound.

WHO SNORES?

• Anyone can snore; doctors estimate that as many as 90 million Americans over the age of 18 do. But the problem is worst among people over sixty (65% of people over 60 snore), especially for males.

• For that matter, men snore more than women in just about every age group. Men have more muscles in their necks and throats than women, which means they have more to go flabby as they age.

• Girth is a factor, too. People who are overweight are three times more likely to snore than people who aren't. Why? Sleep experts point to two causes:

1. Overweight people generally have less muscle tone than people of average weight—including in their mouths. Poorly

toned flesh flaps aroud more than toned flesh, which increases the likelihood of snoring.

2. Overweight people actually gain weight *inside* their mouths; and the more fleshy tissue in the mouth, the more likely you are to have a snore-causing obstruction.

There are also external reasons for snoring:

• Colds, allergies, nasal infections, and anything else that stops up the nose can cause snoring. Why? The sufferer has to breathe more forcefully than normal through the mouth—which increases the chance of blockage.

• People who take depressants—including alcohol and sleeping pills—snore more than people who don't, because of the relaxing effect they have on the body.

• Smoking doesn't usually cause snoring, but can aggravate the condition because it irritates the pharynx and causes mucous membranes to swell.

SNORE CURES
Quick Fixes
• Snoring is usually worst when you sleep on your back, because the soft tissue in your mouth slumps backward, blocking the airway. That's why many traditional cures aim at preventing people from sleeping on their backs. During the Revolutionary War, soldiers forced to bunk together sometimes sewed small cannonballs to the backs of the nightshirts of anyone who snored to keep them off their backs. Not much has changed—a common cure for snoring today is the "snore ball," a tennis ball in a sock that snorers fasten to the back of their pajama tops.

• Another trick that may help: raising the head of your bed four inches by placing bricks, phone books, etc., under the bed. Sleeping with more than one pillow won't do the trick. In fact, it'll probably make snoring worse by bending your body either at the neck or the waist, both of which can increase snoring. (Switching from feather to synthetic pillows can also help, if snoring is caused by allergies.)

• A preventative: Chewing two or three pieces of gum at a time may help, some sleep researchers think, by reducing flab and increasing muscle tone inside your mouth.

• If snoring is really serious, there are plenty of high-tech solutions. Tongue retainers and other appliances are available. Or you can try a "continuous positive air pressure" (CPAP) pump that blows a steady stream of air into your nostrils while you sleep. And if nothing else works, there's surgery: Surgeons can, for example, move your tongue forward and stitch the underlying muscle to the chin bone, so that nothing flops back into the airway during sleep.

DEADLY SNORES

• Snoring can actually be fatal. More than half of all chronic snorers over age 40 suffer from "sleep apnea." In these people, the airway becomes *totally* obstructed, cutting off the oxygen supply to their brain for as long as sixty seconds before they wake up enough to clear the obstruction. Not all sleep apnea sufferers survive. Every year, more than 2,500 of them die from cardiac arrest brought on by the condition.

• Sleep apnea may have other unfortunate side effects. It is believed to cause high blood pressure, an increased pulse, and an enlarged heart, and may also increase the risk of strokes.

• And because it disrupts the deep sleep that provides the most rest, sleep apnea also poses indirect health risks: Sufferers are often physically exhausted during the day, thus more prone to on-the-job accidents and other injuries. More than 20% of sleep apnea victims have been in car accidents caused when they fall asleep at the wheel.

LIFE SAVERS

To be fair, we should also point out that snoring can also *save* lives. This article, reported by Reuters News Service, appeared in newspapers recently:

> A London undertaker was terrified when he heard snores coming from a coffin in which 85-year-old Rose Hanover had been laid out for burial....She had collapsed and apparently died in her home. Two hours after arriving at the parlor, Mrs. Hanover began to snore, even though she had been pronounced dead by a doctor using the normal breathing and heart tests. Last night she was sitting up in a hospital bed and was reported to be much improved.

power lawnmower. (Big surprise: His wife is deaf in one ear.)

SHAKESPEARE'S INSULTS

Shakespeare was a master at hurling off an insult or two.
Here are some of his meanest, wittiest, and cruelest.

"The tartness of his face sours grapes."
—*Coriolanus*

"[You] leather-jerkin, crystal-button, knot-pated, agate-ring, puke-stocking, caddis-garter, smooth-tongue, Spanish pouch!"
—*Henry IV, Part 1*

"You are as a candle, the better part burnt out."
—*Henry IV, Part 2*

"He never broke any man's head but his own, and that was against a post when he was drunk."
—*Henry V*

"[Your] face is not worth sun-burning."
—*Henry V*

"You blocks, you stones, you worse than senseless things!"
—*Romeo and Juliet*

"Your horrid image doth unfix my hair."
—*Macbeth*

"His brain is as dry as the remainder biscuit after a voyage."
—*As You Like It*

"It is certain that when he makes water, his urine is congealed ice."
—*Measure for Measure*

"I durst not laugh, for fear of opening my lips and receiving [your] bad air."
—*Julius Caesar*

"Thy food is such as hath been belch'd on by infected lungs."
—*Pericles*

"[Your] face is Lucifer's privy-kitchen, where he doth nothing but roast malt-worms."
—*Henry IV, Part 2*

"He has not so much brain as ear-wax."
—*Troilus and Cressida*

"Though [he] is not naturally honest, [he] is so sometimes by chance."
—*The Winter's Tale*

"He's a most notable coward, an infinite and endless liar, an hourly promise-breaker, and the owner of no one good quality."
—*All's Well That Ends Well*

When migrating birds fly in a "V" formation, it increases their range by as much as 70%.

MORE TAXING TRIVIA

Here are a few additional ways that income tax has shaped our culture.

H & R BLOCK

Encouraged by their mother to go into business together, Henry Bloch and his brother Richard formed the United Business Company in 1946. They planned to provide bookkeeping, management, and other services to businesses, but they spent so much time helping their customers fill out tax forms that they decided to focus on tax preparation exclusively.

• To give their business a more personal touch, they decided to name it after themselves. But rather than have customers mispronounce their name as "blotch," they changed the spelling to match the way the name is pronounced. Today, H&R Block preparers fill out one of every ten income tax returns filed with the IRS.

BOOSTING THE CREDIT CARD

In 1958, the IRS began requiring taxpayers with expense accounts to list each of their unreimbursed expenses on their tax returns. To avoid this extra record keeping, many employers issued credit cards—which itemize all purchases in the monthly billing statement—to employees with expense accounts. Result: Credit card companies reported the largest sales increases in history.

HISTORIC SWITCH

Ronald Reagan made so much money as a Hollywood actor that he ended up in the 94% tax bracket. In his autobiography *An American Life*, he revealed that the tax was instrumental in converting him from a New Deal Democrat to a conservative Republican.

"The IRS took such a big chunk of my earnings," he wrote, "that after a while I began asking myself whether it was worth it to keep on taking work. Something was wrong with a system like that. When you have to give up such a large percentage of your income in taxes, incentive to work goes down."

25% of the 206 bones in your body are in your feet.

BATHROOM NEWS

Bits and pieces of bathroom trivia we've flushed out over the years.

WORLD NEWS
• **In Paris:** Concerned about the estimated 500,000 tons of poop that Parisian dogs deposit on city streets each year, Pierre Pascallon, Conservative member of Parliament, introduced a bill in the National Assembly requiring the installation of dog *toilets*—to be known as *canisettes*. To pay for it, he proposed that dog owners pay a graduated tax in proportion to how much their dogs weigh.

• **In Malaysia:** The government announced that it is now illegal for restaurants to substitute toilet paper as table napkins. Punishment: $80 in fines (with jail time for repeat offenders).

• **On Mt. Everest:** A state-of-the-art, $10,000 outhouse is being erected about 4 miles up the side of Mount Everest. "Until now, climbers and Sherpas have had to go off and find boulders and bushes to hide behind," a spokesman for the company doing the installation told reporters. The outhouse will help control Mt. Everest's growing waste problem. Since Sir Edmund Hillary first scaled the 29,000-foot summit in 1953, hundreds of Everest climbers have discarded tons of garbage and "other" waste—which decomposes very slowly in the frigid, low-oxygen environment.

AN HISTORIC MOMENT
What was it like to be the second person to walk on the lunar surface? Astronaut Edwin "Buzz" Aldrin, who followed Neil Armstrong moments after Armstrong made his famous first step, described the experience in an interview for British television: "I held onto the near edge of the landing gear and checked my balance and then hesitated a moment....I am the first person to wet his pants on the moon."

THE BATHROOM CRIME BLOTTER
• In 1993, Barry Lyn Stoller, a Seattle drywall installer, took some

Ex-Lax to cure his constipation…and when it didn't work, he wrote the folks at Ex-Lax demanding a refund. The company mailed him a check…with his *zip code* entered as the dollar amount. Stoller deposited the $98,002 in the bank, withdrew it a few days later…and hasn't been seen since.

• In 1994, Milton Ross was videotaped urinating into his office's coffeepot, part of an "an ongoing feud" he had with a co-worker. (Office employees had installed the video camera after noticing that their coffee tasted funny.) Ross's co-workers turned the tape over to the police…*and* the media, which broadcast it all over the world. Ross pled guilty to third-degree assault. He was sentenced to 100 hours of community service, which the judge stipulated had to be spent cleaning public restrooms.

• In October 1995, Gerald Finneran, described as "one of the world's leading authorities on Latin American debt," exploded into rage on a United Airlines flight from Buenos Aires to New York, after a flight attendant refused to serve him another drink. According to witnesses, Finneran assaulted the flight attendants, then "defecated on a serving cart, cleaned himself with the airline's first-class linens, and thus left an odor that remained in the cabin for the remaining four hours of the flight." Ordinarily, such a flight might have been diverted to a closer airport. But the president of Portugal was on board, which made a detour impossible.

PUBLIC SERVICE ANNOUNCEMENT

Do toilet seat covers really protect us against anything? According to David Feldman, in *Why Do Clocks Run Clockwise and Other Imponderables:* "Not only are venereal diseases not spread by toilet seats, but nothing else is, either. Although there was one report suggesting that the herpes virus may survive briefly in such an environment…doctors we spoke to [all said], 'There is no scientific evidence of disease transmitted from toilet seats.' "

THE FINAL FRONTIER

According to *Buzz* magazine, William Shatner, who played *Star Trek*'s Capt. Kirk, had his bathroom remodeled to resemble the bridge of the starship *Enterprise*. *Buzz* reports that he even had his toilet "custom-made in the shape of the fabled vessel."

Normally, says one source, you take about 17 breaths a minute.

RAMBO: THE MOVIE

*Here's the second installment of our story about the fictional
Vietnam vet who became one of the most enduring pop
icons of the 1980s. (Part I is on page 42).*

S AVED!!
First Blood, the story of Rambo, had been bouncing around
Hollywood for years when it was rescued by two film distributors who wanted to be producers. Andrew Vajna and Mario Kassar
were rummaging through unused film properties at the Warner
Bros. lot, looking for an action film they could sell internationally,
when they stumbled on Morrell's story.

They immediately bought the movie rights. Then they hired
Kirk Douglas to direct it, and picked Sylvester Stallone—whose
only commercial success up to that time was *Rocky*—to star.

CHANGING THE STORY

To make the story more suitable for an action film, they changed
the plot. In the novel, Rambo becomes a psychopathic killer, while
the sheriff, also a veteran, is shown in a sympathetic light. For the
film, however, they shifted all the sympathy to Rambo, and made
the sheriff into the villain. "The portrayal of the sheriff bothered
me," Morrell says. "In the novel both the police chief and Rambo
had to die to show how pointless everything was.... My intent was
to transpose the Vietnam war to America, whereas the film's intent
was to make the audience cheer for the underdog."

PROBLEMS

Making *First Blood* quickly became difficult and expensive. Then
Kirk Douglas—whom the producers were counting on to help sell
the film to distributors and investors—dropped out. That left
Stallone as the only well-known person connected to the film...
and all of his non-*Rocky* films had been box-office disappointments. There was no reason to assume his *next* film would make
money either, so no one was interested in the distribution rights.
Kassar recalls, "Here I was $14 million in the red, and nothing was
sold." Things were looking bad.

Every day, Americans use 4.8 billion gallons of water flushing the toilet.

BREAKTHROUGH

In desperation, Vajna and Kassar spliced together 55 minutes of the unfinished film and presented it at the American Film Market convention. "Even today," the *Los Angeles Times* wrote in 1990, "distributors remember the buzz that film clip generated. Within hours, rights to *First Blood* were sold out."

First Blood's timing was perfect. The bad memories of Vietnam were fading, Ronald Reagan was in office, and the country was becoming more conservative and isolationist at the same time. The increasing threat of terrorists was making the country nervous. Morrell says. "Like Rambo, Americans felt backed into a corner by hijackers and terrorists, and they were ready to strike back, if only in fiction."

First Blood, which even Stallone feared would be a flop (he called it "the most expensive home movie ever made"), did $9 million worth of business during its opening weekend in October and went on to gross $120 million in box-office receipts worldwide.

FIRST BLOOD PART II

Two weeks after *First Blood* premiered, Vajna and Kassar decided to make a sequel—*Rambo: First Blood Part II*. In it, Rambo returns to Vietnam to obtain proof that the Vietnamese are still holding American MIAs, and ends up single-handedly liberating an entire prison camp full of U.S. soldiers. Sylvester Stallone, who wrote the script, got the idea for the plot after receiving a letter from a Virginia woman whose husband had been missing for 16 years.

First Blood Part II hit American theaters in the summer of 1985 and was an even bigger hit than the first movie: it was the third most successful launch in Hollywood history. "Sequels usually do about 60% of the original," Vajna told interviewers. "With *Rambo*, we are doing 300%, maybe 400%." By the time it finished its run, *First Blood Part II*, which cost $27 million to make, grossed more than $390 million at the box office.

POP GOES THE SYMBOL

First Blood Part II did more than just make piles of money—it turned Rambo into a household word. This was partly due to the movie, and partly due to merchandising (Rambo posters, T-shirts, action figures, collectors' knives, toy guns, toy bow-and-arrow sets, vitamins...and even Wrigley's Rambo Black Flak bubble gum, black raspberry-flavored gum shaped like shrapnel).

It was also helped along by the Reagan administration's foreign policy, the most assertive and controversial since the end of the Vietnam War. When President Reagan ordered air strikes against Libya, the London *Times* headline screamed "RAMBO JETS BOMB LIBYA"; and when Nicaraguan president Daniel Ortega made a speech at the United Nations, he urged President Reagan to remember "that Rambo exists only in the movies."

U.S. Army recruiting centers hung Rambo posters in their windows, and there was even a poster of President Reagan's head grafted onto Rambo's body. It was a bestseller.

People speculated that Rambo might become as enduring a character as James Bond. But times changed: *Rambo III*, released in 1988, was a critical and box-office flop. Vajna and Kassar's studio, Carolco Pictures, Inc., ran into financial trouble beginning in 1991 and limped along for several years before finally filing for bankruptcy in 1995.

MORE RAMBO FACTS

• Rambo got a first name in *Rambo II*—Johnny, from the song "When Johnny Comes Marching Home Again." By strange coincidence, there really was a John Rambo who fought in Vietnam. But Arthur John Rambo of Libby, Montana, didn't come back—he was killed by enemy fire in 1969.

• Morrell was earning $1,000 a month as a college professor when he sold the rights to his *First Blood* novel in 1971. His lawyer charged him $500 to revise the contract's fine print to include sequels and merchandising rights, and at the time, Morrell felt ripped off. "I told my lawyer, 'What sequels? Everyone's dead at the end of the novel. Merchandise? Who's going to bring out dolls and lunchboxes for a movie about a psychopathic killer?' He said, 'You don't understand Hollywood. They can change anything they want. They could make it into a musical.' " It was the best $500 Morrell ever spent; the contract changes earned him millions.

• How does Morrell feel about the way his anti-war novel was changed to a violent thriller? He likes it. "The *Rambo* films are marvelous special effects movies....like cartoons. When Sylvester comes down the trail with his machine gun, I laugh."

MORGAN'S SWINDLE

"Great is Mr. Morgan's power, greater in some respects even than that of presidents or kings," wrote a British journalist about financier J. P. Morgan in the late 1800s. Did the journalist know that Morgan got his start as a petty swindler?

There have been few businessmen in American history like J. P. Morgan. His bank was the most powerful in America. His financial clout was so great that after the Panic of 1893, his money helped keep the entire U.S. economy afloat. At that point, he was widely regarded as one of America's "saviours."

But when crusading reporters began to look into J. P. Morgan's career, they found that he'd gotten his start in business as a war profiteer, *ripping off* the government…and that he'd jeopardized thousands of American soldiers in order to make his first killing in the marketplace. Here's a little-known story of the great House of Morgan's business beginnings.

A CALL TO ARMS

• In May 1861, the Civil War had just begun…and the U.S. Army desperately needed rifles. It was paying top dollar to anybody who had guns to sell. So when the commander of the Union Army in St. Louis received a telegram from a man in New York offering to sell "5,000 new carbines in perfect condition" for $22 each, the commander accepted—sight unseen.

• When the rifles arrived in St. Louis, the commander found that they had a serious defect: they often misfired, blowing off soldiers' thumbs. The Army refused to pay for them.

• But 24-year-old J. P. Morgan, who was selling the guns, insisted on full payment. When he sued, the Army tried to compromise, offering $13.31 per rifle. Morgan refused to settle. The case went to court, and the judge ruled in Morgan's favor; the government was instructed to pay Morgan in full—$109,912.

• The question remained: Was it a legitimate business deal? Or had Morgan and his cronies conspired to bilk the U.S. government?

The French typing equivalent of "the quick brown fox jumped over the lazy dog" is "Take this

SUSPICIOUS FACTS

• The guns had been bought from an *army arsenal* in New York City for $3.50 apiece. They were the last of a batch that had been there since 1857, when they were condemned as "thoroughly un-serviceable, obsolete, and dangerous."

• The deal was arranged by a speculator named Simon Stevens, who knew exactly what he was buying. Court records later showed that Stevens was working for Morgan.

• After the commander agreed to buy the guns, Morgan borrowed money to purchase them—using the Army voucher as collateral for the loan. So the U.S. Army was buying its own unusable rifles—at a profit to Morgan of roughly 500% per rifle.

• Morgan never even took possession of the guns. When the loan came through, he had the defective rifles shipped directly from the New York arsenal to St. Louis.

WAS IT A CONSPIRACY?

A U.S. congressional committee investigating the arms swindle in 1862 found that Morgan had engaged in a conspiracy to defraud the U.S. government. It reported:

> The proposal actually was to sell the Government at $22 each 5,000 of its own arms, the intention being, if the offer was accepted, to obtain these arms from the Government at $3.50 each....The Government not only sold one day for $17,486 arms which it had agreed the day before to repurchase for $109,912—making a loss to the United States of $92,426—but virtually furnished the money to pay itself the $17,486 which it received.

• Morgan's case set an unfortunate precedent for the thousands of "dead horse claims" that followed, in which wartime swindlers were paid in full for putrid meat, rotting ships, flimsy tents, shoes that fell apart, and weapons that maimed the soldiers who used them.

*   *   *   *

RANDOM THOUGHT

"I don't want a lawyer to tell me what I cannot do. I hire him to tell me how to do what I want to do."

—*J. P. Morgan*

old whiskey to the blonde judge who's smoking a cigar."

ACCIDENTAL HITS

Here are a few improbable-but-true stories that show how musicians can become stars overnight...or write hit songs without knowing it.

GET TOGETHER (1967/1969), by the Youngbloods
Background. In 1967, a group called the Youngbloods put out their first record on RCA, "Grizzly Bear." It was a modest hit. But the follow-up, a peace and love anthem called "Get Together" ("Come on people, smile on your brother / Everybody get together, try to love one another"), bombed. It reached #62 on the charts and died.

Lucky Break. Two years later, the National Conference of Christians and Jews put together a package of information for TV and radio stations to read on the air during National Brotherhood Week. They included a copy of the obscure "Get Together" in each package for the stations to use as background music

It's a Hit! People may not have paid attention to the message, but they listened to the song. Radio stations all over the country were flooded with calls asking what that record was and where they could get it. Stations began playing their copies of "Get Together," turning it into a Top 10 song that sold over 2 million copies.

HUMAN NATURE (1982), by Michael Jackson
Background. Steve Porcaro was a member of the group Toto. One day his daughter came home upset about a fight she'd had with some friends. "Why do they do that?" she asked. "It's just human nature," her father said...and then decided that was a good song title. So he went into Toto's studio and put a melody on tape, occasionally singing the line, "It's just human nature." Then he left the cassette lying around and forgot about it.

Lucky Break. Michael Jackson's producer, Quincy Jones, was looking for material to use on Jackson's new album. He asked another member of Toto, David Paitch, for some songs. Paitch went into their studio, put three tunes on a tape and sent it to Jones...who didn't care for them. But he said he loved the other song at the end of the tape.

What song? It turned out Paitch had accidentally picked up the

---

Pregnant goldfish are known as "twits."

tape on which Porcaro had recorded "Human Nature."

It's a Hit! Jones hired a lyricist to finish the song and included it on Jackson's album—called "Thriller"—which turned out to be the bestselling album in history. Porcaro earned millions for it. On top of that, the single of "Human Nature" reached #7 on its own.

HANKY PANKY (1966), by Tommy James & the Shondells

Background. In 1963, Tommy Jackson, a 16-year-old Michigan high school kid, recorded "Hanky Panky" with his band, the Shondells. It was a regional hit in Michigan, Illinois, and Indiana. Then it disappeared. A year and a half later, Jackson graduated from high school and the Shondells disbanded.

Lucky Break. Jackson was at his family's house one evening in 1965 when he got a phone call from a guy calling himself "Mad Mike" Metro.

"He said, 'I'm a deejay in Pittsburgh, and your record's number one. Can you come here?'" recalls Jackson. "I said, 'What record? Who is this? What's your name?' I thought it was one of my friends pulling my leg." But it was true. A disc jockey had found "Hanky Panky" in a 10¢ bin and started playing it on the air. Soon, every station in Pittsburgh was playing it.

It's a Hit! Jackson's old band wasn't interested in getting back together, so he flew to Pittsburgh alone and began making appearances with a new group. Meanwhile, Roulette Records released "Hanky Panky" nationally. It became the #1 song in the country, and Tommy Jackson—now known as Tommy James—became one of the biggest pop stars of the late 1960s.

OH HAPPY DAY, (1967), The Edwin Hawkins Singers

Background: Edwin Hawkins assembled the 46-piece Northern California State Youth Choir in 1967. To raise money, he picked out eight members of the choir and recorded an album in the basement of a local church. It was never intended for any audience except the limited gospel market. When they sold 600 copies they were pleased.

Lucky Break: A San Francisco rock promoter found the album in a warehouse and gave it to popular S.F. deejay, Abe "Voco" Kesh.

It's a Hit! Kesh loved it. He played it so often that it became a local hit. Then it went national and sold over a million copies.

Ramses condoms are named after Ramses II, an Egyptian pharoah who fathered 160+ children.

MISS AMERICA, PART V: The 1960s

For a brief spell during the '60s, Miss America became a political as well as cultural symbol, caught in the crossfire between forces for change that saw it as an embarrassing relic, and traditionalists who saw it as a comforting connection to the "Leave It to Beaver" years.

MIDDLE AGE

The Miss America Pageant was tremendously popular in the 1950s and early 1960s....But by the late 1960s, it began to show its age. One of the problems was that the various pageant committees had become top-heavy with stodgy Atlantic City businessmen and society matrons, who had virtually nothing in common with the young women of the sixties. After decades of innovation, the pageant officials—many of whom had run the show since the 1930s and were defensively proud of their accomplishments—had become the greatest obstacle to further change.

Out of Fashion

Pageant director Lenora Slaughter's sense of fashion was the most visible manifestation of the problem: She fought nearly every new style in clothing, hair, shoes, and swimsuits that developed in the 1960s, and banned many of them outright, including miniskirts and bikinis. The "fashions" that were permitted were so out-of-date that many were nearly impossible to find in stores, as Miss New York 1969 recounted to Frank Deford in *There She Is:*

> We spent days shopping....There weren't many of the one-piece swimsuits around—I mean, you had no choice—and the shoes with the three-inch spiked heels, they were virtually impossible to find. The clothing styles had to reach within two inches of the knee, and they just weren't selling any dresses like that....All we could do was lengthen the dresses that we bought, but the problem was that we couldn't even find dresses long enough so that when we let them down they were long enough for the pageant.

By 1969 the pageant had gone from a fashion trendsetter to "nearly a complete laughingstock," Deford writes. Contestants "quickly discovered that they were not buying a wardrobe for a pageant; they were buying one for a weeklong costume party."

WHITES ONLY

Like many American cultural institutions, the Miss America Pageant had a history of tokenism and outright racism that caught up with it during the Civil Rights movement. From the very first pageant, Native American and Puerto Rican contestants—when they were allowed to participate at all—had been shunted off to the sidelines in noncompetitive "official guest" roles. Blacks were excluded entirely, except for the 1926 pageant, when a handful of black women played slaves on the King Neptune float in the Fall Frolic.

This began to change in the mid-1950s, when the pageant quietly dropped its whites-only clause—Rule No. 7. But that only applied to the national pageant. Left to their own devices, many state pageants (at least unofficially) continued to discriminate.

A TURNING POINT

Finally in the late 1960s, the pageant began to tackle its problems. This change was partly due to the fact that Lenora Slaughter retired in 1967 after 32 years as Pageant Director, and partly to the fact that the pressures for change had become overwhelming:

• In 1967 civil rights groups threatened demonstrations to protest the fact that there were no black pageant organizers, judges, or contestants more than 10 years after the whites-only rule was abandoned. In response, the pageant agreed to institute reforms.

• A year later Pepsi, a pageant sponsor since 1957, pulled its sponsorship out of concern that the pageant had lost touch with teenagers and young adults. One Pepsi spokesman told reporters, "Miss America as run today does not represent the changing values of our society." (Pepsi's slogan at the time: "Now it's Pepsi for those who think young.")

• Beginning in 1967, the National Organization of Women (NOW) and other feminist groups organized protests at the pageant, charging that the pageant was demeaning to women, racist, and pro-war. Or as one protester put it:

Maine is the only U.S. state with a one-syllable name.

It has always been a lily-white racist contest. The winner tours Vietnam entertaining the troops as a murder mascot. Where else could one find such a perfect combination of American values? Racism, militarism, and capitalism—all packaged in one "ideal" symbol: *a woman.*

The 1968 protests were the most colorful. According to Anne Marie Bivans in *Miss America: In Pursuit of the Crown*, "the feminists...marched on the Boardwalk, where they refused to speak with male reporters, chanted anti-pageant slogans, and tossed bras, girdles, makeup, and hair curlers into a 'freedom trashcan.' " Rumors also circulated that a feminist had infiltrated the pageant and would reveal herself onstage as soon as she was out of the running for the crown, but no one ever did.

The protests generated huge publicity, but after 1969 most feminist organizations backed off, as Deford explains: "The women had received so much serious attention that, practically speaking, they did not need Miss America any more. For one thing, they were beginning to get the uncomfortable feeling that they were becoming part of the show, halfway between the parade and the evening-gown competition."

And now, here it comes...the last section, on page 296.

☛   ☛   ☛   ☛

And Now for Something Completely Different: Ping Pong

• Lawn tennis has been popular with upper-crust Englishmen for centuries, but it can't be played in the rain. That's why someone invented "table tennis" in the 1890s.

• Because it was cheaper than regular tennis, it was also more accessible, and quickly became more popular than tennis had ever been. Parker Brothers brought it to the United States in 1902.

• Thanks to the Doppler effect, which changes the sound of an object as it travels toward or away from you, the sound a table tennis ball makes when it moves away from you is different from the sound it makes when it moves toward you. Because of this, early players nicknamed the game Wick-Wack, Click-Clack, Whiff-Whaff, and Flim-Flam, before they finally settled on Ping-Pong.

Illegible handwriting is known as "griffonage."

MARRIED…WITH CHILDREN

*Married…With Children is one of the longest-running sitcoms in
TV history. Who created it…and how did it become popular?
Glad you asked. Here's the BRI's quick answer.*

BURNOUT
In the mid-1980s, when the Fox TV network was still in
the planning stages, Fox programming chief Garth Angier
approached Michael Moye and Ron Leavitt about creating an
"alternative" sitcom.

• The two men had written for *The Jeffersons*, *Happy Days*, *Laverne
& Shirley*, and other hits. But they were sick of "sappy" sitcoms…
and besides, no network had ever gone up against the Big Three
and survived. Why work for a surefire loser?

• Angier, however, made them an offer they couldn't refuse. "He
said, 'You can do what you want. We'll leave you alone,'" Leavitt
recalls. "It sounded lofty—an alternative network…all this freedom. It was a good incentive, even if the network was going to fold
after the first season." They accepted the job.

ENTER THE BUNDYS
• "At the time," Moye relates, "there was *The Cosby Show* and a lot
of *Cosby*-like clones where everybody was really happy and lived up
to impossibly high ideals. Ron and I felt there was an audience of
people sitting there all that time going, 'Yeah, right.'"

• So they turned that formula on its head and created the Bundys:

✔ Al was a nerdy ex-jock, a hand-in-the-pants shoe salesman
who watched too much TV and bickered constantly with his wife,
Peg, a K-mart fashion queen too proud to work outside the home
and too lazy work inside it.

✔ Their offspring were the slippery Bud (named after the
beer) and the slutty Kelly, whose high school career counselor suggested she was best qualified for a job like "logging camp toy or the
other woman"

• Picked to play Al Bundy was Ed O'Neill, who'd once been draft-
ed by the Pittsburgh Steelers and had tried out for the role of Sam

Malone in *Cheers*. Peg Bundy was played by Katey Sagal, daughter of movie producer Boris Sagal and a former backup singer for Bob Dylan, Bette Midler, and Tanya Tucker.

OPENING NIGHT

• The show premiered on Sunday, April 5, 1987...and not even the people associated with it gave it much chance for survival. "I thought we'd maybe do six episodes and that'd be the end of it," O'Neill says. But it quickly grabbed an audience no mainstream sitcom had been able to reach—young men.

• It turned out to be the sleeper hit of the network lineup. But it wasn't until a crusader named Terry Rakolta turned her attention to *Married* that it became a TV institution. One evening in January 1989, Rakolta tuned in and saw "Her Cups Runneth Over," an episode in which Al searches lingerie shops for Peg's favorite bra.

• She was "so disgusted" that she sent her young children out of the room. In the following weeks she watched more episodes, made note of who the sponsors were, and fired off letters complaining about their support of the show. "I care that there are advertisers out there paying the freight for this," she told reporters. "They're taking my dollars and putting them into soft-core pornography."

GETTING NOTICED

• At first she didn't attract much attention. Then the president of Coca-Cola wrote Rakolta personally, saying he was "professionally, and personally embarrassed" that a Coke ad appeared on the show.

• The story made the front page of *The New York Times* and was covered by *Nightline* and *Geraldo*. The result: A number of companies, including Procter & Gamble, McDonald's and Kimberly-Clark, pulled *their* ads from the show.

• *Married...With Children* toned down its act for a while, but Rakolta's strategy ultimately backfired. The controversy generated so much publicity for the show that ratings went up, and it earned more in ad revenues than ever.

• In fact, the show became so successful that the Big Three networks began dumping *Cosby*-like sitcoms in favor of blue-collar "slob-coms," such as *Roseanne* and *Grace Under Fire*. By 1995, *Married...With Children* had become the longest-running sitcom on the air, and one of the most popular shows in syndication.

Do you dream in color? According to one source, only 5% of Americans do.

GROUCHO GETS ELECTED—ACT II

Here's more from Five Star Theater, the 1933 radio show starring Groucho as Waldorf Flywheel, and Chico as his sidekick, Ravelli.

Outside. Milling crowd. Car noises.

GUARD: You guys can't come in this door. If you wanta hear the Flywheel-Maxwell political debate, you've got to go around to the main entrance.

REPORTER: But we're from the press. We want to talk to one of the candidates, Mr. Flywheel, about tomorrow's election.

GUARD: Okay, come on in. Waldorf Flywheel's in that room down the hall. First door to the right.

PHOTOGRAPHER: Thanks.

REPORTER: Funny how this man Flywheel has jumped into prominence so suddenly.

PHOTOGRAPHER: Well, when Big Boss Plunkett gets behind a candidate, he's as good as elected.. Here's the room.

Knocks.

GROUCHO: Come in.

Door opens, closes.

PHOTOGRAPHER: Good evening, Mr. Flywheel, we're from the press.

GROUCHO: Good. You can press my pants.

REPORTER: No, we're from the newspapers. We want your views on tomorrow's election.

RAVELLI (runs in): Hey boss!

GROUCHO: What's the matter, Ravelli?

RAVELLI: There's some big crowd outside. When I tried to come in here, a policeman wanted to hit me.

GROUCHO: How do you know he wanted to hit you?

RAVELLI.: Because he hit me. Whatta you gonna do about it, boss?

GROUCHO: I'm busy now, but I'll thank him later.

REPORTER: Mr. Flywheel, our paper would like to get a record of all that you've done in this town.

RAVELLI: Come on, don't bother my boss. You can get his record at the police station.

GROUCHO: Shut up, Ravelli. Reporter, I'd like to say that everything I am I owe to my great-grandfather, old Cyrus Tecumseh Flywheel. If he were alive today, the whole world would be talking about him.

REPORTER: Why, Mr. Flywheel?

GROUCHO: Well, if he were alive today, he'd be a hundred and forty years old.

REPORTER: But...

RAVELLI: Excuse me, please, Mrs. Reporter. I got-a someting important to ask my boss. Hey, Flywheel, was that hair tonic you had in the bottle on your desk?

GROUCHO: No, it was glue.

RAVELLI: Glue? (Laughs) No wonder I can't get my hat off! ... Hey, here comes Big Boss Plunkett. He looks-a mad.

PLUNKETT: Flywheel!

GROUCHO: Just a minute, old boy, I want you to meet the reporters. Reporters, this is my friend and manager, Big Boss Plunkett. There are two things I want to say about Plunkett. First, he's never been in prison. And second, I don't know why.

PLUNKETT: See here...

PHOTOGRAPHER: Sorry to interrupt, but we've got to get back to the paper. And we'd like a photograph of Mr. Flywheel. Hold that smile, Mr. Flywheel. Here goes...Thank you! Goodbye!

Door shuts...followed by a knock.

PLUNKETT: Come in.

GUARD: Time for the debate.

PLUNKETT: Come on, boys . . . right through this door. This is a shortcut to the platform. Remember, Ravelli, I had a tough time getting you the job as chairman of this debate. Do you know anything about a debate?

RAVELLI: Ah-h, sure! I explain it to you. When you wanta catch de fish, you use-a debate.

GROUCHO: There you are, Plunkett. You'd have to go pretty far to find a better chairman than Ravelli. And I wish you had!

PLUNKETT: Come on!—right through this door.

Door opens, crowd is cheering, "We want Flywheel," "Hooray for Maxwell," etc.

ANNOUNCER: Ladies and gentlemen. The debate on judicial reform between Judge Herbert Maxwell and Waldorf Tecumseh Flywheel is about to begin. I now present the chairman of the meeting, Mr. Emmanuel Ravelli.

(Applause.)

RAVELLI : (in formal speaking voice): Alright, everybody...The foist guy I want to introduce is a man *everybody* is-a crazy about. A man who's good to little kids— and to big kids too... And he ain't afraid of nothin'! Ladies and gentlemen, that man is... *me!*

(Crowd claps loudly.)

What's up, Doc?: First uttered by Bugs Bunny in the 1940 cartoon "A Wild Hare."

Now I gonna call on Judge Maxwell.

JUDGE: Mr. Chairman, ladies and gentlemen. I was born in this city forty-eight years ago. I studied law here. I married here. And in all my forty-eight years, I…

GROUCHO: Just a minute, chairman.

RAVELLI: What you want, boss?

GROUCHO: If this guy's gonna talk only about himself, I'm going home.

JUDGE: Please, Mr. Flywheel, you'll get your chance later. Ladies and gentlemen, my candidacy is being fought by a group of men who are dishonest, grafting and meretricious!

RAVELLI: Tanks, judge. I wish you da same.

JUDGE: Wish me what?

RAVELLI: A meretricious. A meretricious and a Happy New Year!

JUDGE (furious): Mr. Chairman, will you let me go on with my speech? Fellow citizens, I…

RAVELLI (pounds gavel): At's-a all, Judge. Your time is up.

JUDGE : My time is up? Why, how long have I talked?

RAVELLI: I don't know. I haven't got a watch. You sit down. And now, people, you're gonna hear from my boss, Mister Flywheel, the winner of this debate.

GROUCHO: Well, folks, I'm sorry my speech had to be delayed, but Maxwell insisted on talking. (*Formal voice*) Fellow citizens, I'm here to tell you that a vote for Flywheel means a vote for free speech, free press, free-wheeling and free cheers for the red, white and blue. (*Crowd claps.*)

My esteemed opponent…is all steamed up. And why? Because I broke a few promises. Well, I can make new ones just as good. And to you women in the audience, I can only say that there's one thing I'll never forget, as long as I can remember it… and that is, that the mothers of some of our greatest men were women. (*Crowd claps.*)

JUDGE: Flywheel, I'd like to ask a question. Is it true your organization has bought 20,000 votes to swing tomorrow's election?

GROUCHO: I'm glad you brought that up. We did buy 20,000 votes.

JUDGE: What?

GROUCHO: But don't get excited. I've got good news for you.

JUDGE: Good news?

GROUCHO: Yes, we bought five thousand more votes than we need, and we'll sell 'em to you at cost price.

Who's the new judge? For election results, turn to page 294.

"Gilligan's Island" was inspired by Daniel Defoe's Robinson Crusoe.

CELEBRITY TAX TROUBLES

*It's not easy being famous, particularly if you haven't been paying
your taxes properly. Here's a look at some rich and famous people
who have fallen to earth with a thud, courtesy of the IRS.*

WILLIE NELSON

Tax Troubles: In 1990, the IRS slapped the country
singer with a bill for $32 million in delinquent taxes,
penalties, and interest—one of the biggest in history—after it disallowed his heavy tax shelter investments. Nelson blamed his Price
Waterhouse accountant, saying that their bad advice caused the
underpayments.

What Happened: Nelson's lawyers argued that since the accountants were to blame for his troubles, he should only be required to
pay the original taxes owed. The IRS ultimately agreed to charge
Nelson only $9 million, and gave him three years to pay it. He
raised the money by auctioning off property, signing over the rights
to an album called *Who'll Buy My Memories: The IRS Tapes*, handing over the proceeds from his lawsuit with Price Waterhouse, and
accepting donations from fans. "Willie is happy to be done with it,"
his lawyer told reporters after the last payment was made. "He has a
very good relationship with the IRS now."

PRESIDENT BILL CLINTON

Tax Troubles: In December 1993, the *Washington Post* revealed
that then-Governor Clinton had donated his underwear to the Salvation Army and claimed the donations as charitable deductions
on his income taxes. The deductions included $1 apiece for undershorts donated in '84, $2 apiece for 3 pairs of underwear donated in
'86, and $15 for a single pair of long underwear donated in '88.

What Happened: Making deductions for underwear donated to
charity is perfectly legal, provided you don't claim more than the
"fair market value" of the garments in your taxes. That's where
Clinton ran into trouble: he claimed too large a deduction on his
knickers. The actual fair market value of underwear for tax purposes is 5¢-6¢ a *pound*, even for skivvies worn by governors. (No
word on whether he ever made good on the overstated deductions.)

LEONA HELMSLEY

Tax Troubles: A few years after telling an employee that "only the little people pay taxes," the hotel queen was indicted on charges that she and her husband, hotel magnate Harry Helmsley, evaded $1.2 million in income taxes by billing their business for "personal items ranging from a marble dance floor to girdles."

What Happened: Harry was eventually deemed too incompetent to stand trial because of failing health, but Leona was convicted of tax evasion in December 1989, fined $7.1 million, and sentenced to four years in federal prison. She was paroled in October 1993 and began three years of probation, which included 250 hours of community service per year.

In 1995, Helmsley's employees complained to reporters that *they* were the ones performing community service. Helmsley, they said, forced them to do the court-assigned work—wrapping gifts and stuffing envelopes for charity. "We sat around our staff dining table like field hands shucking peas," one anonymous employee complained, "but instead of shucking, we were wrapping presents in between our regular duties." The judge tacked an additional 150 hours of community service on to Helmsley's sentence.

JOE LOUIS, "THE BROWN BOMBER"

Tax Troubles: Louis was heavyweight boxing champ from 1937 to 1949, a national hero who held the title longer than any boxer in history. Like many of us, he didn't fill out his own tax forms. His manager did…and he underpaid Louis's taxes so much that by the time the champ retired in 1949, he owed more than $1.25 million. Louis was forced to come out of retirement in 1950 and try to box his way out of his IRS troubles.

What Happened: Louis fought 10 times over the next year, but never recaptured his title and never made enough money to pay off the IRS. The agency filed liens against all of his assets, and even seized the $667 he inherited from his mother when she died. But it didn't come close to paying what he owed; he had to stoop to pro-wrestling to pay the bill. This helped him settle the tax issue, although not in the way he'd expected. As *Sports Illustrated* recounted in 1985:

Sympathy for him grew as the public came to believe that the IRS had hounded the former heavyweight champion into a degrading career in wrestling. After considerable frustration, the IRS agreed in the early 1960s to limit its collections to an amount [that] did not even cover the interest on his debt.

The IRS never officially closed the books on the case, it just stopped trying to collect. As the commissioner of the IRS explained it, "We have gotten all we could possibly get from Mr. Louis, leaving him with some hope that he can live." Nearly bankrupt, Louis spent much of the 1970s working as a "greeter" at Caesar's Palace in Las Vegas. He died in 1981.

MARVIN MITCHELSON

Tax Troubles: When Mitchelson, divorce attorney to the stars and Hollywood's "Prince of Palimony," dumped a client-turned-lover, she got revenge by contacting the IRS. In 1993, he was formally indicted for filing false returns between 1983 and 1986, during which he allegedly hid more than $2 million in income.

What Happened: Mitchelson filed for bankruptcy and was convicted on charges of tax fraud, for which he was sentenced to 30 months in prison and ordered to pay more than $2 million in back taxes. "This is the second-saddest day of my life," he told the judge on the day of sentencing. "My mother's death was the first."

JERRY LEE LEWIS

Tax Troubles: The IRS nailed the '50s rock star for non-payment of back taxes in the late '70s. They seized real estate, vehicles, and other assets, but his tax bill continued to grow. By 1994, the amount due had grown to $4.1 million.

What Happened: Lewis worked out a deal to pay only $560,000, less than 15¢ on the dollar. His secret: He didn't have any money.

Lewis raised the cash through a concert tour, a record, a biography, and by temporarily opening his home in Nesbit, Mississippi, to tourists. The tours were conducted by friends or Lewis's wife and included visits to the living room, den, and piano-shaped swimming pool in back—but not the bedrooms. Price of admission: $5, not bad considering that every once in a while the tour offered something Graceland didn't—a live rock star. "At least once a week," Mrs. Lewis explained, "Jerry Lee forgets they're there and walks out in his robe or wearing jeans and a T-shirt."

UNCLE ALBERT SEZ...

Albert Einstein had a few things to say that even we bathroom readers can understand. Like these....

"If a cluttered desk is a sign of a cluttered mind, of what, then, is an *empty* desk?"

"Only two things are infinite, the universe and human stupidity, and I'm not sure about the former."

"Sometimes one pays most for things one gets for nothing."

"Problems cannot be solved at the same level of awareness that created them."

"To make a goal of comfort or happiness has never appealed to me; a system of ethics built on this basis would be sufficient only for a herd of cattle."

"Education is what remains after one has forgotten everything he learned in school."

"Common sense is the collection of prejudices acquired by age eighteen."

"When the solution is simple, God is answering."

"What does a fish know about the water in which he swims all his life?"

"Knowledge is limited. Imagination encircles the world."

"My religion consists of the humble admiration of the illimitable superior spirit who reveals himself in the slight details we are able to perceive with our frail and feeble minds."

"Peace cannot be achieved through violence, it can only be attained through understanding."

"Gravitation cannot be held responsible for two people falling in love."

"He who joyfully marches to music in rank and file has already earned my contempt. He has been given a large brain by mistake, since for him, the spinal cord would fully suffice."

"The answer is 'yes' or 'no,' depending on the interpretation."

"Nothing will benefit human health and increase the chances for the survival of life on Earth as much as the evolution to a vegetarian diet."

Believe it or not: If a man's tie is too tight, his vision gets worse.

"LIFE" AFTER DEATH

Here's an interesting question: If you make it big after you're dead, is it really you who's succeeding? After all, you—at least theoretically—don't exist anymore. Woody Allen, reflecting on this, said: "I don't want to achieve immortality through my work...I want to achieve it through not dying." Our sentiments exactly. Here are 4 examples of folks who hit it big after death. Enjoy it...while you can.

JONATHAN LARSON

In 1992, Larson wrote a musical about New York artists struggling with AIDS. He sent the script and songs to the New York Theater Workshop. The artistic director was so impressed that he spent the next four years helping Larson develop the work, called *Rent*, for the stage. It was finally scheduled to open on January 26, 1996, and would have been the biggest moment of Larson's life. But he couldn't make it—he was found dead in his apartment on January 25, a few hours after the final dress rehearsal. Cause of death: an aortic aneurysm. He was 35.

Life After Death: The show opened to rave reviews and quickly became the hottest theater ticket in town; within weeks, the New York press was printing lists of celebrities—including Woody Allen—who wanted tickets but couldn't get them. *Rent* later moved to Broadway and won the 1996 Pulitzer Prize for drama.

JOHN KENNEDY TOOLE

During the 1950s, while he was in the army, Toole wrote a novel called *A Confederacy of Dunces*. For years he tried to get it published. Finally, in 1967, Simon and Schuster expressed some interest; he was ecstatic. Unfortunately, in 1969—after Toole had spent two years on rewrites—the publisher rejected it. Toole, 31, didn't wait to see what happened next. He committed suicide.

Life After Death: Toole's mother found the manuscript among his belongings and spent the next seven years trying to get it published. In 1976, she convinced novelist Walker Percy to read it...and he convinced Louisiana State University to print 2,500 copies. An inauspicious beginning...but the novel got glowing reviews, and a major publisher picked it up. It went on to sell more than 650,000 copies and win the 1981 Pulitzer Prize for fiction.

Why did Napoleon lose at Waterloo? Among other things, he was bedridden with hemorrhoids.

OTIS REDDING

One of pop's great singers, Redding had never had a Top 10 hit, and he was determined to break into the mainstream market. So in 1967 he went to the Monterey Pop Festival and triumphantly performed with people like Janis Joplin and Jimi Hendrix. Afterward, Redding spent a week on a houseboat outside of San Francisco, "just wastin' time." He dreamed up a little pop tune called "Dock of the Bay," brought it back to Memphis, and put it on tape, planning to get back to it when he returned from a tour. Three days later, he died in a plane crash.

Life After Death: Redding's co-writer, guitarist Steve Cropper, went back into the studio and finished the record. It became the first posthumous #1 record in history.

HANK WILLIAMS

In 1952, a singer named Big Bill Lister got his first contract with a major record company. He knew country star Hank Williams, and asked if Williams had any songs he could use. To help Lister out, Hank gave him "There's a Tear in My Beer," a song he'd just written and recorded on a single acetate demo record. Lister included the tune on his album. A few months later, the 29-year-old Williams died from alcohol poisoning.

Life After Death: Lister lost track of Williams's acetate recording until 1988, when he found it while cleaning out his house. He sent it to Hank Williams, Jr. The younger Williams, now a country star in his own right, had been only three years old when his father died, so he'd never had the chance to record with him...until now. He took "There's a Tear in My Beer" into the studio, cleaned it up, and created a duet by mixing his own vocals with his father's.

Hank Jr. even made a video of "There's a Tear in My Beer." He took a film of his father singing a different song and superimposed someone else's lips onto the face. Both the song and the video became huge bestsellers, even winning the Country Music Association's Vocal Event of the Year award.

Note: Since then, other "direct from the grave" duets have been hits. Natalie Cole even won a Grammy singing with her dead father, Nat "King" Cole.

The song "You're a Grand Old Flag" was originally called "You're a Grand Old Rag."

WEIRD DOLLS

*Here are a few more unusual dolls that you could have
bought at your local toy store…but probably didn't.*

EARRING MAGIC KEN

In 1993, Mattel decided to give Barbie's boyfriend a new
look: it introduced "Earring Magic Ken" to its line of Ken
dolls, complete with two-tone hair, a pink mesh shirt, a lavender
"leather" vest, a plastic ring around his neck, and a single earring
in one ear. "Ken's still a clean-cut guy," a Mattel spokesman explained to reporters. "He's just a little more contemporary."

Yeah, sure. "You can't look at Earring Magic Ken and *not* think
gay," Chicago gay rights advocate Rick Garcia told reporters. "He's
stereotypically gay—it's what you saw men wearing a few years
back. And that plastic ring that Ken wears around his neck looks
an awful lot like what gay men were buying at sex shops."

Retailers agreed. "We sold out in less than a month and we had
to reorder them," one toy salesperson told reporters. "And it's primarily gay men who are buying them. Most customers just ask specifically for 'The Gay Ken Doll.' "

Mattel was shocked. "We gave him an earring and two-tone hair
to make him look cool and hip," protested one company official,
"and lavender clothing because it's a girl's second favorite color
after pink."

THE J. J. ARMES DOLL

Ideal Toys had a big success with its Evel Knievel line of toys in the
mid-1970s, so in 1976, they based another toy on a real-life human
being—Jay J. Armes, a multimillionaire Texas private eye.

The real Armes was the James Bond of El Paso, complete with
a karate blackbelt, a bomb-detecting Cadillac, a smokescreen-
spewing Corvette, and a walled-in estate that he patrolled himself
with a 750-pound Siberian tiger on a leash. He'd built one of the
most successful detective agencies in the country, commanding fees
as high as $250,000 per assignment from clients like Elvis Presley,
J. Paul Getty, and Marlon Brando.

Perhaps even more interesting to the folks at Ideal was the fact that the real Armes had no hands—he had lost both of them at the age of 11 playing with dynamite blasting caps in his backyard and had worn prosthetics ever since. Most of the time he wore steel hooks, but he also had custom-made prosthetic guns that shot real bullets. Ideal figured that Armes would make a perfect action figure, and sold the J. J. Armes doll with a large suitcase full of interchangeable prosthetic machetes, magnets, suction cups, and other gadgets.

It was a flop. Ideal speculates that the doll bombed for a number of reasons: (1) kids had never heard of Armes; (2) the adventures of a real-life detective can actually be pretty boring; and (3) a lot of youngsters were spooked by the idea of pretending to be a man with hooks for hands. "Kids would find it very difficult to role-play a man with two artificial arms," one (former) Ideal executive admitted afterwards. "I don't even think you'd want to. I would be kind of squeamish about it myself."

THE PET CONGRESSMAN

Described in press reports as a "fuzzy little bow-tied lawmaker doll," it was introduced in 1992 by a Maryland businessman after he noted the similarities between his pet dog and his representatives in government. "I realized congressmen are like pets," he told interviewers. "They wet the rug, and you get mad at them. But you still elect them and keep them."

The dolls were packaged in a "dome-shaped wire cage" designed to resemble the U.S. Capitol and came with a 15-page owner's manual that explained that the pint-sized politico "expects to be entertained frequently by his owner, but will rarely offer to pick up the tab." Not surprisingly, former President Ronald Reagan bought one for his Los Angeles office. But not everyone thought the dolls were funny. One chain store refused to carry them because they were "an inappropriate way to recognize a congressman."

MARYBEL GET WELL

The hypochondriac doll from Madame Alexander. Came with crutches, a cast for her leg, bandages, pills, quarantine signs, and measles spots.

COURT TRANSQUIPS

We never imagined that court transcripts would make good bathroom reading. But that was before we read Humor in the Court *and* More Humor in the Court, *by Mary Louise Gilman, editor of the* National Shorthand Reporter. *Here are a few excerpts from these two funny volumes of "courtroom bloopers." Remember—these are actual courtroom transcripts.*

THE COURT: "Now, as we begin, I must ask you to banish all present information and prejudice from your minds, if you have any."

Q: "What is your brother-in-law's name?"
A: "Borofkin."
Q: "What's his first name?"
A: "I can't remember."
Q: "He's been your brother-in-law for years, and you can't remember his first name?"
A: "No. I tell you I'm too excited."
[Rising from the witness chair and pointing to Mr. Borofkin.]
"Nathan, for God's sake, tell them your first name!"

Q: "Did you ever stay all night with this man in New York?"
A: "I refuse to answer that question."
Q: "Did you ever stay all night with this man in Chicago?"
A: "I refuse to answer that question."
Q: "Did you ever stay all night with this man in Miami?"
A: "No."

Q: "What is your name?"
A: "Ernestine McDowell."
Q: "And what is your marital status?"
A: "Fair."

Q: "Doctor, how many autopsies have you performed on dead people?"
A: "All my autopsies have been performed on dead people."

Q: "Are you married?"
A: "No, I'm divorced."
Q: "And what did your husband do before you divorced him?"
A: "A lot of things I didn't know about."

Q: "How did you happen to go to Dr. Cherney?"
A: "Well, a gal down the road had had several of her children by Dr. Cherney, and said he was really good."

Q: "Do you know how far pregnant you are right now?"
A: "I will be three months November 8th."
Q: "Apparently then, the date of conception was August 8th?"
A: "Yes."
Q: "What were you and your husband doing at that time?"

Q: "Doctor, did you say he was shot in the woods?"
A: "No, I said he was shot in the lumbar region."

Q: "Mrs. Smith, do you believe that you are emotionally unstable?"
A: "I should be."
Q: "How many times have you committed suicide?"
A: "Four times."

Q: "Were you acquainted with the deceased?"
A: "Yes, sir."
Q: "Before or after he died?"

Q: "What happened then?"
A: "He told me, he says, 'I have to kill you because you can identify me.' "
Q: "Did he kill you?"
A: "No."

Q: "Mrs. Jones, is your appearance this morning pursuant to a deposition notice which I sent to your attorney?"
A: "No. This is how I dress when I go to work."

On just one square inch of your skin, there are 20 million microscopic animals.

JESSE'S BIG NUMBERS

Uncle John's six-year-old son, Jesse, has been asking questions about numbers lately, like "What comes after a trillion?" and "What's a billion billion?" We'd never thought much about that before, but it's pretty interesting. Here's a page that Jesse will enjoy.

HOW MUCH IS A BILLION?
Depends on where you are. In the United States, 1,000 is used as a multiplier for big numbers: a million is 1,000 thousands; a billion is 1,000 millions; a trillion is 1,000 billions, and so on.

But in many other places (Britain, Spain and Latin America, for example), they use 1,000,000 (one million) as the multiplier. A million is still 1,000 thousands. But a billion is *one million* millions; a trillion is *one million billion*, and so on. Big difference.

WHAT COMES AFTER A TRILLION?

Uncle John's standard answer: a trillion and one. But there's a whole universe of numbers that most of us have never heard of which follow a million, a billion, and a trillion. Here are some, in U.S. numerical terms:

Quadrillion: 1,000 trillion
Quintillion: 1,000 quadrillion
Sextillion: 1,000 quintillion
Septillion: 1,000 sextillion
Octillion: 1,000 septillion
Nonillian: 1,000 octillion
Decillion: 1,000 nonillion
Undecillion: 1,000 decillion
Duodecillion: 1,000 undecillion

Tredecillion: 1,000 duodecillion
Quattuordecillion: 1,000 tredecillion
Quindecillion: 1,000 quattuordecillion
Sexdecillion: 1,000 quindecillion
Septendecillion: 1,000 sexdecillion
Octodecillion: 1,000 septendecillion
Novemdecillion: 1,000 octodecillion
Vigintillion: 1,000 novemdecillion

• How do these numbers look on paper? To give you a sense of scale:

Trillion: 1,000,000,000,000
Quadrillion: 1,000,000,000,000,000
Septillion: 1,000,000,000,000,000,000,000,000
Quattuordecillion:
1,000,000,000,000,000,000,000,000,000,000,000,000,000,000,000

The word "furniture" originally applied to portable military equipment.

WHAT'S THE BIGGEST NUMBER?

Theoretically, you could probably keep going forever. But practically speaking:

• According to *The Mathematics Calendar 1996*, by Theoni Pappas, the "illions" haven't really been used beyond vigintillion. Why? "Perhaps," suggests one mathematician, "most everyday phenomena can be covered by these huge numbers."

• Nonetheless, books list some bigger numbers. Among the "illions," for example, is the number *centillion*—1,000, followed by 300 zeroes, or:

1,000,000,000,000,000,000,000,000,000,000,000,000,000,
000,000,000,000,000,000,000,000,000,000,000,000,000,000,
000,000,000,000,000,000,000,000,000,000,000,000,000,000,
000,000,000,000,000,000,000,000,000,000,000,000,000,000,
000,000,000,000,000,000,000,000,000,000,000,000,000,000,
000,000,000,000,000,000,000,000,000,000,000,000,000,000,
000,000,000,000,000,000,000,000,000,000

• To deal with the "biggest number" question, one mathematician created a sort of catch-all number that has come into general use—the *googolplex*. By his reasoning, a googol is a one followed by 100 zeroes. And a googolplex is a one followed by a googol of zeroes. Presumably, we don't need any number larger than that.

HOW MUCH IS A ZILLION?

As one mathematician writes: "A zillion falls into the same category as a few, some, a lot, many. A zillion is deceiving since it ends in -illion, but it is no more specific than saying 'a tremendous amount.' "

WHERE DOES INFINITY FIT IN?

When exact numbers aren't big enough, there's always infinity, defined as "a concept of limitlessness." Or, practically speaking, a number too big for our minds to grasp or our language to describe.

When Uncle John was a kid, his sister asked: "What's bigger than infinity?" This stumped Uncle John. The answer was "infinity, +1." That sounded pretty clever, and Uncle John repeated it for years. But the truth is that since infinity goes on forever, you can't stop it at a single digit. Infinity + 1 still equals infinity.

According to the Bible, there were two windows on Noah's Ark.

THE MONSTER LIVES!

*When Universal Pictures coined the term "horror movie" in 1931,
it was because of this film…and Boris Karloff, the actor who brought the
monster to life. As one critic puts it: "Just as the monster of the story was
stitched together from pieces of the dead, Universal's cinematic Monster was
stitched together from the genius of Jack Pierce's makeup, James Whale's
direction, and Boris Karloff's performance. The results were so perfect
that the image of the Frankenstein monster, as seen in this classic
film, has become ingrained into the fabric of our culture."*

LUCKY BREAK

Have you ever heard of William Henry Pratt? Most people haven't. In late 1920s he was an unemployed actor, making ends meet by driving a truck for a lumber yard. In 1931, he landed a small part playing a gangster in a movie called *The Criminal Code*. It happened to premiere just as director James Whale began his search for someone to play the monster in *Frankenstein*.

A friend of Whale's saw the film, noticed Pratt, and suggested that the director take a look at him. So Whale went to see *The Criminal Code*. He was impressed with Pratt's work…but more important, he recognized that Pratt's gaunt features, exaggerated with lots of makeup, would make an excellent monster-face.

Whale drew some preliminary sketches of Pratt as the monster and showed them to Jack Pierce, head of Universal's makeup department. Then he approached Pratt about playing the part. Years later, Pratt recalled how he learned about the role:

> I'd spent 10 years in Hollywood without causing the slightest stir. Then one day I was sitting in the commissary at Universal, having lunch, and looking rather well turned out, I thought, when a man sent a note over to my table, asking if I'd like to audition for the part of a monster.

THE NAME GAME

Pratt took a screen test and got the job on the spot. But he didn't get public *acknowledgment* for the role until much later. He wasn't

---

What do pediatricians do when their kids get colds? 63% say they "let them run their course."

considered an important member of the cast, so the studio didn't even bother to list his name in the credits. Only a question mark appears next to the words "The Monster"

Within a year, however, Pratt's name would become a household word....Or at least his *stage* name would: Universal Pictures thought that "William Henry Pratt" sounded too ordinary for such an exotic monster and asked him to change it to something a little more unusual. Pratt picked a name that would be synonymous with horror for over 35 years—*Boris Karloff*.

MAKEUP

Universal put Jack Pierce, head of the studio's makeup department, in charge of creating Karloff's makeup. He prepared for the job by studying anatomy, surgery, electrodynamics, and criminology. It was this research that led to the monster's unusual flat-topped skull, as Pierce later related to *The New York Times*:

> My anatomical studies taught me that there are six ways a surgeon can cut the skull in order to take out or put in a brain. I figured that Frankenstein, who was a scientist but no practicing surgeon, would take the simplest surgical way. He would cut the top of the skull off straight across like a pot-lid, hinge it, pop the brain in, and then clamp it on tight. That is the reason I decided to make the Monster's head square and flat like a shoe box and dig that big scar across his forehead with the metal clamps holding it together.

Pierce also added a caveman-like protruding brow to suggest de-evolution, and Karoly Grosz, a Universal poster illustrator, came up with the idea of putting steel bolts in the monster's neck.

FACE FACTS

Karloff had several false teeth on the right side of his mouth; these were removed to give his already gaunt face an even more hollow appearance. This look was further accentuated when Karloff himself suggested to Pierce that his eyelids be heavily puttied with embalmers' wax, which gave the monster a sense of pathos.

The rest of the facial makeup was applied to *accent* rather than cover up Karloff's natural features, so that his face would retain its expressiveness. "We were all fascinated by the development of Karloff's face and head," Mae Clarke later recalled. "White putty on the face was toned down to a corpse-like gray. Then there was a sudden inspiration to give the face a green tint. It awed us and gave Boris and the rest of us a different feeling about the whole concept." The movie was filmed entirely in black and white (that's all there was back then) but in some prints of the film, Universal had Karloff's face tinted green by hand before they were distributed to theaters.

BODY LANGUAGE

"Karloff's face fascinated me," James Whale would recall years later. "His physique was weaker than I could wish, but that queer, penetrating personality of his, I felt, was more important than his shape, which could be easily altered." And alter it they did:

• Karloff's frame was stiffened by a five-pound spinal brace that ran up his back and steel struts in his legs.

• He also wore platform asphalt spreader's boots, which weighed twelve and a half pounds apiece.

• On top of the braces, Karloff wore padding and on top of that a thick, double-quilted suit that added tremendous bulk to his frame; its sleeves were cut short to make his arms appear longer than they really were. All in all, the braces, struts, boots, and costume weighed more than forty-eight pounds.

TEST RUN

Even after Karloff was fully made up, he wasn't sure whether the makeup was truly scary or not—would it frighten people, or just make them laugh? As he recounted years later,

> I was thinking this while practicing my walk, as I rounded a bend in the corridor and came face-to-face with this prop man. He was the first man to see the monster—I watched to study his reaction. It was quick to come. He turned white—gurgled and lunged out of sight down the corridor. Never saw him again. Poor chap, I would have liked to thank him—he was the audience that first made me *feel* like the monster.

IN THE THEATER

When Universal previewed *Frankenstein* before test audiences in

One ounce of gold can be beaten thin enough to cover an entire acre of ground.

Santa Monica, they noticed two important things:

1. It was Karloff's monster, not the other characters, who made the film work. This was real horror for panicked Universal execs. They'd considered Karloff unimportant and neglected to put him under contract. They quickly called his agent and signed him up. Karloff's response: "After more than 20 years of acting, for once I'll know where my next breakfast is coming from."

2. The film made people fidgety and squeamish. Rather than downplay the response, the studio decided to publicize it. They added a prologue, warning filmgoers what they were in for. Edward Van Sloan, who played Dr. Frankenstein's mentor, Dr. Waldman, told audiences:

> Mr. Carl Laemmle [head of Universal] feels it would be a little unkind to present this picture without a word of friendly warning.... [Frankenstein] is one of the strangest stories ever told....It will thrill you,...It may shock you. It might even—horrify you! So, then, if you feel that you do not care to subject your nerves to such a strain, now is your chance to—well, we've warned you!

Theaters around the country added to the hype by posting nurses in the lobby, making free "nerve tonic" available to those who needed it, and other gimmicks. One movie house in Texas even hired a woman to sit in the empty theater and watch the film alone. But the publicity wasn't necessary—*Frankenstein* was one of the biggest hits of 1931 and went on to become one of the all-time classic Hollywood films. To this day, Boris Karloff's sensitive portrayal of the monster is the performance by which all other monster movies are measured.

GONE TO PIECES

By the late 1930s, it seemed like *Frankenstein* might finally be dying. Boris Karloff, who'd played the monster in *Frankenstein* (1931), *Bride of Frankenstein* (1935), and *Son of Frankenstein* (1939), hammered the first nail in the creature's coffin when he announced that he'd grown weary of the role. As David Skal writes in *The Monster Show*, Karloff "suspected that the monster would be increasingly relegated to the role of prop or buffoon" and didn't want to be part of it.

What do Pompeii, Niagara Falls, and Shakespeare's birthplace have

It didn't take long for Karloff's prediction to come true. With each new film Universal released—*Frankenstein Meets the Wolf Man* (1943), *The House of Frankenstein* (1944), and *The House of Dracula* (1945), the monster became less frightening. The studio finished the job in 1948, when it ended its Frankenstein series with *Abbott and Costello Meet Frankenstein*. Karloff agreed to help promote that film...as long as he didn't have to watch it.

KID STUFF

But even as familiarity worked against Frankenstein films, demographics were working in their favor. Thanks to the post-World War II baby boom, younger viewers were making up an increasingly large share of the movie audience. By 1958, 72% of all moviegoers were between the ages of 12 and 25.

Hollywood started making movies especially for teenagers—and they quickly found out that teenagers loved horror films. Sticking a monster, vampire, or werewolf into a film became an easy way to increase ticket sales.

Low-budget studios like American International Pictures (*I Was a Teenage Werewolf*) couldn't use Karloff's familiar monster because Universal Studios owned a copyright on *that* Frankenstein "look." But they could use the *name* Frankenstein because it was in the public domain (which means no one owns it).

And they did use it—hundreds of times. "Frankenstein" became a generic term for any manmade monster. He showed up in theaters as an alien, a sex fiend, a "demon of the atomic age," a resurrected teenage auto wreck victim, and so on; 65 years later, the Frankenstein movies keep on coming. As *The Videohound's Complete Guide to Trash Pics and Cult Flicks* says:

> Frankenstein lives in the movies better than anywhere else. With dozens of films based directly on characters from the novel, not to mention the hundreds with at least a tenuous connection to it, it may be the single most adapted work in all of cinema. No other name draws audiences so well.

Boris Karloff, the man who made Frankenstein—and horror films—a part of our culture, died in 1969. But he's been granted a weird kind of immortality. Every time a mad scientist builds a monster onscreen, it's an homage to Karloff's genius.

FRANKENSTEIN MEETS THE SPACE MONSTER

Some of these Frankenstein films are pretty watchable. Others are so bad, only a dedicated fan could even consider sitting through them. These are real movies—we didn't make them up!

1. *Frankenstein Meets the Space Monster* (1965)
NASA builds a robot named Frank and sends it into space, where it meets a space monster and goes berserk.

2. *Assignment Terror* (1971)
An alien lands on Earth, brings Frankenstein, Dracula, the Mummy, and other monsters to life, "but is thwarted by the socially aware Wolf Man."

3. *Jesse James Meets Frankenstein's Daughter* (1965)
Frankenstein's granddaughter, Maria, tries to capture Jesse James and his sidekick to turn them into monsters.

4. *I Was a Teenage Frankenstein* (1957)
A descendant of Dr. Frankenstein moves to America, where he sets up a lab and begins building monsters out of the bodies of hot rod racers killed in car accidents.

5. *Frankenhooker* (1980)
After a woman dies in a freak lawnmower accident, her mad-scientist boyfriend brings her back to life by sewing her head onto body parts taken from prostitutes on New York's 42nd Street.

6. *Frankenstein General Hospital* (1988)
Frankenstein's 12th grandson tries his experiments in the basement of a modern hospital.

7. *Frankenstein Conquers the World* (1964)
"A boy eats the radioactive heart of the Frankenstein monster and begins to grow into an ugly giant that watches Japanese teenagers do the Twist" (*The Frankenstein Movie Guide*). Japanese title: *Frankenstein vs. the Giant Crab Monster*.

Elephants can run 20 miles per hour; hummingbirds can fly 60 miles per hour.

8. *Frankenstein on Campus* (1970)
A college student plots to turn his fellow-students into monsters.
"If you can sit through this tripe, go to the head of the class."
(*Creature Features Movie Guide*)

9. *Frankenstein Island* (1981)
"A group of balloonists crash on a mysterious island populated by
bikini-clad warrior-women descended from aliens....Frankenstein's
great-great granddaughter Sheila, is around...experimenting on
captives." (*Frankenstein Movie Guide*)

10. *Frankenstein Created Woman* (1966)
"Male spirit is transplanted into the body of a beautiful woman
with heaving bosom, who then goes around stabbing respectable
folks with a knife." (*Creature Features Movie Guide*)

11. *Frankenstein 1970* (1958)
A descendant of Dr. Frankenstein sells the TV rights to his famous
ancestor's story and uses the money to build an atomic-powered
Frankenstein monster. The studio thought a futuristic-sounding
title would help at the box office.

12. *Frankenstein's Daughter* (1958)
Frankenstein's grandson tests a drug called *degeneral* on a teenage
girl, and it "degenerates her into a bikini-clad creature running
through the streets."

13. *Frankenstein '80* (1979)
Dr. Otto Frankenstein puts together a sex-crazed monster who goes
on a killing spree. Lots of blood, including real surgical footage.

14. *Frankenstein's Castle of Freaks* (1973)
Using his "Electric Accumulator," Count Frankenstein brings back
Goliath the caveman, Kreegin the Hunchback, and Ook the Nean-
derthal Man! *South Pacific* star Rossano Brazzi—"sounding like a
cross between Chico Marx and Bela Lugosi"—plays the Count.

15. *Frankenstein's Great-Aunt Tillie* (1983)
Victor Jr. and his 109-year-old aunt "search for the family fortune
and become involved with women's emancipation." (*The Frankenstein Movie Guide*)

Long wait: The "longest recorded interval" between the birth of twins was 136 days.

THE WORLD'S MOST FAMOUS CORPSE

More people have seen Lenin's mummy than any other mummy in history. It's a tourist attraction, a cultural artifact, and as you'll see, a political gimmick. How did this weird monument—denounced by Lenin's official historian as an "absurd idea"—come into being? Here's the full story.

L enin's tomb in Moscow's Red Square is the best-known landmark in the Soviet Union, as well as the spiritual center of Soviet political ideology. Some 150 million people have visited the mausoleum since it was first built….

There are always long lines, but you should expect to be descending the gloomy stairs into the tomb within 20-30 minutes. Without stopping, you walk around three sides of the glass case in which Lenin lies, stubbly and ashen-faced, wearing a jacket and polka-dot tie.

—*Travel Guide to the Soviet Union*

DEATH OF A LEADER

At 6:50 p.m. on January 21, 1924, Vladimir Ilyich Lenin, first leader of the Soviet Union and father of his country, suffered a stroke and died.

No one was sure how to handle it. Lenin had asked for a simple funeral. He wished to be buried next to his mother and sister in the family burial plot. But when Soviet leaders met to discuss the matter, they came up with another idea—turn the funeral into a "propaganda event" that could help legitimize the Communist regime. They decided to embalm him so he could lie in state for a while.

Then, only three days after his death, the Politburo began discussing the idea of saving the body "a little longer." Lenin's relatives balked at the idea…but Joseph Stalin insisted. As Dmitri Volkogonov writes in *Lenin: A New Biography*, Stalin "came to see [preserving Lenin's body] as the creation of a secular Bolshevik relic with huge propaganda potential." A short time later, the Politburo issued the following orders:

1. The coffin containing V. I. Lenin's corpse is to be kept in a vault which should be made accessible to visitors;

2. The vault is to be formed in the Kremlin wall on Red Square among the communal graves of the fighters of the October Revolution. A commission is being created today for the construction of a mausoleum.

A burial vault was dug along the Kremlin wall, a wooden hut was built over it to keep out the elements, and Lenin's body was placed inside following the funeral.

CORPSE OF ENGINEERS

Meanwhile, the secret police were rounding up the country's top scientists to put them to work figuring out how to embalm Lenin for eternity. A streetcar was towed into Red Square and fitted with beds, hot plates, and washbasins; it served as the terrified scientists' home for the rest of the winter.

But restoring Lenin to his former glory was not so easy. Illness had ravaged him in the final years of his life, leaving him frail-looking and emaciated. And since permanent, *lifelike* embalming had never been attempted before, research on how to accomplish such a task had to begin from scratch. In the meantime, the body continued to deteriorate.

Lenin's cadaver was packed in ice to slow the decay, and by June the scientists finally succeeded in "stabilizing" the body. By then, however, it was a mess. "In those four and a half months," historian Robert Payne writes in *The Life and Death of Lenin*, "remarkable changes had taken place: he was waxen gray, wrinkled, horribly shrunken." Nonetheless, by August 1924, Lenin's body had been cleaned up enough to put on public display.

STAYING IN SHAPE

Work on *improving* Lenin's after-death appearance would continue for more than 25 years. The task was handled by the Research Institute for "Biological Structures" (a Soviet euphemism for cadaver) and its Lenin Mausoleum Laboratory—both of which were so secret that the West did not learn of their existence until after the

Every 7 years, your body grows the equivalent of an entirely new skeleton.

collapse of the Soviet Union. Part of the routine that was worked out over the years:

• To prevent Lenin from decomposing, the temperature in the mausoleum is kept at precisely 59°F. The humidity is also kept constant.

• Every Monday and Friday, the mausoleum is closed and a senior official of the institute's "body brigade" (most of whom log 20 years or more on the job before they are allowed to touch the corpse) removes Lenin's clothing and examines the cadaver for any signs of wear and tear. Any dust that has accumulated is carefully brushed away; then a special preservative ointment is applied to the skin. The corpse is then re-dressed and put back on display.

• Every 18 months, the cadaver is bathed in preservatives and injected with chemicals, which displace both water and bacteria in the cells and prevent the tissues from decomposing. Which chemicals are used in the process? Hardly anyone knows—even today, the "recipe" is as closely guarded a secret as the formula for Coca-Cola. Only the eight most senior members of the institute know the precise formula. When the process is completed, the cadaver is given a brand-new, hand-tailored suit.

KEEPING THE FAITH

As of 1996, more than five years after the collapse of the Soviet empire, Lenin's body was still on display in Red Square. Keeping the mausoleum open is no empty gesture—the corpse requires constant attention and a lot of money to keep it in good condition. But for many, it has become the political shrine that Stalin envisioned…and the Russian government fears that giving Lenin a regular burial will create a political backlash. Seventy-two years after he died, Lenin is still—literally—a political presence to be reckoned with.

MUMMIFIED FACTS

• **Wasted effort.** Soviet scientists continued perfecting their embalming techniques until the 1950s…just in time for the death of Joseph Stalin. He, too, was embalmed, then laid to rest alongside Lenin. But *that* turned out to be a waste of time. Eight years later, Nikita Khruschev ordered Stalin's body removed and buried in a more modest grave along the Kremlin wall.

A giraffe's neck has 7 vertebrae; a bird's has 14; a person's has 26.

• **Mummies for sale.** Budget cuts brought on by the collapse of the Soviet Union have forced the Research Institute for Biological Structures to make its services available to the public. The mummification process takes a full year, requires the removal of all organs, and costs around $500,000. "The precise cost depends on the condition of the body," an official explains. "But our work is the best." The $500,000, by the way, only covers the cost of the embalming—you still have to build a mausoleum with temperature and humidity controls, which the institute estimates will cost as much as $5 million...not including the cost of staffing it forever.

• **No-brainer.** In 1924, Lenin's brain was removed and handed over to the Soviet Brain Institute—an organization founded specifically to determine whether the Leader's brain was superior to other human brains. Not surprisingly, they reported in 1936 that the brain "possessed such high organization that even during Lenin's illness, it continued to function on a very high level." Alas, it was just propaganda. In 1994, the Brain Institute's director admitted that "in the anatomical structure of Lenin's brain, there is nothing sensational."

CADAVER CONSPIRACY?

Is the body on display in Lenin's Tomb really *his* body? The official word is yes. But throughout the late 1920s and 1930s, rumors spread that the embalmers had actually failed in their task. According to the story, the body in the mausoleum is a wax dummy.

This rumor is so widely accepted that the Soviet government opened an official "investigation" into the matter and invited a German doctor to participate and report his findings to the world. But the inquiry only heightened suspicions. As Payne reports, the German doctor

> was not permitted to make more than a cursory examination. He reported that he had observed frostbites on the skin, felt the cheeks, and lifted one of Lenin's arms....He inquired about the techniques and was told they were secret but would be fully revealed in three or four years' time when they had been proved effective; and nothing more was ever heard about the secret formula.

Even after the fall of Communism in Russia, no one (except for the government) knows for sure whether the corpse is real.

KNIFE-STYLES OF THE RICH AND FAMOUS

BRI member Erik Linden sent us this amazing article on plastic surgery in L.A. It's from Marie Claire *magazine, written by Sally Ogle Davis.*

At Hollywood's Oscar show, filmland's biggest night of the year, you can count on three things: tearful acceptance speeches, over-the-top gowns, and a TV audience that includes every L.A. plastic surgeon worth his or her scalpel. It's their award ceremony too. Where else can they see their carefully crafted handiwork displayed to over one billion people worldwide?

Plastic surgeon Dr. Frank Kamer, who's lifted more famous faces than the elevator at CAA—Liz Taylor, Cher, Jane Fonda, Dolly Parton, and Joan Rivers, to name a few—sits in his elegant pastel-hued clinic in Beverly Hills, smiling wryly. "They're happy their careers are going well," he says of his celebrity patients. "Whether I had something to do with that I don't know. But I think I did."

Others agree. At the bar at the Four Seasons Hotel, agents talk about the two plumped-up reasons why Demi Moore, 33, is worth a million more per picture than Julia Roberts, while the plastic surgeons at the next table prefer to focus on Demi's nose. "She had it done right after her Vanity Fair cover," said one. "Her's was the rounded kind that doesn't age well," sniffed another. "It's surprising she got as far as she did with the original."

GETTING STAR TREATMENT

Welcome to L.A.….without question, the plastic surgery capital of America. Every year, four times as many breasts are enlarged in L.A. as on the entire eastern seaboard. Twice as many faces are lifted there as in New York….Los Angelenos flock to surgeons' offices…demanding "Kim Basinger's lips," "Cher's cheekbones," "Demi's breasts."

Today in L.A., you need never be fat, flat chested, or, God forbid, old.…The magazines on the newsstands are chockablock with ads for liposuction artists, chemical peelers, laser surgeons, and eye debaggers, [and] hairdressers around town are experts at hiding scars.…

You can't take it with you: When Empress Elizabeth of Russia died in 1762, she owned 15,000 dresse

"It's pretty routine to us," says…the 66-year-old wife of a wealthy building contractor. She's had her neck redraped, her eyes de-bagged, and her upper lip chemically peeled. Only two weeks after her third face-lift, she looks 50. "We all sit around at my country club and compare doctors, prices, and pain stories like we used to discuss childbirth."

THE SECRET WORLD OF SURGERY

In the tight little world of nip-and-tuck intelligence, plastic surgeons take more oaths of secrecy than a CIA candidate. But who's done what to whom is as much grist for the Hollywood gossip mill as the weekly movie box-office returns. Dishers on divas whisper that Jessica Lange, 47, had a really terrific lift just before making *Losing Isaiah*, that 38-year-old Sharon Stone's famous frontage has been oh-so-subtly enhanced, and that 55-year-old Faye Dunaway's lift is too tight, making her look, according to one Hollywood producer, as if she has "erased her own face."

"More celebrities are having surgery than the media knows, by a mile, because if it's good you can't tell," says Dr. Kamer. There are a few holdouts in the celebrity ranks. Cybill Shepherd, 46, has so far resisted the knife; so has Meryl Streep, also 46—but don't be surprised if they succumb soon. Even the legends have gone the surgery route: Joanne Woodward, 66, and Katherine Hepburn, 88, finally bit the bullet and were lifted.

PLASTIC HISTORY

Los Angeles has been marketing eternal youth since the 1950s, thanks to Dr. Franklin Ashley, La-La Land's plastic surgery pioneer. When he opened his clinic on western L.A.'s Pico Boulevard in the early 1960s, Hollywood greats raced to his operating table. Susan Hayward came in looking like hell and went out looking like, well, Susan Hayward. Even the leathery icon John Wayne had a career-extending face-lift. (True to western code, he refused to take his boots off during the procedure.)

But it was comedienne Phyllis Diller, now 78, who changed plastic surgery in Los Angeles forever—by proving that you don't even have to start out as a Hollywood beauty to end up looking like one. The haggard hausfrau had her first face-lift by Ashley in the early 1970s, becoming a smooth-cheeked belle overnight. And, remarkably, she not only admitted it but boasted about it to the press.

Suddenly, the whole town wanted the miracle Diller treatment.

RECOVERY ZONE

Today, on tree-shaded streets all over L.A., there are unassuming houses with names like Halcyon or The Hidden Garden where bandage-swathed guests in dark glasses come to recover under the watchful eyes of private nurses. Since California law restricts patients of private surgical clinics to a stay of only 23 hours and 59 minutes, a lucrative trade flourishes in post-plastic surgery care....

Some doctors offer service even more personal. Dr. Kelly O'Neil, a dermatologist celebrated by celebs for his wrinkle-erasing chemical peels, ships recovering clients to his...five-acre ranch in Temecula. There, bandaged like mummies, they take their food through straws so as not to disturb their new, freshly smoothed faces.

BRING ON THE BOOBS

Not surprisingly, in the industry town that spawned Marilyn Monroe and houses Hugh Hefner's Playboy mansion, Boobs are BIG. And the business of enlarging them is even bigger. "We can make better breasts than God," declares Dr. Maja Ruetschi, an elegant Swiss-born surgeon....

After notorious silicone implants were banned from cosmetic surgery practice in 1992, there was a lull in the U.S. demand for breast enhancement, while die-hard wanna-haves got used to the new saline substitutes. However, surgeons expect that soon they'll be able to use Europe's most popular implant, which contains a gel that feels more natural than saline and comes with a built-in lawsuit repellent: If the jelly leaks, it's excreted by the kidneys.

"With the breast, you're talking about sexual fantasy," explains the soft-spoken Dr. Barbara Hayden. "It's as individual as the patient herself. I can give the breast a mushroom shape, or make it flatter so it's like a little trampoline. If she wants more cleavage, I can suction the sides."

ADDICTED TO PERFECTION

But having a little plastic surgery is like doing a little decorating work on your house; every improvement makes the rest look bad....

Celebrities are particularly susceptible to plastic surgery addiction, says Dr. Pam Lipkin...."These are not the world's most secure

The Nobel Prize was first awarded in 1901.

people. When you have cosmetic surgery and it goes well, there's a tremendous psychological reassurance. And when cost is no object, the more you have the more you want." Mary Tyler Moore, 59, is rumored to be a can't-stop patient. The actress has reportedly had two face-lifts, breast implants, and collagen injections.

And they're coming in younger and younger. "Melrose Place" 's Josie Bisset, 26, and 22-year-old Tiffani-Amber Thiessen of "Beverly Hills 90210" both sport bigger breasts these days. But the current junior plastic-surgery champion is Tori Spelling, 22, a continuing work-in-progress who has that what-age-is-she-anyway look that comes from too much surgery too soon. "I've worked with her several times," said a Hollywood photo editor, "and her breasts have changed twice. She's also had her nose done twice, and had cheek and chin implants." But the daddy of all plastic surgery junkies is, of course, Michael Jackson, 37, who could afford the very best but ended up with an "amputated nose." "There were a lot of people involved with that nose," one surgeon said. "One doctor would tell him 'No,' and he'd say, 'All right, I'll go somewhere else.' "...

CELEBRITY SILENCE

Yet, despite the pervasiveness of cosmetic surgery in L.A., stars still don't like to admit that their extravagant frontage is more a tribute to their surgeon's skill than God's. Some refuse comment altogether: Jane Fonda, now 58, once preached, "We should learn to love our wrinkles"—then got rid of hers and inflated her chest. Some stars have always white-lied through their neatly capped teeth: Elizabeth Taylor, 64, had admitted only to a tiny little tuck under the chin, done after she lost over 100 pounds. In fact, local surgeons say, she has had four face-lifts....

And while the rest of the country may believe that Sophia Loren, 61, came by her ageless beauty from good genes and thinking kind thoughts, Los Angelenos gossip about eye work and face-lifts done on several continents.... Michelle Pfeiffer, 39, keeps quiet about her rumored cheek implants and nose work, and there has been no peep from model Lauren Hutton, 52, who left her gap-toothed smile untouched but lifted her face some time ago. "Hairdressers everywhere have seen those scars," says one Hollywood insider. Priscilla Presley, 50, does not talk about the chemical peels she reportedly has to get of wrinkles and brown spots. Even Barbra Streisand, 54, has allegedly undergone some subtle surgical enhancement. "She still has her famous nose," says an expert. "But look at her early pictures. It's not the *same* nose."

Some celebs are only a little bit honest: Cher, 49,...owns up to her breast augmentation but says nothing about her cheek implants, tummy tuck, buttock lift, new nose, navel surgery, or liposuction. Dolly Parton, 50, admits to a face-lift but neglects to mention the silicone in her fabulous frontage and the liposuctioning of virtually every other part of her lavish anatomy....

WHAT ABOUT COMPLICATIONS?

"We don't run beauty shops," cautions Dr. Kamer. "This is not something you drop in and do on your lunch hour, whatever the advertisements claim."

More usual complications run the gamut from blood clots...to lumpy postliposuction skin...to droopy eyelids....Infections happen; so do poor healing, scarring, rejection of implants, nerve damage, rock-hard breasts, and, of course, wind-tunneled faces.

In fact, prominent botches are on display at your local theater; being rich and famous doesn't guarantee you good surgery. For every Liza Minnelli (age 50) and Susan Lucci (47), whose lifts are terrific, there's a Carol Burnett (63)—who, post-lift, looks like an entirely different person—or a Paul Hogan (56), who came up from down under for a lift. "He lost his distinctive tanned cragginess," says local surgeon. "Now he looks bland and creaseless." Another cosmetic casualty is 46-year-old actor Don Johnson, say the tongue waggers: Johnson's new eye job makes him look Oriental. "They just took away too much skin," explains another local doctor. And then there's Roy Scheider, 63, who emerged from his lift with a lop-sided face. "I think they damaged a nerve," an expert says.

No wonder Robert Redford, 59, finally showing his age from all that exposure to the Utah sun, is looking carefully before he leaps. "He's shopping around here and in Manhattan," said a Beverly Hills surgeon. "With that great face, he can't afford to take chances."

Meanwhile, it's springtime in L.A. On the streets of Beverly Hills, tanned ladies of leisure in tiny miniskirts strut their stuff.... Everything is on display. "Centuries from now," muses Dr. Novack, "when archaeologists dig up our civilization, they'll find dust, bones, and a collection of implant bags."

Medical update: Men get more ulcers; women get more migraine headaches.

ACT III:
JUDGE GROUCHO

Here's the final episode of a 1933 radio show starring Groucho as newly elected Judge Waldo Flywheel, and Ravelli (Chico) as his sidekick.

BRUMMET: Well, Plunkett, Judge Flywheel owes a lot to you.

PLUNKETT: Yeah, we ran away with the election.

BRUMMET: It's lucky for you that your trial's coming up in his court.

PLUNKETT: Lucky? What do you think I got him put in office for? Judge Maxwell would've given me twenty years on this bribery charge. But with Flywheel on the bench, I ought to get off in a couple of hours.

BRUMMET: What about that lawyer you got—Ravelli? He don't look too smart to me.

PLUNKETT: Oh, Ravelli's all right. Flywheel asked me to hire him. I guess they got the whole thing worked out between them. I ain't even demandin' a jury. I'm leaving it all in Judge Flywheel's hands. Let's go in. The courtroom's filling up.

BAILIFF: Hear ye, hear ye. Court is now in session. Everybody rise. His honor, Judge Flywheel.

GROUCHO: Never mind. Where's the court stenographer?

I want him to take a letter to my wife.

BAILIFF: Why, he can't do that.

GROUCHO: He can't? Better look for a new stenographer. What's the first case?

BAILIFF: It's the case of Steve Granach, charged with making too much noise in his apartment, and operating a poolroom within three hundred feet of a schoolhouse.

GROUCHO: A poolroom three hundred feet from a schoolhouse? That's a disgrace. Have them move the schoolhouse. I don't want those little kiddies walking that far. Now then, it's time I went to lunch.

BAILIFF: But Judge Flywheel, you haven't tried any cases yet.

GROUCHO: All right, bring one on. I'll try anything once.

BAILIFF: Next case is the trial of John H. Plunkett, charged with bribing public officials.

GROUCHO: Where's your lawyer, Plunkett?

RAVELLI: Here I am.

GROUCHO: Ravelli, are you the

When asked what they think is the most stressful event of the year, 20% of Americans

lawyer for the defendant?

RAVELLI: No, I'm the lawyer for this crook, Plunkett.

PLUNKETT: Say! What do you mean saying I'm a crook?

RAVELLI: Alright, alright. I didn't know it was a secret.

DISTRICT ATTORNEY: Your honor!

GROUCHO: What is it?

DISTRICT ATTORNEY: The state is prepared to proceed with the trial of John H. Plunkett. Our first witness is Leo Greenbury.

GROUCHO: Greenbury can't be a witness in this court.

DISTRICT ATTORNEY: Why not, your honor?

GROUCHO: Well, he told my wife's butcher that he didn't vote for me. The sneak!

DISTRICT ATTORNEY: I regret to say, your honor, that I consider your remark most unbecoming to a judge.

GROUCHO: What did you say?

DISTRICT ATTORNEY: I said your remark was most unbecoming to a judge.

GROUCHO: Hey, that's the second time you said that. Just for that I fine you a hundred bucks. I dare you to insult me again.

DISTRICT ATTORNEY: Oh, never mind.

GROUCHO : Oh, come on. I'll let you have this insult for fifty bucks.

RAVELLI: Come on, Plunkett, get on the witness stand, I ask you questions.

PLUNKETT: Alright, Ravelli. (*gets on stand*)

RAVELLI: How old are you?

PLUNKETT: I'm forty-five.

RAVELLI: Hey, Judge, I object.

GROUCHO: You object to your own witness's answer? On what grounds?

RAVELLI: I dunno. I couldn't think of anything else to say.

GROUCHO: Objection sustained!

DISTRICT ATTORNEY: On what grounds?

GROUCHO: I couldn't think of anything else to say either. Ravelli, proceed.

DISTRICT ATTORNEY: If your honor pleases, the state...

GROUCHO: Oh, pipe down and give somebody else a chance. You talk more than my wife. That's why I never got married.

DISTRICT ATTORNEY: The state objects, your honor. This is not a divorce case! John H. Plunkett is charged with bribery!

GROUCHO: Bribery? Why wasn't I told about that? I don't count, do I? Oh, no. I'm just the judge here, that's all. Plunkett, I'm going to give you your choice of sentences: 10 years in Leavenworth, or 11 years in twelve-worth.

PLUNKETT: What?

GROUCHO: All right. We'll make it 5 & 10 in Woolworth.

PLUNKETT: Wait a minute, your honor. The state ain't proved that I'm guilty of bribery.

GROUCHO: The state doesn't have to. I know you're guilty.

PLUNKETT: Say, how do you know I'm guilty?

GROUCHO: Are you kidding? Don't you remember? You bribed me. That's how I became a judge.

PLUNKETT: You double-crosser!...

RAVELLI (Looking at the door): Boss, here comes Judge Maxwell.

MAXWELL: Mr. Flywheel, we have just come from the election board. Your sitting on the bench is absolutely illegal. We've just discovered that Emmanuel Ravelli voted more than once.

GROUCHO: Is that right, Ravelli? Did you vote more than once?

CHICO: Well, let me see. (*Thinking*) Mm-m. Maybe I did.

GROUCHO (Upset): Well, did you or didn't you? Think, man

RAVELLI (Still thinking): I voted one...two...three...YEP, I voted three thousand times.

☆   ☆   ☆   ☆

MORE "TRANSQUIPS"

Real courtroom conversation from Humor in the Court *and* More Humor in the Court, *by Mary Louise Gilman.*
(see page 273 for more)

Q: Now, Mrs. Johnson, how was your first marriage terminated?
A: By death.
Q: And by whose death was it terminated?

Q: And who is this person you are speaking of?
A: My ex-widow said it.

Q: Officer, what led you to believe the defendant was under the influence?
A: Because he was argumentary and he couldn't pronunciate his words.

Literary pretensions: The TV show *The Love Boat* was based on a novel.

MISS AMERICA TODAY, PART VI

Like all social institutions, the Miss America Pageant has had to become a bit of a cultural chameleon to survive. It doesn't change drastically—it has to be true to its roots as a traditional beauty contest, after all. But when the pressure gets strong enough, it seems to creak forward. Here's an update on the state of the pageant today:

NEW AND IMPROVED

The protests of the late 1960s and early 1970s over the Miss America Pageant's alleged anti-feminist and racist attitudes launched an era of gradual change for the pageant that continues to this day. For example:

✓ In 1968, the pageant named a black clergyman to its board of directors and nominated two African American women to the hostess committee; a year later Dr. Zelma George became the pageant's first African American judge. The first African American contestant was Cheryl Brown, Miss Iowa 1970.

✓ The most crassly sexist components of the pageant (except the swimsuit contest, of course) were quietly done away with. The "Neat as a Pin Award," created in 1969 to reward $250 to the tidiest contestant, was abandoned in 1973; the Miss Congeniality Award bit the dust two years later. In 1986 the pageant abandoned the practice of publishing contestants' bust, waistline, and hip measurements.

✓ Contemporary issues were given greater attention beginning in 1974. Contestants had to answer "controversial, issue-oriented questions dealing with topics ranging from rape to prostitution." But the questions were asked offstage, away from the audience and TV cameras, to avoid the possibility of embarrassing the contestants or the pageant. The TV audience had to settle for short rehearsed issue speeches, which were made during the evening gown competition. Eventually, the pageant came up with a "platform" that the new Miss America agreed to support.

How long does it take a frozen sandwich to thaw at room temperature? Our sources say about 3 hours

THERE HE GOES...

By the 1980s, nothing was sacred. In its endless quest for relevance and higher ratings, the pageant began leading its most sacred cows to slaughter. In 1980 it was announced that Bert Parks, who'd hosted every broadcast since 1955, was "retiring." (Pageant chairman Albert Marks later claimed that sponsors had been urging him to get rid of Bert for more than a decade.)

The move was handled shabbily—Parks learned of the firing from a reporter—and the publicity that resulted was disastrous. Miss America fans bombarded the pageant's Atlantic City headquarters with thousands of angry phone calls and letters, and "Tonight Show" host Johnny Carson, no spring chicken himself, waged an on-air campaign to have the crooner reinstated.

It didn't work. Marks stuck to his guns and replaced Parks with actor Ron Ely in 1980...then with Gary Collins in 1982...then with Regis Philbin and Kathie Lee Gifford in 1991. So far, however, no one has been able to fill Parks's shoes. (Parks made a guest appearance at the 1990 pageant—which some insiders claim was possible only because Marks had died in September 1989—but he made a lot of gaffes during the live broadcast and did not return in subsequent pageants. He died in 1992.)

There It Ain't

The axe fell again in 1982, when the Miss America Pageant failed to agree with composer Bernie Wayne on a price for using the song "There She Is" in the pageant. Wayne wanted a 15-year, $25,000 contract, but pageant officials refused, and the song was cut. As with Parks's firing, public response was negative and overwhelming...and this time it actually worked. Three years later, the pageant put "There She Is" back in the show.

THE HOLY OF HOLIES

But the biggest change of all came in 1994, when the Miss America Pageant—after suffering the lowest TV ratings in 20 years—announced that it was considering dropping the swimsuit competition altogether. This idea was hardly a new one; in fact, the swimsuit competition was as unpopular with top officials at the Miss America Pageant as with the pageant's protesters. Lenora Slaughter had spent years lobbying behind the scenes to dump the swimsuits, but pressure from traditionalists and swimsuit fans had proved too great.

Now, rather than make the decision itself, the pageant left it up to viewers. And to milk the maximum amount of publicity from the event, the vote was held *during* the 1995 Miss America broadcast. Viewers could call a 900 number and cast their votes while watching the show. The vote was updated throughout the program; the final tally was to be announced toward the end of the show. Just in case the vote was in favor of axing the suits, the pageant had another "mystery" event waiting in the wings to take its place.

The mystery event wasn't needed—the suits won 60% to 40%. The live vote was the biggest pageant publicity stunt since the 1920s, and it had the desired effect: 2.1 million more people watched the broadcast in 1995 than did in 1994.

THE END?

Will the pageant survive? Maybe not as the major cultural institution that it was in the 1950s, but if the pageant's ability for reinventing itself in a crisis is any guide (and the TV ratings don't slip much further), it will probably be around for decades to come.

☞ ☞ ☞ ☞

MISS AMERICA BEAUTY SECRETS

How do makeup artists affiliated with the Miss America Pageant keep America's beauties beautiful? Here are a few of their tricks.

Dirty hair. One of the pageant's hairstylists admits, "Dirty hair is more manageable. I can make a style fuller and stay better."

Face Putty. Used to cover up lines, scars, and pockmarks, and to create "porcelain" complexions. One makeup artist says: "I've even gone so far as to use mortician's wax mixed with the makeup."

Vaseline. Smeared on the teeth so that contestants can smile easily—even if their mouths dry up from nervousness.

Preparation H. The hemorrhoid ointment is smeared on eyelids and under the eyes. According to one makeup artist, "It smells pretty bad, but it removes puffiness."

There are ten million bricks in the Empire State Building.

MISS AMERICA SCANDALS

*The Miss America Pageant has never had a scandal big enough
to destroy it...but a bunch of middle-sized controversies have
made headlines over the years. Here are a few of the juicier
ones that we haven't already covered.*

VANESSA WILLIAMS, *Miss America 1984*
Scandal: It was a big deal when Williams became the first
African American Miss America. And there was just as
much publicity when, 10 months later, *Penthouse* magazine announced that it had obtained a series of nude pictures Williams had
posed for years earlier (including photos in suggestive poses with
another woman)...and was planning to publish them in its September 1984 edition. Pageant officials immediately pronounced the
photos "inconsistent with the Miss America image" and gave Williams 72 hours to resign her crown.
What Happened: It was the biggest scandal ever involving a reign-
ing Miss America. But if anything, it *boosted* Williams's career.
Since 1984, she's appeared on Broadway and recorded million-
selling singles and Grammy-winning albums. Ironically, she's now
the most successful ex-Miss America in the history of the pageant.

VENUS RAMEY, *Miss America 1944*
Scandal: A few days after she won the title, Ramey, 19, revealed
that she'd forged her mother's name on the contract binding her to
the pageant's scheduled promotional appearances—so it was legally
unenforceable. Her reason for the stunt: She wanted to negotiate
her own deals directly with advertisers.
Pageant officials "invited" Ramey to New York's Waldorf-
Astoria hotel, where they held her while they tried to persuade her
to honor the contract. When that failed, they flew in Ramey's
mother to sign the contract for real. She also refused to cooperate.
What Happened: Ramey never did honor the contract. She em-
barked on her own tour—which bombed. She earned only $8,500
for an entire year on the road. (By comparison, Miss America 1941
earned an estimated $150,000 during her reign.) "I wanted to get
into show business," Ramey complained afterward. "I thought the

pageant would be a good entree. It is, all right—an entree into oblivion. Forever afterward, you're like a broken-down actress trying to make a comeback."

CLAIRE JAMES, *Miss California 1938*

Scandal: James made it all the way to First Runner Up, then lost out to Marilyn Meseke, Miss Ohio, when judges "disapproved of her use of mascara."

What Happened: James was furious. Her promoter, theatrical producer Earl Carroll, denounced the judges as "incompetents," and the day after the pageant called a press conference to crown James the "people's choice" for Miss America. It was a publicity stunt, but James took it seriously, often identifying herself as Miss America in commercials and in speaking tours around the country. She finally backed off after Meseke, the real Miss America, took her to court.

B. ("BILLY") DON MAGNESS, *Chairman of the Board, Miss Texas Pageant, 1970-1990*

Scandal: In September 1990, *Life* magazine alleged in an article on Magness—whose nicknames included "Mr. Miss Texas" and "God"—that, among other things, he:

- Held private swimsuit modeling sessions with Miss Texas contestants at his house.
- Made "very pointed hints" to a number of contestants over the years.
- Regularly kissed contestants on the lips.
- Telephoned contestants and asked them questions like "Wanna get nekkid?"
- Gave contestants obscene T-shirts, including one that read, "In case of rape, this side up."
- Referred to contestants as "sluts" during the *Life* magazine interview.

"While I make an attempt at appearing to be a dirty old man," Magness explained during the interview, "I make double that attempt to be sure that I'm not. Does that make sense? It's just kind of fun. You can be too clean and pure. Some of the girls just need to be dirtied up a little. It's just a continuance of their education."

The federal government owns about 20% of the land in America.

What Happened: The article quoted Miss America CEO Leonard Horn as saying Magness "has lots of elegance and class. I think B. Don really cares about these kids." But after reading the *Life* article, Horn quickly changed his tune. He ordered Texas pageant officials to investigate Magness, then threatened to keep the next Miss Texas out of the Miss America pageant unless Magness resigned.

YOLANDE BETBEZE, *Miss America 1951*

Scandal: The day after her coronation, Betbeze announced at a breakfast meeting that she would not pose in swimsuits during her reign. An earlier Miss America had taken the same stand and gotten away with it, but this time the Catalina Swimsuit Company was sponsoring the pageant, and had already booked Betbeze on a nationwide swimsuit tour.

What Happened: "The coffee cups rattled, let me tell you," Betbeze recalled years later. "The man from Catalina bathing suits stood up and fumed. He was furious. He looked at me and said, 'I'll run you off the news pages. I'll start my own contest. You'll see.' "

"I said, 'That's splendid. Good luck to you.' Anyway, he did, indeed, start the Miss USA and Miss Universe Pageants. So people can thank me—or blame me—for that."

BESS MYERSON, *Miss America 1945*

Scandal: In 1987, Myerson, then New York City's Commissioner of Cultural Affairs, was indicted for conspiracy, bribery, and fraud after she allegedly helped her boyfriend, a millionaire sewer contractor with reputed mob ties, lower his alimony payments by giving a judge's daughter a $19,000-a-year job in city government.

That was only the beginning of Myerson's legal troubles: In May 1988, she was arrested for shoplifting after she walked out of a New York department store without paying for the six bottles of nail polish, five pairs of earrings, one pair of shoes, and the flashlight batteries she'd stuffed into her purse and shopping bag. "I was leaving the store to lock my car and come back and pay for the merchandise," she explained to reporters after her arrest. Total value of the merchandise: $44.07. (Myerson was carrying $160 in cash.)

What Happened: Myerson was eventually acquitted on the alimony fixing charges, but pled guilty to shoplifting and paid a $100 fine, plus court costs.

SUSAN AKIN, *Miss America 1986*

Scandal: Within a month of her crowning, the story broke that Akin's father and grandfather had been arrested in connection with the Ku Klux Klan murders of three Mississippi civil rights workers in 1964. Neither man was convicted.

What Happened: Miss America officials didn't learn of the story until it was reported in the media, but insisted that Akin had no responsibility to disclose the family connection. Akin—who was born a month *after* the murders—admitted she was hurt by the revelations, but refused to let her family's past prevent affect her reign. "They're not Miss America," she told reporters, "I'm Miss America. …You're not going to hold it against me.…I don't even know the facts about these things because I don't want to know."

TONI GEORGIANA, *Miss New Jersey 1985*

Scandal: Shortly after Georgiana won the New Jersey title, first-runner-up Laura Bridges filed a lawsuit saying that Georgiana was actually a Pennsylvania resident, had competed twice in the Miss Pennsylvania pageant (and lost), and that she wasn't really a New Jersey student because she'd only enrolled in a single two-week education course at a state college, had not attended a single class, and had failed the course.

What Happened: New Jersey pageant officials sided with Georgiana, arguing that even if it was true, she had met minimum residency requirements set by the national pageant. Bridges lost the case.

STACY KING, *Miss Louisiana 1989*

Scandal: In 1989, the Miss Louisiana pageant director filed a protest, alleging that King was unfairly excluded from the Top 10 contestants in the national pageant because she was white and non-disabled. "It appeared that if you were black, ethnic, or had some kind of medical problem you had overcome, you stood a better chance of getting into the Top 10," he told reporters. "Two of the Top 10 were ethnic—one black and one Oriental—and there was one contestant who had a kidney transplant and another one who was deaf.…It was just awful odd the way it worked out."

What Happened: The media had fun with the "anti-politically correct" protest, but pageant officials ignored it.

THE PUPPET-MASTER

*Edward Bernays was one of the most influential people of the 20th century.
A nephew of Sigmund Freud, he applied psychology to the art of publicity
and became America's first "public relations" expert (a term he coined).
What he was able to accomplish was both fascinating and frightening—sort
of like a train wreck. The way he was able to manipulate cultural forces
behind the scenes is amazing; but he was (and his successors are) doing it to
us...which is pretty scary. This selection, taken from Bernays' book
Engineering Consent, should give you an idea of the way commercial
interests quietly get us to do their bidding...without ever letting us know it.*

NOTE: In the 1920s, one of Bernays' main clients was the
American Tobacco Company, whose president, George
Washington Hill, was dedicated to one goal: get more people to smoke Lucky Strikes. Women were a prime market. He had
already gotten Bernays to instigate a "women's freedom" movement
that linked liberation with smoking. (Bernays anonymously encouraged debutantes to march down New York's Fifth Avenue
smoking, in "protest" of the fact that women weren't allowed to
smoke like men. The ensuing publicity brought women smokers
out of the closet all over the United States). Now Hill decided to
influence the fashion world, so his green Lucky Strike package
would be in style. Bernays knew just how to do it. Here's his account of what happened.

A NEW PROJECT

Hill never stopped thinking about the huge potential Luckies market—the women of America. New surveys showed him that wom-
en were now smoking in and out of the house; they also disclosed
that many women objected to Luckies because the green package,
with its red bulls-eye, clashed with the colors of the clothes they
wore. Some time in the spring of 1934 Hill called me.

"Women aren't buying Luckies as they should. What do you suggest, Mr. Bernays?" he asked.

"Change the Lucky package to a neutral color that will match
anything they wear," I replied.

This was a logical suggestion, but Hill became emotional at the thought of changing the color of his package. "I've spent millions of dollars advertising the package. Now you ask me to change it. That's lousy advice."

"If you don't change the color of the package, change the color of fashion—to green."

"Change the fashion—that's a good idea. Do it," Hill shouted enthusiastically, adding as an afterthought, "What will it cost?"

I knew that money alone couldn't change a fashion. Such a change depended on setting forces in motion that would influence others forces, and these in turn might change the fashionable color. I plucked a round figure out of the air.

"Twenty-five thousand."

"Spend it!" yelled Hill.

That was the beginning of a fascinating six-month activity for me—to make green the fashionable color. My work had shown me that fashions seldom happen fortuitously; they follow trends. A planned event of importance can play a part in affecting these trends. The costumes and decor of the Bal de l'Opera in Paris held French fashion trends—so why not a Green Ball in New York? Why shouldn't an American ball planned along comparable lines influence fashion trends here, particularly if it was linked with Paris fashion influences?

SECRETS OF SUCCESS

Some years before, I had asked Alfred Reeves, of the American Automobile Manufacturers Association, how he had developed a market for American automobiles in England, where roads were narrow and curved.

"I didn't try to sell automobiles," he answered. "I campaigned for wider and straighter roads. The sale of American cars followed."

This was an application of the general principle which I later termed the "engineering of consent." Like an architect, I drew up a comprehensive blueprint, a complete procedural outline, detailing objectives, the necessary research, strategy, the ends and timing of the planned activities. I wanted to be sure the money Hill had authorized was spent effectively.

THE MEANING OF "GREEN"

Next, I researched the impact of green on society. The future always holds within it something of the past and present. I wanted to know the values embraced in the color green. Green had psychological, health and aesthetic values. Green was "the color of spring, an emblem of hope, victory and plenty," "the springtime of life and recuperation"; it suggested calm, peace and serenity. Many universities used green as their school color; graduate students in physical education and pharmacy wore jade-green hoods.

A statistical analysis disclosed that green was featured in 5 percent to 50 percent of the current lines of the great French fashion houses; the average was almost 20 percent, an encouraging base on which to build. I also studied the part played by fashion magazines, socialites, top dress houses and manufacturers, newspapers and women's magazines in influencing the popular colors in the country.

Soon we were at work on two continents, making contact with a variety of social and economic groups.

THE "GREEN BALL"

First I talked to Mrs. Frank A. Vanderlip, a friend, chair of the Women's Infirmary of New York, wife of the former chairman of the National City Bank. Mrs. Vanderlip's imaginative fund-raising efforts kept this voluntary hospital going. I suggested that a Green Ball be held in November under the Infirmary's auspices for the hospital's benefit. I explained that a nameless person would defray the costs up to $25,000; our client would donate our services to promote the ball; the color green would be the ball's motif and the obligatory color of all the gowns worn at the ball. I added, "I can assure you the cause is not Paris green—a poison."

AS SMOOTH AS GREEN SILK

I now approached Philip Vogelman, the enterprising president of the Onondaga Silk Company, and suggested his firm become the spearhead for color leadership in the United States. He listened to the program I outlined, and then agreed to bet on green.

This was somewhat of a speculation on his part, but not financially, because green would have been in his line anyway. He was risking at most a wrong prediction. If he lost, it would not hurt much; such miscalculation was a part of the textile business. But if he was right—with our help—it would raise him to leadership.

Vogelman gave a "Green Fashions Fall" luncheon that spring for fashion editors and fashion trades at the Waldorf-Astoria to induce these industries to follow his lead in picking green, and to stimulate public acceptance of the color. We printed the menus on green paper and served green food—green beans, asparagus-tip salad, pistachio mousse glace, green mints and creme de menthe. Joseph Cummings Chase, a portrait painter and the head of Hunter College's Art Department, discussed green in the work of great artists; Dr. Joseph Jankrow, the psychologist, discussed the psychological implications of green.

SPREADING THE GREEN

Widespread publicity followed the lunch. The New York *Sun* headlined its story, "It Looks Like a Green Winter"; the New York *Post* stressed a "Green Autumn." One press service reported "Fall fashions stalking the forests for their color note, picking green as the modish fall wear."

Vogelman invited buyers to a showing of his new green fall silks. We supplied Onondaga with green letterheads, and green sheets of paper for press releases and organized a Color Fashion Bureau, which sent authentic fashion data from New York and Paris to editors of feature and women's pages. It alerted the fashion field to green's leadership in the whole women's clothing and accessories area. The bureau also promoted green in interior decoration.

Nothing stands by itself. There is an interrelationship between the elements of fashion. House decors affect dress colors; if green dresses clashed with prevailing decors, women might not wear them. Costume accessories need to match the basic fabrics. In May, 1,500 letters on the dominance of green were sent to interior decorators, home-furnishings buyers, art-in-industry groups and club-women; 5,000 announcements were sent to department stores and merchandise managers.

THE GREEN TEAM

Throughout the summer the bureau maintained its barrage. We were encouraged to note that green pencils and green writing paper followed the accelerating trend to that color. Without a nudging, other firms got on the green bandwagon. Peggy Sage announced a new emerald nail polish to be worn with green costumes; Lilly Dache designed a special green hat; Prosper McCallum introduced green stockings. McGibbon & Company arranged a green window display in their Fifth Avenue shop. The women's-page editor of a Philadelphia newspaper wrote: "Let me know what you are plugging. It is so adroit that even I, a hard-boiled old she-dragon, can't detect it."...

Thousands now asked to be put on the Onondaga bulletin mailing list. Department stores, theatrical producers, radio fashion commentators, art editors, pattern companies and trade papers added to the spreading enthusiasm for green. The praise of green in newspapers rose in a crescendo through the summer.

An Infirmary Green Ball Committee of prominent social leaders sold Green Ball tickets....The ball committee held a series of luncheons with representatives of the accessory trades to encourage them to make available green accessories for the green gowns the ball guests would wear. At my suggestion, the committee started a news bulletin of its own about the ball. Emphasis by repetition gains acceptance for an idea, particularly if the repetition comes from different sources.

GREEN-TIME IN PARIS

In 1934, high fashion in the United States still needed Paris backing. At my suggestion, Mrs. Vanderlip sailed for France. We wanted the *haute couture* of Paris to supply the green dresses that would be modeled by American society women in the fashion show at the ball. We also wanted official...support of the French government.

In Paris our publicity woman arranged a tea for Mrs. Vanderlip. Forty French fashion VIPs, plus Marian Taylor of *Vogue* and Carmel Snow of *Harper's Bazaar*—attended and agreed to support the campaign. The *haute couture* people and the French government agreed to co-operate. The *haute couture* was dependent economically on the purchasing power and good will of American women. Because of her husband's standing, Mrs. Vanderlip was recognized by the French as a formidable spokesperson for American women, their customers. The French government, too, acted in recognition of the place luxury goods occupied in their international trade.

GREEN BALL-GAME

Next, the committee engaged a consultant to handle the mechanics of the ball. Debutantes flocked to her call; society editors followed her lead. As early as August the New York *Herald Tribune* carried a full page headlined "Charity Benefit to Stress Fashion Importance of Green," showing pictures of the costumes to be worn and the paintings that inspired them. Newspaper interest mounted.

Meanwhile, we trod gingerly through the political mazes of the American fashion world. Experts had advised us to await the return of Edwin Goodman, of [the] Bergdorf Goodman [department store], from a trip abroad before we approached other New York high-fashion houses for co-operation. If he played along, they would too. We waited; Goodman liked the idea, and his competitors came along, as predicted.

In September, Altman's Fifth Avenue windows were filled with green dresses and suits. Women's magazines were featuring green fashions on their covers. The November issue of *Vogue* carried two pages of sketches of the green dresses to be brought from Paris to New York. We knew now that green had arrived.

THE WEARING OF THE GREEN

The unsuspecting opposition gave us a boost: the November magazine advertisements for Camel cigarettes showed a girl wearing a green dress with red trim, the colors of the Lucky Strike package. The advertising agency had chosen green because it was now the fashionable color.

As the ball's date approached, the green publicity moved ahead on its own momentum. Editors were now asking the ball committee for dress photographs and descriptions. The dress rehearsals for the event aroused sufficient interest for *Hearst Metrotone* and *Universal Newsreel* to film them and run them through the country.

I did not attend the ball itself. If the plans worked out, I was delighted; if not, I could do little. The ball was a great success, from the social and fashion viewpoint, and it firmly established green's predominance.

Your tongue has 9,000 taste buds.

HOLLYWOOD SCANDAL: 1921

A woman is found dead…a well-known celebrity is charged with
murder… the whole world follows the trial. O. J. Simpson?
Nope—Fatty Arbuckle. In its day, the Arbuckle trial
was as big as the Simpson trial. Here's the story.

A KNOCK AT THE DOOR
On the morning of Saturday, September 10, 1921, two men from the San Francisco sheriff's office paid a visit to Roscoe "Fatty" Arbuckle, then Hollywood's most famous comedian, at his home in Los Angeles. One of the men read from an official court summons:

"You are hereby summoned to return immediately to San Francisco for questioning…you are charged with murder in the first degree."

Arbuckle, thinking the men were pulling a practical joke, let out a laugh. "And who do you suppose I killed?"

"Virginia Rappé."

Arbuckle instantly knew that this was no joke. He'd just returned from a trip to San Francisco, where he'd thrown a party over the Labor Day weekend to celebrate his new $3 million movie contract—then the largest in Hollywood history—with Paramount Pictures. A 26-year-old bit actress named Virginia Rappé had fallen ill at the party, presumably from drinking too much bootleg booze. Arbuckle had seen to it that the woman received medical attention before he returned to L.A., but now Rappé was dead—and Arbuckle had somehow been implicated in her death. Whatever doubts he may still have had about the summons vanished the following morning as he read the three-inch headlines in the *Los Angeles Examiner*:

ARBUCKLE HELD FOR MURDER!

The autopsy report showed that Rappé died from acute peritonitis, an inflammation of the abdominal lining brought on by a ruptured bladder. Why was Arbuckle a suspect in the death? Because Maude

---

A woman can detect the odor of musk—which is associated with

"Bambina" Delmont, another woman at the party, had filed a
statement with San Francisco police claiming that she had seen
Arbuckle drag Rappé into his bedroom against her will and assault
her. As she later explained to newspaper reporters,

> I could hear Virginia kicking and screaming violently and I had to
> kick and batter the door before Mr. Arbuckle would let me in. I
> looked at the bed. There was Virginia, helpless and ravaged. When
> Virginia kept screaming in agony at what Mr. Arbuckle had done,
> he turned to me and said, 'Shut her up or I'll throw her out a win-
> dow.' He then went back to his drunken party and danced while
> poor Virginia lay dying.

The 265 pound comedian had supposedly burst Rappés' bladder
with his weight during the assault. And because the injury had
gone undiagnosed and untreated, it developed into a massive
abdominal infection, killing Rappé.

Pressing Charges
After Delmont's statement was filed, San Francisco District Attorney Matthew Brady had ordered Arbuckle's arrest and had issued a
public statement to the press:

> The evidence in my possession shows conclusively that either a rape
> or an attempt to rape was perpetrated on Miss Rappé by Roscoe
> Arbuckle. The evidence discloses beyond question that her bladder
> was ruptured by the weight of the body of Arbuckle either in a rape
> assault or an attempt to commit rape.

FALSE WITNESS
Brady's case was based almost entirely on Delmont's police statement. And the case certainly *appeared* substantial—at least until
Brady looked into Maude Delmont's background after she gave her
statement. Then he discovered a police record containing more
than 50 counts of bigamy, fraud, racketeering, extortion, and other
crimes (including one outstanding bigamy warrant, which Brady
would later use to his advantage).

WHAT REALLY HAPPENED
Brady later learned from other guests at the party that a very drunk
Maude Delmont had actually been locked in a bathroom with Low-
ell Sherman, another party guest, during the entire time that she

claimed to have witnessed Arbuckle with Rappé. She could not have seen any of the things she claimed to have seen—and if that were not bad enough, Brady later discovered that on Wednesday, September 7, Delmont had dashed off the following telegram to two different friends as Virginia Rappé lay dying at the St. Francis Hotel:

WE HAVE ROSCOE ARBUCKLE IN A HOLE HERE
CHANCE TO MAKE MONEY OUT OF HIM

Blind Ambition

District Attorney Brady had no case—there wasn't a shred of physical evidence to indicate that Arbuckle had committed any crime against Rappé; his only "witness" was a woman with a long criminal record; and the telegrams demonstrated clearly that Delmont's police statement was part of an attempt to blackmail Arbuckle.

Despite all this, Brady decided to bring the case to trial. Why? One theory: Brady, whom acquaintances described as a "self-serving, arrogant, ruthless man with blind ambition and a quick temper," was gearing up to run for governor of California. He probably figured that winning a murder conviction against Hollywood's biggest comedian would score points with the public.

Judge Not

Still, the case could not have gone to trial if the police judge, Sylvain Lazarus, had dismissed the case due to lack of evidence. But Judge Lazarus refused to throw it out, citing the "larger issues" surrounding the case:

I do not find any evidence that Mr. Arbuckle either committed or attempted to commit rape. The court has been presented with the merest outline....The district attorney has presented barely enough facts to justify my holding the defendant on the charge which is here filed against him.

But we are not trying Roscoe Arbuckle alone; we are not trying the screen celebrity who has given joy and pleasure to the entire world; we are actually, gentlemen, trying ourselves.

We are trying our present-day morals, our present-day social conditions, our present-day looseness of thought and lack of social balance....

I have decided to make a holding on the ground of manslaughter.

The judge suspected Arbuckle was innocent, the district attorney *knew* Arbuckle was innocent, and yet the case still went to trial.

EXTRA!

Much like the Menendez brothers trials and the O. J. Simpson trials of the 1990s, the media—which in the 1920s consisted mostly of newspapers—had a field day with the Arbuckle trial. Unlike the Simpson trial, however, the lack of evidence in the Arbuckle trial led most newspapers to conclude that Arbuckle was innocent. *Most* papers, that is, except for those owned by media baron William Randolph Hearst. His papers loudly attacked Arbuckle's character, insinuated his guilt, and ran as many as six special editions per day to keep readers up-to-date on the latest developments in the case.

The Hearst papers published the most lurid accounts of the crime and the trial, and even stooped to publicizing totally unsubstantiated rumors about the case—the most famous of which was that Arbuckle, supposedly too impotent from booze to rape Rappé himself, had used a Coke bottle (some accounts said it was a champagne bottle) instead, causing her bladder to rupture. "Nowhere in any testimony in the court transcripts, police reports, or personal interviews did this story appear," Andy Edmonds writes in *Frame Up! The Untold Story of Roscoe "Fatty" Arbuckle*. "Everyone connected with the case vehemently denied it, yet it is the most popular story, and one of the most ugly lies, still connected with the ordeal. The fabrication haunted Roscoe throughout the remainder of his life."

GOING TO COURT

As Brady prepared his case, one of the first things he did was see to it that Maude Delmont would not be able to testify. He knew that the other witnesses would prove she had lied in her police statement. Furthermore, Delmont had changed her story so many times that Brady knew she would be caught in her own lies during cross-examination. Rather than let that happen, Brady had her arrested on an outstanding charge of bigamy. Delmont—the only person who claimed that Arbuckle had committed a crime—spent the next several months in jail, where Arbuckle's attorneys could not get at her.

THE TRIAL

The People v. Arbuckle lasted from November 14 to December 4, 1921. More than 60 witnesses were called to the stand, including 18 doctors. According to Bernard Ryan in *Great American Trials*,

> Through defense witnesses, lawyer Gavin McNab revealed Virginia Rappé's moral as well as medical history: As a young teenager, she had had five abortions in three years, at 16, she had borne an illegitimate child; since 1907, she had had a series of bladder inflammations and chronic cystitis; she liked to strip naked when she drank; the doctor who attended her in the several days before she died concluded that she had gonorrhea; when she met Arbuckle for the first time on Monday, she was pregnant and that afternoon had asked him to pay for an abortion; on Wednesday, she had asked her nurse to find an abortionist....Medical testimony proved that Virginia Rappé's bladder was cystic—one of the causes of rupture of the bladder.

Arbuckle Takes the Stand

The climax of the trial came on Monday, November 28, when Arbuckle testified in his own defense. He recounted how he had found Rappé in his bathroom vomiting into the toilet, and how he had helped her into the next room when she asked to lie down. Arbuckle testified that he spent less than 10 minutes alone with Rappé before summoning Maude Delmont, who took over and asked him to leave the room. He stood up well under cross-examination; and the final testimony, in which expert witnesses testified that the rupture of Ms. Rappé's bladder was not caused by external force, seemed to cinch the case for Arbuckle.

THE VERDICT

As the case went to the jury, both sides appeared confident of victory. But on December 4th, after 44 hours of deliberation, the jury announced that it was hopelessly deadlocked, and the judge declared a mistrial.

One juror, a woman named Helen Hubbard—whose husband was a lawyer who did business with the D.A.'s office—held out for a conviction throughout the entire deliberations.

The Second Trial

The case went to trial a second time, beginning on January 11 and lasting until February 3. The second trial was much like the first, only this time the defense introduced even more evidence concerning Ms. Rappé's shady past. But Arbuckle's lawyers, confident they would win handily, did not have Arbuckle take the stand in his defense. That was a huge mistake—this time the jury deadlocked 9-3 in favor of *conviction*.

The Third Trial

The case went to trial a third time on March 13. This time, Arbuckle's defense left nothing to chance: it provided still more evidence questioning both Rappé's physical health and her moral character, and it brought Arbuckle back to the stand to testify on his own behalf.

FINAL VERDICT

The case went to the jury on April 12, 1922. They deliberated for less than 5 minutes, then returned to court and read the following statement:

> We the jury find Roscoe Arbuckle not guilty of manslaughter.
>
> Acquittal is not enough for Roscoe Arbuckle. We feel that a great injustice has been done him. We feel also that it was only our plain duty to give him this exoneration, under the evidence, for there was not the slightest proof adduced to connect him in any way with the commission of a crime.
>
> He was manly throughout the case, and told a straightforward story on the witness stand, which we all believed.
>
> The happening at the hotel was an unfortunate affair for which Arbuckle, so the evidence shows, was in no way responsible.
>
> We wish him success....Roscoe Arbuckle is entirely innocent and free from all blame.

THE AFTERMATH

Roscoe Arbuckle was a free man, but his life was in tatters. The trials had cost him more than $750,000, wiping out nearly his entire life savings (the $3 million Paramount contract had fallen through when the scandal broke). As if that wasn't bad enough, the IRS went after him a few months later, when it seized the remainder of his estate to collect more than $100,000 in back taxes. It also obtained a court order to attach whatever wages he earned in the future until the entire tax debt was paid back.

THE HAYS OFFICE

Things got even worse for Arbuckle. Largely because of the scandal, 12 of Hollywood's top studio moguls hired William Hays, chairman of the Republican National Committee and a former postmaster general, to become America's "movie czar." His job: Keep Hollywood's image clean. His first task: Deal with Arbuckle.

Hatchet Job

Six days after Arbuckle was acquitted, the "Hays Office" (as it came to be known) banned him from the screen. The public was led to believe it was a moral issue. Actually, Hays was doing the bidding of Paramount heads Adolph Zukor and Jesse Lasky, who no longer wanted to work with Arbuckle, out of fear that he was box office poison. But they didn't take any chances; rather than risk losing Arbuckle to a competing studio, they lobbied the Hays Office to ban him from the film industry entirely.

COMEBACK

The ban was lifted eight months later, but the taint remained and Arbuckle had trouble finding work. He began work on a short subject film called *Handy Andy*, but was so hounded by reporters that he gave up on the project.

Over the next decade he appeared in stage shows, ran a Hollywood nightclub, and directed a number of films under the pseudonym William B. Goodrich (Will B. Good). But it wasn't until 1932—more than 10 years after the trials—that he had a chance to return to the screen. Studio head Jack Warner hired him to act in a film called *Hey, Pop!* It was a box office success, and Arbuckle was signed for six more films. He only completed three—*Buzzin' Around, Tamalio,* and *In the Dough.* The evening *In the Dough* finished shooting, Arbuckle celebrated at dinner with his wife and went home to bed. He died in his sleep at about 2:30 a.m., leaving an estate valued at less than $2,000.

THE
ANSWER PAGES

THE ELVIS ANSWERS
(FROM PAGE 33)

1. c. He thought he could heal the sick. For example: One time Dean Nickopolous, son of Dr. Nick (Elvis' personal physician), injured his leg sledding in the snow. It hurt so badly that he thought it was broken. Elvis's bodyguard recalls: "Then old psychic healer Elvis comes along. He starts 'laying on the hands' and grabbing the leg. Poor old Dean is nearly passing out with pain." Later in the hospital, the doctor told Elvis and his friends that the leg was only bruised, not broken.

"When Elvis heard from the doctor that the leg wasn't broken, he gave one of those satisfied little know-all smiles," the bodyguard says. "He said, 'I know, it isn't broken. It's okay now.' He was taking credit for the fact that the leg wasn't broken."

2. b. Elvis' vegetarian friend Larry Geller recounts in *If I Can Dream: Elvis' Own Story:*
> Out went the brownies, the ice cream, the chicken-fried steak, the burgers. Elvis ate only fresh, nutritious, healthy foods—for two days. Then it was back to the same old nonsense.

3. c. Elvis hated the show because Karl Malden's character was named Mike Stone. When Priscilla Presley separated from the King, she left him for a karate instructor named Mike Stone. A different Mike Stone to be sure, but that didn't matter to Elvis.

4. a. "Dr. Nick said he didn't recommend the surgery, merely mentioned it as a possibility," Jerry Hopkins writes in *Elvis: The Final Years,* but "Elvis, no stranger to rapid and extreme weight loss schemes, said he wanted the operation that night." Dr. Nick finally talked the King out of the procedure by explaining that if he had it, Elvis would have to stick to a strict diet for the rest of his life. "To celebrate the decision not to have the operation," Hopkins writes,

Elvis "had one of his boys go to a fast-food place in the neighbor-hood and sneak back with a sack of bacon cheeseburgers and fried potatoes."

5. b. Elvis loved mortuaries. As we told you in *Uncle John's Sixth Bathroom Reader*, Elvis liked to wander through the Memphis funeral home where his mother had been laid out before her burial. "I don't mean he would just go there during the day and look around," Elvis' friend Sonny West recounted to Steve Dunleavy in *Elvis: What Happened?* "I mean he would go there at three in the morning and wander around the slabs looking at all the embalmed bodies. It scared the sh— out of me."

When his friend on the police force died, the King wanted to be there at the mortuary when they worked on him. "I'm sure Elvis was sad about the whole thing, but do you know what he did, man?" says a member of the Memphis Mafia. "He watched the mortician embalm his friend....Can you imagine that? Someone watching someone else slicing into the body of a friend....Elvis could tell us details about embalming that would impress a doctor."

6. a. A friend recalls: "I remember Jimmy Dean, a nice guy, was waiting for him one night. Elvis came out of his bedroom after keeping Jimmy out there for an hour. Jimmy greeted Elvis with a big hello and said jokingly, 'I oughta rip a yard from your ass, keeping me waiting.' And Elvis whipped out his .22 revolver and stuck it under Jimmy's chin and said, 'And I ought to blow your head off for talking to me like that.'"

7. b. His manager, Colonel Tom Parker, botched the invitation by demanding $25,000 for the King to appear. As Jerry Hopkins writes, "The man in the White House was dumbfounded. Finally he regained his composure and said, 'Why, Colonel Parker, no one ever gets paid to perform in the White House.'

"'Well,' said the Colonel, 'no one ever asks Elvis to play for free.'" Elvis lost the gig...and was never invited back.

8. b. "There's all kinds of speculation about what book Elvis was reading when he died," says his cousin Billy Smith. "It was *The Scientific Search for the Face of Jesus*, the Shroud of Turin book, by Frank Adams."

In 1979, a South African boy was found to have a marigold seed growing from his left eye.

ANSWERS TO "WOULD YOU BELIEVE..."
(FROM PAGE 89)

1. b) North was testifying before the Iran-Contra investigating committee, and in a supremely cynical gesture, presented the incident as an example of why Congress can't be trusted with secrets. It was too much for *Newsweek*, which had been the recipient of the leaked information. They revealed that the source of their info had been "none other than North himself."

2. c) In an interview with Norman Mailer in *Esquire*, she said: "I think you get to a point with a person that you say, 'I love this person...enough that I don't give a damn what happens to me, I'm willing to take the chance.' "

3. a) Lightner, who was fired by MADD in 1985, began work for the American Beverage Institute—which represents restaurants and breweries. "I assume some people will say, 'Gee, what's she doing working for the industry, the other side,' " she told a reporter, adding: "I don't see it was the other side. They're just as affected by drunk driving as anyone else." Lightner's first project, according to *The New York Times*, was "working against state laws tightening the standards for drunk driving."

4. c) "Her beliefs remain unshaken," said news reports, "even though she had a baby during spring break." The report went on:

> The baby's father was a short-term boyfriend....and the athletic teenager gained only seven pounds during her pregnancy. So she was able to conceal her condition from family and friends until she went into labor during a trip with her present boyfriend. He had planned to take her hang-gliding, but ended up rushing her to a hospital maternity ward at 3 a.m. She told her mother the news the day after the baby was born.
>
> Danyale plans to attend college next year and the child probably will live with her grandmother. When the time comes, the baby will be taught about abstinence. "I still believe in it," Danyale said.

5. a) When Rashwan didn't show up to receive his Fair Play Trophy, David Wallechinsky, author of a definitive book on the Olympics, "went back and looked at the tape of the match and discovered that Rashwan had attacked the injured leg. In fact, it was his first move, 10 seconds into the match."

6. c) "Football and family values—a great marketing concept," wrote columnist Joe Urschel in *USA Today*. "Too bad David Williams was dumb enough to fall for it." He went on:

First, they threatened to fine and suspend him. Then they decided to withhold $111,111 of Williams' pay instead.

Williams' immediate supervisor, offensive line coach Bob Young, took a more personal view of the situation....."Shoot, I had a baby when I was playing," Young said. "Ninety percent of the guys have babies when they are playing, but you never miss games. My wife told me she was having a baby, and I said, 'Honey, I've got to play a football game.' "

7. b) Scot Morris writes in *The Emperor Who Ate the Bible*: "Benjamin Franklin saved his well-earned pennies at Philadelphia's Bank of America. In 1940, accountants audited all of the bank's records —including the earliest transactions. According to their findings, Benjamin Franklin…was overdrawn on his account at least three times each week."

8. b) In 1994, the General Accounting Office of Congress did an audit of the IRS and found that "the agency did things with its books that would put ordinary people in jail." According to one news report, for example:
• The IRS's "inventory records are so poorly maintained that it said a $752 video display terminal had cost $5.6 million."
• "Auditors couldn't account for two-thirds of the money [the IRS] spent in one recent year."
• "When federal investigators wanted to see records for several billion dollars' worth of transactions, the paperwork couldn't be found. So [IRS] employees doctored files to fit."

9. a) According to an account in *If No News, Send Rumors*: "In a summary of Supreme Court actions in 1973, *The New York Times* omitted one Court decision. The Justices had announced that they would not revive a paternity suit in which the defendant was *Times* publisher Arthur Ochs Sulzberger."

THE GRAMMY QUIZ ANSWERS (FROM PAGE 147)

1. b) The Beach Boys. They were nominated for Best Vocal Group in 1966, along with the Association and the Mamas & the Papas. But all lost to the Anita Kerr Quartet, a nondescript middle-of-the-road group. (Anita Kerr just happened to be the vice president of the Nashville chapter of the National Academy of Recording Arts and Sciences—the organization that gives out the Grammys.)

"Good Vibrations" was nominated for 1966's best rock & roll recording...but lost to "Winchester Cathedral." In 1988, the Beach Boys were nominated (and lost) again—this time for "Kokomo."

On the other hand: The Chipmunks won in 1958, for Best Comedy Record and Best Children's Record. Aerosmith was named Best Rock Group in 1990.

2. a) Vaughn Meader did a great impersonation of President John F. Kennedy, and his *First Family* record, which gently spoofed life at the Kennedy White House, was Album of the Year in 1962. In fact, at one point it was certified by the *Guinness Book of World Records* as the fastest-selling album in history. Thomas O'Neil writes in *The Grammys:*

> Meader is remembered in comedy circles today as one of its most tragic figures. He was clearly America's leading political satirist of his day, but [his] career was...shot down the same day that gunfire made history in Dallas on November 22, 1963....

> When Kennedy was assassinated in Dallas, the album was tossed out of homes and record stores across America. While other comics [who] lampooned Kennedy in the past...were able to prevail professionally after his death, Meader was unable to rescue his career, despite countless comeback tries that even included changing his name.

3. c) Yep, it's the Anita Kerr Quartet again, for their immortal album, *We Dig Mancini*. Probably the most scandalous award in Grammy history, because they beat out the Beatles, who were in their prime. The Beatles were nominated for nine awards—and got none. Bob Dylan didn't even get a nomination.

4. c) 1967, for *How Great Thou Art*. In fact, the only Grammys Elvis ever won were for religious music. He was given the 1972 and 1974 Best Inspirational Performance awards, too.

5. c) Sinéad O'Connor. In 1990, she was nominated in four categories, and said: "If I win, I won't accept it and I wouldn't want it near me. As far as I'm concerned, it represents everything I despise about the music industry." She did win a Best Alternative Music award, and turned it down.

6. a) John. George and Ringo won in 1972 for their performances on the *Concert for Bangladesh* album; Paul won one in 1972 for *Uncle Albert* and one in 1974 for *Band on the Run*. Remarkably, the most creative of the quartet got nothing for his solo efforts while he was alive. After (and perhaps because) he was assassinated, he and Yoko won an Album of the Year award for *Double Fantasy*.

7. b) The Rolling Stones. But the Who and the Doors never won anything, either.

8. a) Roseanne Cash. She was nominated for 1982's best female country singer, and didn't get it. After the show, driving down Hollywood Boulevard, she wrote a "tongue-in-cheek...little ditty" that went, "I got my new dress, I got my new shoes / I don't know why you don't want me." She recorded it, and it won her the award for Best Female Country Vocalist in 1985. "I wrote it out of self-pity," she said in her acceptance speech. "How ironic to win with it!"

9. c) Frank Zappa. When he was nominated in 1987 for *Jazz from Hell* (which won Best Rock Instrumental), he said: "I have no ambiguous feelings about the Grammys at all. I know they're fake. I find it difficult to believe that Whitney Houston is the answer to all of America's music needs."

10. a) What Grammys? Each was nominated once—Hendrix in 1970 for an instrumental of "The Star Spangled Banner" and Joplin in 1971 for "Me & Bobby McGee." And that's it.

11. d) Natalie Cole, 1975. It took 17 years. Among the winners in that stretch: Tom Jones, the Carpenters, and Marvin Hamlisch.

12. b) He couldn't afford to rent a tux to go to the awards ceremony. It's a bizarre story. Clark, a blind Nashville street singer, record-ed one album for RCA, called *Blues in the Street*. It didn't sell well, but did get a Grammy nomination. For some reason, RCA wasn't interested in promoting it; they didn't even *loan* him the money to go across town and attend the ceremony. So he wasn't there when he beat out Peter, Paul & Mary and Ravi Shankar for Best Folk Re-cording. In fact, he never recorded again.

According to Thomas O'Neil in *The Grammys*:

> The day after the Grammy ceremony, he was seen still hus-tling spare change on the sidewalks of the honky-tonk capi-tal. Two years later, he died when a kerosene stove exploded in his trailer home.

13. a) "I tore a ligament in my leg, jumping out of my seat," Popper said; he had to limp up to the stage. What was he going to do with his trophy? "I got a lovely spot for this," he said, as he waved it around. "There's this door that keeps closing…"

DOCTOR'S ORDERS

Recently, BRI member Jack Miller sent us this amusing story.

"My friend's dad was an ear-nose-and-throat doctor on the upper West Side, in New York City. He treated a lot of well-known sing-ers, including many from the Metropolitan Opera. He was a very proper old Viennese gentleman.

"One day in the late 1960s, who should walk into the office but Janis Joplin. Dr. Reckford doesn't know her from Adam, but he examines her and delivers his diagnosis:

'Young lady, I don't know what you do for a living, but you've got to stop drinking and shouting so much.' "

include the phrase "to honor and obey" in their wedding vows.

THE LAST PAGE

FELLOW BATHROOM READERS:
The fight for good bathroom reading should never be taken loosely—we must sit firmly for what we believe in, even while the rest of the world is taking pot shots at us.

Once we prove we're not simply a flush-in-the-pan, writers and publishers will find their resistance unrolling.

So we invite you to take the plunge: Sit Down and Be Counted! by joining The Bathroom Readers' Institute. Send a self-addressed, stamped envelope to: BRI, 1400 Shattuck Avenue #25, Berkeley, CA 94709. You'll receive your attractive free membership card, and a copy of the BRI newsletter (if we ever get around to publishing one), and earn a permanent spot on the BRI honor roll!

ထ   ထ   ထ

UNCLE JOHN'S NEXT BATHROOM READER (OUR 10TH ANNIVERSARY EDITION) IS IN THE WORKS!

Don't fret—there's more good reading on its way. In fact, there are a few ways *you* can contribute to the next volume:

1. Is there a subject you'd like to see us cover? Write and let us know. We aim to please.

2. Got a neat idea for a couple of pages in the new *Reader*? If you're the first to suggest it, and we use it, we'll send you a free copy of the book.

3. Have you seen or read an article you'd recommend as quintessential bathroom reading? Or is there a passage in a book that you want to share with other BRI members? Tell us where to find it, or send a copy. If you're the first to suggest it and we publish it in the next volume, there's a free book in it for you.

Well, we're out of space, and when you've gotta go, you've gotta go. Hope to hear from you soon. Meanwhile, remember:

Go with the flow.